Industrial efficiency and state intervention

In *Industrial Efficiency and State Intervention* Nick Tiratsoo and Jim Tomlinson describe and assess the Labour Party's development of a policy for improving industrial efficiency between 1939 and 1951. The authors concentrate on the debates and initiatives of the wartime period and on the subsequent implementation of policy aimed at raising productivity under Attlee.

The book provides two major modifications to existing historiography. First, it shows that the prevailing view of Labour between 1945 and 1951, with its emphasis on the creation of the Welfare State, is wrong. Labour saw the correction of social ills as vital, but it also recognised the crucial need for industrial modernisation. Second, this reading demands the re-evaluation of wider theories about Britain's economic decline. If the key difference between Britain and, say, Japan is Britain's lack of a 'developmental state', then, as the book shows, any explanation of this situation is impossible without consideration of the country's political parties and the context within which they have operated. Given this twin purpose, the book should appeal to both specialists interested in party politics and those who are interested in wider questions about Britain's overall contemporary history.

Nick Tiratsoo is Lecturer in Social History at the University of Warwick and Visitor in the Business History Unit at the LSE. **Jim Tomlinson** is Reader in Economic History at Brunel University and Visitor in the Business History Unit at the LSE.

Books published under the joint imprint of LSE/Routledge are works of high academic merit approved by the Publications Committee of the London School of Economics and Political Science. These publications are drawn from the wide range of academic studies in the social sciences for which the LSE has an international reputation.

Industrial efficiency and state intervention: Labour 1939–51

Nick Tiratsoo and Jim Tomlinson

ROUTLEDGE
LSE
London and New York

First published in 1993
by Routledge
11 New Fetter Lane, London EC4P 4EE

Simultaneously published in the USA and Canada
by Routledge
29 West 35th Street, New York, NY 10001

Typeset in Times by LaserScript Limited, Mitcham, Surrey
Printed and bound in Great Britain by
TJ Press (Padstow) Ltd, Padstow, Cornwall

British Library Cataloguing in Publication Data
A catalogue record for this book is available from the British Library.

ISBN 0-415-08810-0

Library of Congress Cataloging in Publication Data
has been applied for.

ISBN 0–415–08810–0

Harold [Wilson] said he had invented the concept of output per man-shift and even the concept of productivity which had been a theoretical concept before but he had got it extended over all industry. A terrible thing to have on his conscience.

(Tony Benn, *Against the Tide: Diaries 1973–76*, London: 1989, p. 506)

instead of fussing about glaring and conspicuous evils, squalor and injustice and distressed areas . . . [democratic socialists] have to fuss about the balance of payments, and incentives, and higher productivity.

(C.A.R. Crosland, *The Future of Socialism*, London: 1956, p. 99)

Contents

Tables

Acknowledgements

The research on which this book is based was partly financed by a grant from the London School of Economics. We should like to thank the Governors of the LSE, Mr Gus Stewart and Dr Terry Gourvish (Director of the Business History Unit) for arranging this support. We would particularly like to acknowledge the considerable encouragement that Terry Gourvish has given us over the last few years: he has gone far beyond the normal call of duty in facilitating the completion of this work.

Second, we should like to thank the various archival experts who have helped us in locating documents, especially Sharon Barker and Jennie Butters at the British Institute of Management library, Corby; Dr Sarah Street at the Conservative Party archive, the Bodleian Library, Oxford; Stephen Bird at the Labour Party archive, the Museum of Labour History, Manchester; Dr Richard Storey and staff at the Modern Records Centre, University of Warwick; and the staff at the Public Records Office, Kew.

Finally, we are most grateful to James Hinton, Helen Mercer, Neil Rollings, Deborah Spring and Jonathan Zeitlin for providing advice at different points along the way.

Chapter 1

British industry, state intervention and Labour politics, 1900–39

The theme of relative industrial and economic decline dominates the historiography of twentieth-century Britain. Whilst there is little agreement on the precise character, scope, timing, let alone causes, of this decline, its central importance in shaping British society seems indisputable.[1]

Explanations for this process have ranged over almost every feature of the economy and wider society, these interpretations seemingly being themselves subject to cycles of support and disavowal. Indeed, historical explanations have also frequently been linked to contemporary ideological and political concerns. In the 1960s and 1970s, for example, much emphasis was put on low investment rates as a key problem, in turn often related to the alleged focus of British ruling groups on external economic goals (such as foreign investment and a strong currency) at the expense of the interests of industry.[2]

In the 1980s two kinds of hypothesis tended to dominate. On the one hand 'cultural' explanations, especially those associated with the names of Martin Wiener and Corelli Barnett, created a 'Thatcherite' history of economic decline, linked to the alleged atrophying of entrepreneurial spirit and an excessive political concern with social welfare at the expense of industry.[3] Accompanying this a less politically fashionable but more firmly historically grounded literature emerged, which saw economic failure as a consequence of political blockage, the absence of a state giving priority to industrial modernisation. This view was best summarised by Marquand, who concluded that 'Unlike its counterparts on the mainland of Europe and in Japan, Britain's political class had never managed – even in its interventionist periods – to create an entrepreneurial or developmental state',[4] though similar views, albeit with varying ideological glosses, appeared in a range of work.[5] Some of the themes raised here could be found in earlier investigations, which argued that throughout the twentieth century policy had been excessively either externally oriented or attuned to domestic macroeconomic goals. However, the originality and insightfulness of the new writing stemmed from its emphasis on the political conditions for a shift to a potentially more successful industrial policy. Much literature on British decline soon collapses into 'grand themes' of cultural malfunction, imperial grandeur and supersession or the dominance of finance capital, with politics read-off as simply a reflection of these over-arching designs or misadventures.[6] In contrast, Marquand, Hall, Newton and Porter, and others underlined the specifics of party strategies, ideologies and organisation in explaining the absence of the political will and capacity to create a 'developmental state'. Such an emphasis on the importance of political parties and their policies is pursued in this book.

It is useful to begin by sketching in the kind of history of British economic decline before 1939 that this approach would suggest. First, it is clear that economic decline begins to emerge as a serious political issue around the turn of the century, mainly linked to worries about Britain's waning relative strength as a Great Power. The threat to this position came from a number of sources including perceived failures in competitiveness, largely registered through the trade figures.[7]

This initial period of concern saw the emergence of a cross-party alliance of those wanting to address 'efficiency' issues, the Co-Efficients. But this group was essentially a small coterie of metropolitan intellectuals whose claim to fame was precisely their novelty and exceptionality, rather than their position as the spearhead of a mass movement. In addition, whilst the Co-Efficients were certainly mindful of industrial efficiency, their focus was in fact very different from that which marked later 'industrial policy', except in regard to the issue of technical education. Their central concerns were, on the one hand, governmental efficiency and, on the other, the efficiency of the worker, thought of largely as a question of physical health.[8]

Above all, the issue of efficiency lost political resonance because it cut across the linked major economic debates of the pre-1914 period – tariff reform and public finance. On tariff reform, the Co-Efficients were divided, though many regarded it as a diversion from the 'real' issues. Equally, on the question of whether higher government expenditure should come from tariff revenues or from higher direct taxes, the Co-Efficients' position did not fit in with the Conservative/Liberal party divide. Consequently, they failed to become major contributors to the economic arguments of the period.[9]

Of course, and as always, this failure may be traced back to 'deeper' forces at work in the British political economy. Undoubtedly one of the difficulties of making industrial efficiency a prime political goal was the strikingly *rentier* character of the economy, with large parts of the country drawing income as tribute from foreign investment. Perhaps 10 per cent of National Income came from this source immediately before 1914. In addition, Britain depended in its foreign trade to a large extent on earnings from shipping and financial services, which had no direct links with industrial competitiveness.[10]

These factors in turn may be linked (though not in an over-determinist fashion) to weakness in the organisation of the main industrial producer groups. Crucially, industrial employers had failed to establish a 'peak association' to fight for their aims and interests, most of their organisations being oriented to either industrial relations or technical, trade issues. This lack of a unified voice in turn partly reflected the divisions amongst employers on the big political issues of tariffs and public finance.[11]

But an adequate account of the absence of a developmental state prior to 1914 must refer to more than these structural factors. Politics, it must be insisted, has an independent character and must be discussed in its own terms. On this basis it is clear that neither of the two main parties, the Liberals or the Conservatives, was plausible as a vehicle for policies of industrial modernisation in this period.

On the one hand, the Liberals, partly under the influences of New Liberalism and partly through straight electoral calculation, were shedding major elements of their Gladstonian heritage and committing themselves to a much more active state in the field of welfare. But this activism was on a clearly limited front. In particular, a commitment to private ownership and competition in industry remained largely unchallenged, with much of the radicalism of the New Liberalism coming from its attacks on the *abuses* of private ownership and the monopolistic supersession of competition, rather than any questioning of the desirability of these two kinds of institution. Hence the Liberal agenda encompassed higher taxation and greater state expenditure but resisted the idea of seeing the state as pivotal in the strategic and economic rivalry of the period. In economic terms it remained committed to the priority of consumer interests – free trade, cheap food and competition – over those of domestic producers.[12]

On the Conservative side, concern about threats to Britain's Great Power status led to a sharper break with Victorian orthodoxy. Tariff reform was at least in part about defending domestic producer interests against foreign competition. But the Conservatives, more than the Liberals, were committed to the sanctity of private property and free enterprise. Whilst Conservative concerns with industrial efficiency as an aspect of the general problem of Empire efficiency could encompass better education and more state expenditure on research and development, what was increasingly the party of business was hardly likely to emerge as an initiator of intervention in the private industrial sector.[13]

By 1914 the traditional *laissez-faire* state had, therefore, undoubtedly been altered from its Victorian heyday. Public spending was significantly higher than 40 years earlier and tax levels reflected this. The state's role in the labour market was much expanded in the 1906–14 period. But the broad parameters of Britain's political economy had been sustained. The gold standard, free trade and the (relatively) low and balanced budget remained in place, constraining in their different ways the emergence of a state aiming to break with 'market forces' in the name of industrial efficiency.

The First World War, like the Boer conflict, put the efficiency of British industry once more on the agenda. Dependence on imported (especially German) war materials exposed some of the weaknesses of Britain's industrial structure, whilst analyses of post-war prospects highlighted the problems of a number of key industries.[14] In many areas the exposure of British industry to the glare of state scrutiny during the First World War matched that which was to come with the war of 1939–45. But the key difference was the very limited continuity between wartime and post-war policy on the earlier occasion.

Broadly speaking, the state machine rolled into industrial intervention in the First World War, but was then rolled back afterwards. Some permanent changes survived the ebb and flow. The 'safeguarding' of certain key industries against import competition continued and indeed expanded post-war. Employers' peak associations, drawn into existence by the wartime state, became a permanent feature of the political landscape.[15] But these were untypical developments, exceptions to the rule. Post-1918 politics (especially after 1920) saw a concerted attempt to return to the norms of the pre-1914 political economy.

At the core of this policy stance was a continued adherence to economic internationalism – to varieties of a (very mildly qualified) free trade and the gold standard. This in turn was related to an economic analysis which saw post-war economic problems as largely the result of wartime disruption to established financial and trade patterns. The priorities were therefore to restore exchange rates, defeat inflation and secure the conditions for a revival of trade.[16] These broad positions, it should be noted, were shared by most Labour politicians as much as by the Liberals and Conservatives – a point returned to in a later section.[17]

Economic policy in the 1920s was dominated by this desire to restore 'normalcy', a factor which underlay the return to gold in 1925. It also fitted in with an emphasis on *relieving* unemployment, as an acceptable means of dealing with the problem until the 'real' solution of expanded world trade arrived. Only slowly did disillusion with this approach emerge. Of course, Keynes and his Liberal allies attacked the priority given to the external value of the pound and the impact of this on the staple export industries. But this was in many ways a marginal as well as an ineffective attack on policy. Whilst Keynes might note the 'end of *laissez-faire*', his major concern in the 1920s was with monetary management not industrial modernisation.[18]

Nevertheless, alongside the dominant orientation, change was beginning to occur. Thus, whilst remaining resistant to the calls for proto-Keynesian public works policies, the overwhelmingly Conservative Governments of the decade did begin to accept that the old staples would not regain their former scale and employment levels, and that some degree of change in industrial structure and organisation was desirable. The change of approach was signalled by the Industrial Transference Act of 1928, which encouraged workers to move from the old staple regions to work elsewhere in the country. In practical terms this achieved little, but symbolically it suggested an acceptance that financial stability, however much it might be secured, would be insufficient to revive significantly the fortunes of coal, steel, shipbuilding and cotton.[19] Even more significant for the development of policy on industry was the widespread if inchoate and often inconsistent enthusiasm for 'rationalisation' in industry. Like so many economic fashions in Britain, this was imported from Germany, and usually denoted in some general sense the need to reorganise industry into larger units to secure greater efficiency via economies of scale.[20]

Enthusiasm for such a change went across the political spectrum albeit with different ideological glosses. For many in the late 1920s it seemed obvious that British industry must reorganise or be re-organised in order to revive, and this was supported by much of the material presented to, and reproduced in official form by, the Balfour Committee.[21]

But widespread support for the principle of rationalisation was insufficient to generate much policy to that end, especially before the slump of 1929–32. The enforced amalgamation of the railways in 1921 might be seen in this context, though it basically made permanent the wartime arrangements. More innovatory was the creation of the Central Electricity Board (CEB) in 1926, which very much reflected the idea that industrial efficiency required cheap large-scale generation of electricity.[22] The most active body in the area of rationalising the staples was the Bank of England, drawn in by the problems of its own customers and by the threat posed to the banking system of bad debts arising in the older industries. The Bank had also acted to pre-empt more radical action by an incoming Labour Government in 1929.[23]

As in the pre-war period, the Conservative Governments of the 1920s were hardly *laissez-faire* in attitude, and were not averse to expanding the frontiers of state intervention in certain directions (e.g. industrial transference). But rationalisation suggested a direct role in the private sector and its prerogatives which most Conservatives still found anathema. Hence, for example, intervention in the coal industry in the 1920s, a prime industry for rationalisation, allowed for state compulsion in amalgamations, but only if the initiative came from a majority of owners in an area. The impact was quite limited.[24] A more radical measure of state intervention was embodied in the cartel and compulsory amalgamation provisions of the Coal Mines Reorganisation Act of 1930, the product of a parliamentary alliance between Labour and the Liberals, but again its results were limited.[25]

The collapse of the gold standard and the ending of free trade in 1931 mark a kind of watershed in the development of British economic policy. The liberal, cosmopolitan arrangements of the pre-1914 era had rested on three pillars – the gold standard, free trade and low and balanced budgets.[26] Two of these were now defunct. At the same time the cause of their demise – the world slump – gravely exacerbated the problems of the staple industries, problems which had largely initiated the tentative movements to state intervention in the 1920s. There was now both an economic and a political 'space' for a more dirigistic role from government.

But this role took a largely defensive form. The tariff imposition obviously shielded British industries from competition and so reduced the need to reorganise. The Government proved unable to replace such an incentive by any other, so that in iron and steel, for example, official enthusiasm for rationalisation as a quid pro quo for protection in the end achieved very little.[27] Overall, the picture of the Conservative Governments and industry in the 1930s is one of support for cartelisation and market sharing within a protectionist framework. This is not to argue either that protectionism is always harmful to industrial efficiency or that cartelisation combined with forced amalgamations might not have yielded some benefits. But in the circumstances of the 1930s it is difficult to escape the conclusion that the administration's role was largely unhelpful to any notion of a state-sponsored industrial modernisation.[28]

First, these were Conservative Governments which drew substantial support from owners in the private sector, who were not only ideologically an unlikely source of proposals for major state intervention but, perhaps more important, ill-organised to produce any consistent policy positions. The impression that employers presented, even within individual industries, was usually one of fragmentation and disagreement rather than unity. This seems to have led to a persistent 'lowest common denominator' attitude of defensiveness and minimal change, with which the politicians went along in the absence of a viable alternative.[29]

This 'safety first' stance was reinforced by the Tories' conception of overall economic policy. Alan Booth has persuasively argued that the Conservatives had a fairly coherent approach to economic policy in the 1930s, which involved managing the economy in a new way. The party's package revolved around taking advantage of the departure from gold by using a programme of cheap money and maintaining a low exchange rate for the pound. These measures were (eventually) envisaged as means of reviving the economy by raising the price level, and hence profits, but this required, in the Government's eyes, tight fiscal control to prevent any loss of confidence which would threaten the compatibility of the two central policies.[30] This strategy not only ruled out Keynesian-style fiscal 'extravagance' but also militated against any innovative policy on the economy. The defensiveness and negativism of industrial policy was, therefore, on a par with the general stance as regards economic policy.

As a consequence of these factors, by the outbreak of the Second World War Britain had little more of a 'developmental state' than in 1900. The Government had intervened in new ways after the First World War exposed some of the shortcomings of British industry. Certain 'key' industries had been given protection, and this was extended to all of manufacturing and some of agriculture in the 1930s. But whilst protection may have been a necessary condition to allow space for the reorganisation of certain of Britain's industries, or the growth of new ones, it was not a sufficient condition. The simple fact was that the Government remained reluctant to intervene directly and systematically in industry. There were examples of such intervention – railways, electricity and coal have been noted above. There were also such cases as the official encouragement given to the creation of ICI, particularly stimulated by the strategic significance of some of its products. But in no sense could this be said to amount to an industrial strategy, and it only added up in the end to a set of *ad hoc* interventions which failed to address the real magnitude of British manufacturing weakness. Furthermore, though some general 'supply-side' initiatives were made, such as the wartime creation of the Department of Scientific and Industrial Research (DSIR), their impact was insubstantial. Typically, the DSIR focused its efforts on prodding the private sector to expand research, rather than acting as a major player itself. It does not seem to have succeeded in shifting the low levels of R. & D. prevalent throughout British industry.[31]

In sum, whilst by the 1930s there had been a decisive break with the political economy of Victorian liberalism in the sphere of international economic policy (the gold standard and free trade), confidence in the capacity of private industry to deliver efficient production and employment had been replaced not with an aggressive programme of modernisation but with a defensive, even defeatist, alignment, which arguably managed to combine the worst features of private enterprise and state intervention.

What of Labour's role in this story? Up until 1939 the party never achieved a parliamentary majority. It became the main challenger to the Conservatives after the First World War, but was only able to form two short-lived governments in 1924 and 1929–31. Hence Labour's direct impact on state policy was limited. But the party's views on industry and industrial policy were undergoing significant changes, and these form an important background to its later role in the 'years of influence', 1939–45, and years of power from 1945 to 1951. These developments also deserve some detailed consideration as there is currently a striking dearth of material on this important topic.

From its foundation in 1900 (as the Labour Representative Committee) until 1918 the Labour Party was a body whose programmatic and policy-making side continued to be extremely underdeveloped. The basis for the foundation of a distinct Labour Party was a desire to form a body to represent the interests of the working class, where that representation was seen largely in sociological terms (i.e. giving a voice to a class) rather than as involving a distinct set of policy objectives. Initially this situation even precluded political goals beyond working-class representation. In 1908 common ownership of industry became a general objective, but was simultaneously rejected as a *programme*. The dominant view was that the party consisted of a fragile alliance of trade unionists and socialists, a unity which would not survive detailed statements of intention. The most that should be done was to establish principles, and let the Parliamentary Party turn them into practical activity. Policies that did emerge were largely *ad hoc* responses to events of the day.[32]

Alongside this programmatic vacuum there was the development of a definite approach to industry, largely from Fabian sources. Whilst the Independent Labour Party dominated the 'ethos' of Labour at this stage, it was the Fabians who seemed to give the most serious consideration to policy issues, on industry as in so many other areas.[33]

In the first significant Fabian publication, the *Fabian Essays* of 1889, two chapters were devoted to industry, the most substantial by William Clarke, the other by Annie Besant. Both had a similar line. Above all they shared a highly evolutionary analysis of industry, describing an ineluctable movement from handicraft to machine production, and an ever increasing massing of capital and grouping of workers. This process was now reaching a new stage in which the 'ring' and the 'trust' more and more replaced previously free competition. Such developments were seen as both inevitable and efficient: 'Those combinations can be shown to be the most economical and efficient methods of organising production and exchange. They check waste, encourage machinery, dismiss useless labour, facilitate transport, steady prices and raise profits.' The socialist aim should therefore be not to break up the combinations but to 'absorb and administer' them:

> Instead . . . of attempting to undo the work which the capitalists are unconsciously doing for the people, the real reformer will rather prepare the people, educated and organised as a true industrial democracy, to take up the threads when they fall from the weak hands of the possessing class.[34]

Annie Besant carried the argument a logical step further by noting that the development of industry had separated the industrial population into a proletarian majority and a tiny owning class, and that this laid the basis for a straightforward expropriation of the trusts' owners. In addition she spelt out a further highly significant practical consequence of the new configuration of industry:

> There is no practical difficulty in the way of management of the ordinary productive industries, large or small. The Trusts and

Co-operatives have, between them, solved or put us in the way of solving, all problems connected with these.[35]

These two essays defined a position which was both widespread and long-lived. Other Fabians wrote on similar lines, and the approach seems to have become close to an official Labour position.[36] But the perspective employed clearly drew on much wider Left traditions. Besant's essay, especially, employs an almost Leninist tone, whilst on the other hand closely paralleling the views of the most important 'New Liberal' economic theorist, J.A. Hobson.[37] In other words, this position on industry illustrates the pervasiveness of evolutionary modes of thought across the ideological spectrum at this time, with Fabians and Labour sharing a common intellectual heritage.

Such views remained the bedrock of Labour's thinking on industry up to the First World War. Whilst such an approach, as already noted, was not translated into a programme during these years, it was compatible with the largely *ad hoc* policies which did emerge at this time. In particular, Labour's accretion of commitments to nationalise particular areas, such as the railways, was fully in line with the judgement that this would represent a further step along the path which industry was already following, rather than a fundamental break in its development. Thus, the case for railway nationalisation (parallel to that for land) was founded upon the belief that the employers in this industry were currently exacting a monopolistic surplus which distorted the distribution of income, rather than any allegations about their supposed inefficiency.[38]

In other words, nationalisation did relate to efficiency but not in the sense of the efficiency of industrial organisation. The private ownership of land, railways and mining royalties was seen as imposing inefficiency on other sectors by exacting monopoly rents from them. Secondly, the maldistribution of income which resulted from such monopolies, it was argued, lowered the incomes of workers, and so made them inefficient.

This latter sense of efficiency, relating to the physical health of the worker, was a predominant one in discussions of this period, again uniting Labour and the New Liberals. But such a focus highlights the *absence* of attention to the details of corporate performance, an absence explained by the continuing popularity of the evolutionary view that private ownership, whilst it might be a problem in some respects, did *not* involve any problems as regards efficiency. This is also evident in the programme of the 'Co-Efficients' whose concern with efficiency involved no criticism whatever of current forms of industrial organisation.[39]

Faith in the productive efficiency of current capitalist forms of industrial organisation remained pervasive until the First World War. Then, like many across the political spectrum, Labour thinkers were shaken by wartime revelations of British incapacity and lack of organisation. In later writing, the Webbs pointed to the Board of Trade Reports as demonstrating 'the gross inefficiency in processes, mechanical plant and organisation within each of the staple trades'.[40] Whilst many were unwilling to give up entirely the idea of the advantages of economies of scale made possible by industrial concentration, the overall view of the capabilities of industry soon became vastly more qualified than pre-war.

Thus, in the *Constitution for a Socialist Commonwealth of Great Britain* of 1920, the Webbs argued that 'it was one of the unexpected discoveries of government during the Great War that the system of capitalist profit-making, as a method of producing commodities and services, habitually fell so enormously short of the maximum efficiency of which it was capable'. Accordingly, they came to the conclusion that there was need for a 'Standing Committee on Productivity' as part of a new scheme of government, to aid all industries to conduct themselves more efficiently.[41]

This was not just Fabian eccentricity. A loss of faith in the conduct of industry was part of the whole recasting of the Labour Party's political and ideological orientation at the end of the First World War. As is well known, in 1918 the Labour Party adopted a new constitution, which embodied Clause Four, committing it to a programme of common ownership as the central long-term goal. In some ways the significance of this latter goal can be exaggerated. On the one hand, it was not seen as a major issue in the Labour Party at the time, attention being paid much more to other parts of the constitution. On the other hand, it can be seen as simply a logical development of the pre-war stance, coupled to an invigorated desire to give Labour a distinct political position.[42]

Perhaps more important than the new constitution and Clause Four was the adoption by Labour of a new programmatic statement, written by Sidney Webb, called *Labour and the New Social Order.* This included some sections very much following pre-war assumptions, including an argument for nationalisation because private ownership involved a 'perpetual private mortgage on the annual product of the nation'. But beyond this, and marking a new departure, was a case for public ownership based on the inefficiency of the private sector. Webb put this as follows:

> the Labour Party refuses absolutely to believe that the British people will permanently tolerate any reconstruction or perpetuation of the disorganisation, waste and inefficiency involved in the abandonment of British industry to a jostling crowd of separate private employers. ... What the nation needs is undoubtedly a great bound onward in its aggregate productivity. But this cannot be secured merely by pressing the manual workers to more strenuous toil, or even by encouraging the Captains of Industry to a less wasteful organisation of their several enterprises on a profit-making basis. What the Labour Party looks to is a genuinely scientific reorganisation of the nation's industry no longer deflected by individual profiteering, on the basis of Common Ownership of the Means of Production.[43]

This emphasis on the pursuit of efficiency as a basis for nationalisation was carried over into particular cases. For example, the advocacy of railway and electricity nationalisation was related to the importance of efficiency in these industries for the economy as a whole, and the obstacle presented by private ownership to the realisation of the economies of scale available in each of the two cases.[44]

In sum, the war had significantly shifted Labour's approach to the economy. It had increased belief in the efficacy of government planning, as Oldfield emphasises. Conversely, it had reduced the evolutionist faith in general, and especially in relation to industry. Nationalisation was nothing new, but the grounds for its advocacy had significantly shifted, and was coupled to a new 'productionist' emphasis in Labour thinking. At the June 1918 Labour Party conference, Ramsay Macdonald put forward what seems to have been the first ever resolution calling for increased production as a priority. This was amended, not to deny the objective but to stress that it was acceptable only in the context of public ownership.[45]

How did this position develop between 1920 and 1939? Most discussion of Labour's economic policies during these years has been dominated by questions about the party's resistance to adopting whole-hearted Keynesianism as a response to the mass unemployment of the period.[46] During the post-1945 boom, which was assumed to have been caused by the adoption of such Keynesianism, it was perhaps natural to assume that this might well have been the path to solving the inter-war slump. More recent work has distanced itself a little from such perspectives, though still tending to focus on macroeconomic rather than industrial policy.[47]

Unemployment did dominate Labour's economic agenda in the

interwar period, but overall the record of policy ideas from the party on this issue is not an impressive one. Skidelsky's suggestion that there was an 'obvious' solution, which only Labour's combination of Utopian rhetoric and practical conservatism obscured, requires substantial qualification.[48] But his point that the Labour Party, especially in the 1920s, was not geared up to formulate a plausible reformist strategy for economic management is surely right. Labour's continued adherence to pre-1914 radical internationalism, involving support for free trade, the gold standard and financial conservatism, was not a framework likely to produce the necessary re-orientation of British economic policy. Equally the leadership of the Labour Party desired neither to overthrow capitalism nor to lose its claims to political responsibility by adopting unorthodox economic doctrine.[49]

The orthodoxy of the Labour Party was challenged by elements within it. Most importantly, the Independent Labour Party in the 1920s continued to produce impressive initiatives on unemployment. The most detailed of these was the 1925 *Revolution by Reason*, which embodied neo-Keynesian proposals for an expansion of demand via a nationalised banking system coupled to a floating exchange rate. The following year another group of ILP members published *The Living Wage*, which drew much on J.A. Hobson's underconsumptionist theories to argue for a minimum wage and large-scale redistribution of income via steeply progressive taxation. Such views were widely debated on the Left, and restated in a weaker form by Oswald Mosley in his famous memorandum of 1930. But their impact on official Labour policy, whether the party was in or out of government, remained minimal.[50]

During Labour's first period in office in 1924 the watchwords were financial orthodoxy and general economic caution. Labour still looked to the revival of the international economy as the only sure way of guaranteeing trade regeneration and a fall in unemployment.[51] But the concern with unemployment was also reflected in Labour's approach to industry. Whilst carefully eschewing any strong commitment to nationalisation in its 1923 Election manifesto, in government Labour did revive the idea of much greater expenditure on and standardisation of electricity generation, with many arguing that this could be secured only by nationalisation. Nothing directly came of this during the period of office, though it gave impetus to the pressures which eventually led to the creation of the Central Electricity Board in 1926. Here was a classic case where private enterprise seemed simply incapable of achieving the potential economies of scale, and where a technical and non-political case for nationalisation could have wide appeal.[52]

Labour's approach to industry also developed in the context of the debates about rationalisation during the late 1920s. One way of viewing these debates is as signalling a loss of faith in the revival of trade as the only real remedy for unemployment, and a desire to see greater industrial efficiency as a way of expanding Britain's markets.

Before the election of the second Labour Government in 1929 enthusiasm for rationalisation was more apparent in the Trades Union Congress (TUC) than in the Labour Party. For example, in Labour's 1928 statement of policy, *Labour and the Nation*, rationalisation was urged as a solution to 'the waste and inefficiency of private ownership in industries which, whether called private or not, are essentially public in character'. But beyond this rhetoric there was little in the way of practical policy proposals, and the extent of the government's role in efficiency remained, to say the least, obscured by the statement that 'employers . . . will be well advised to begin by setting their own house in order, to modernise their organisation, improve their technique, eliminate waste, and apply more intelligently the resources which science has revealed'.[53]

Labour's reply to Lloyd George's *We Can Conquer Unemployment* in 1929 argued that unemployment necessitated 'drastic reorganisation' of the staple export sectors, but it also recognised that unemployment was being caused by rationalisation of other industries. The potential difficulty in advocating a policy which was at once both apparently a cause of, and a panacea for, unemployment was not, however, addressed. Rather, there was just a broad statement emphasising the need for the state to be involved in the necessary industrial reorganisation, 'not by uniform measures applied to them all, but by a variety of steps designed to eliminate waste and wasteful competition, to improve and co-ordinate methods of marketing, purchase of materials, and production, and to adapt business structure to the changed economic conditions of the post-war world'.[54]

The TUC involvement in the debate over rationalisation came about essentially because of its involvement in the Mond–Turner talks, which flowed from a general desire on both sides of industry to move on from the conflict of 1926 and seek a more consensual pattern of industrial relations (Mond was the head of ICI, Turner a Trade Union leader and the TUC president in 1927). A major incentive to talk here was the issue of rationalisation. The employers involved mainly represented 'progressive' firms which wanted to rationalise but were worried about union opposition. On the union side there was a significant fear that rationalisation would go ahead without them and at their cost.[55] Initially the talks achieved some success, with the participants outlining an agreement which included a 'deal' on rationalisation, where the unions would offer to assist the process if they were given a role in designing it. But this agreement ultimately came to nothing, essentially because of opposition from many employers to giving unions an enhanced role either in wage negotiation or, even more, in discussing firms' policies.[56] Nevertheless, it is significant that the unions, as distinct from the Labour Party at this stage, were willing to countenance substantial industrial reorganisation as a way of trying to restore the fortunes of British industry.

The 1929–31 Labour Government is chiefly remembered for its failure to deal with the unemployment problem, and for its ignominious collapse in the face of the counter-claims of financial 'prudence' and the living standards of the unemployed.[57] Reasonably enough, perhaps, these events have obscured other aspects of the economic policy pursued by the Government. In particular it is important to recognise that the Government did attempt to raise efficiency in both the public and private sectors. In the former case, the major monument that was created was the London Passenger Transport Board (LPTB) which, like the CEB, reflected the view that private competition was inefficient and that significant economies of scale could be achieved by an amalgamation under public ownership.[58] The LPTB owed much to Herbert Morrison, whose work on it reflected what were to become the dominant themes in Labour's nationalisation programmes of the 1930s and 1940s. The Morrisonian corporation, as it came to be called, would be largely autonomous of government, run by experts, and bereft of workers in any direct managerial role. This was a model which was grounded on a technocratic belief in the efficacy of large-scale administration and an ethos of public service. In economic terms it represented the belief that efficiency sprang largely from a combination of economies of scale and technical expertise, though Morrison himself also held that public ownership would unleash an enthusiasm for production from the workers.[59]

A similar set of ideas underlay the Labour Government's support for the rationalisation of coal. Here the 'rationalisation' of forced amalgamations with consequent increases in unemployment clashed with the 'rationalisation' of allowing the industry to create a cartel and hoping this would protect output and jobs.[60] As noted above, the outcome was an amalgamation of both approaches, but one which essentially emphasised the protection of the industry against competitive pressures.

Rationalisation figured quite largely in the rhetoric of the 1929–31 Government, but the obvious difficulty with such an approach, given the unemployment prevailing, was that it had to be an essentially long-run measure. In the short-run rationalisation could only exacerbate unemployment, and such a prospect was hardly attractive as the unemployed grew month by month in 1930 and 1931. But apart from this compelling short-run political problem, Labour did little to involve itself actively in policies of rationalisation except in the coal industry. By and large it abdicated its role to the Bank of England whose priorities remained essentially financial rather than those connected with industrial modernisation.[61]

Labour was out of power from August 1931 until the Second World War. Its impact on economic and other policy areas in the 1930s was minimal, perhaps less than might have been the case even given the lack of a parliamentary majority.[62] This long absence from power led to a major shift in thinking amongst many Labour supporters, and to some degree this was reflected in the Party's programmatic development.

One area of change involved the Morrisonian corporation. After fierce debates in the early years of the decade this became unchallenged as Labour's approach to public ownership.[63] The model outlined here was linked to a clear identification of priorities as regards the sectors to be nationalised, creating a 'shopping list' which was close to the industries actually taken over in 1945–51.[64] In the current context what is striking about the discussion of nationalisation in this period is the emphasis on efficiency. In the key document, *For Socialism and Peace*, the case for public ownership is grounded on the fact that it was to enable industrial reorganisation to take place. 'Reorganisation from the point of view of productive efficiency' was in turn to aim at six objectives:

(a) The introduction of efficient methods of production;
(b) The organised purchase of raw materials;
(c) The establishment of effective selling agencies;
(d) The elimination of all unnecessary charges;
(e) Reasonable wages and conditions for the producers;
(f) Reasonable prices for the consumers.[65]

Booth and Pack[66] are critical of this focus on efficiency, as inappropriate to the immediate unemployment problem, but nevertheless it does demonstrate the extent to which nationalisation was seen as a pragmatic, quasi-technical response to the failings of the private sector, rather than as an 'ideological' objective linked to control over industry. Finally, *For*

Socialism and Peace can be seen to have accepted that the need for reorganisation went beyond those industries that were likely to come quickly into the public sector, and there was some talk of the need to 'enforce' such a policy. But no details of what this might involve were given.[67] Here, perhaps, we can see the development of an attitude that the private sector need not be seriously addressed as in need of reform because nationalisation would *eventually* be appropriate for almost all industries – though this remained implicit in Labour's discussions rather than explicit.

Amongst Labour's economic intelligentsia, three strands of opinion became evident in the 1930s. Many of the party's thinkers became converted to versions of Keynesianism, which gave a priority to demand management in economic policy, but they also argued for significant measures of nationalisation in the name of efficiency where there existed natural monopoly. The most important of such thinkers was James Meade.[68] A second group, including G.D.H. Cole, were not hostile to Keynesianism but were keen to distinguish it from socialism, and to assert the *political* importance of social ownership. They tended also to make planning a central feature of their socialism, though the content of this planning was ill-defined.[69] Finally there were those, especially Evan Durbin, who were much keener on the orthodox tools of economic analysis than Cole and his supporters, but who were sceptical of Keynesianism. Above all, they saw the key socialist objective as equality and believed that economic policies should be subordinated to such inescapably *political* objectives.[70]

All of these approaches were influential when Labour came to address seriously economic policy issues from inside government during the 1940s. They represented a major step forward in the sophistication of Labour's economic thinking. But this had its limits. Broadly speaking, economics as a discipline focuses its attention on the efficiency of resource allocation, not the efficiency of production. Labour's economists of the 1930s tended to accept this traditional demarcation: hence, for example, the discussion on the need to nationalise natural monopolies, which hinged on the argument that in such industries the realisation of economies of scale led to monopolistic units and the misallocation of resources; hence, too, the discussion on the applicability of marginal cost pricing rules to public sector industries.[71]

The point about these debates is not that they were irrelevant, but that they largely 'crowded-out' thinking about the determinants of productive efficiency. Indeed, they rested on the orthodox economists' usual assumption, that productive efficiency will be assured as long as firms have to compete. In terms of Labour's priorities, the economists tended to have the effect of switching attention away from the examination of how efficiency is attained, except in so far as this was linked to the existence of competition or monopoly.

To a degree the new economic thinking of the 1930s was in fact compatible with the 'old' emphasis on public ownership. Most of the industries that were listed as to be nationalised in *For Socialism and Peace* could be characterised as natural monopolies or as sectors having other characteristics which limited competition. Hence quite orthodox economic arguments might be advanced for their nationalisation, though this necessarily contradicted the idea that beyond this list the scope of nationalisation was more or less unlimited.[72]

Some escaped this framework. In particular Durbin, despite a great attachment to economic orthodoxy, appears to have set the agenda of efficiency in much wider terms. He saw that agenda embracing issues of motivation, training, personnel selection, production organisation, forms of accountancy, and investment levels.[73] In this way he may be seen as at least recognising many of the issues which were to come to the fore in the 1940s.

This survey, in conclusion, allows two major observations about the broad position prior to 1939. It is apparent, firstly, that industrial modernisation and efficiency had never been the primary goal of any British government before this date. Equally, it is quite clear that Labour had been by no means indifferent to such issues, contrary to those accounts which characterise the party as having been only ever interested in distributive questions.[74] Labour did not have, of course, well developed plans, only some fairly general ideas; but the important point is that it had generated at least an aspiration to intervene at a micro level in the economy.

The aim of this book is to explain what happened after 1939, and in particular how the whole efficiency issue was handled when Labour was in power between 1945 and 1951. There is already a body of literature on this subject and it will be as well to conclude this introduction by reviewing what others have argued, in order to indicate how the following text differs from the existing interpretations.

Historians, it should be noted at once, have not judged the Attlee Governments' policies on industrial modernisation very highly. Labour, the consensus would have it, came to office essentially determined to pursue welfare reform, an object that shaped macroeconomic policies and fuelled the nationalisation programme. Trading and financial difficulties subsequently necessitated a closer relationship with the private sector, but there was little attempt by the Government to force reform here or to pursue modernisation because of the overwhelming need to obtain exports at all costs. Industrial policy as a whole thus remained, as even the otherwise sympathetic Morgan has to admit, 'half-hearted, indirect, and in many ways unsuccessful'.[75] What makes this particularly irritating for many is that, as they claim, it all could and indeed should have been so very different. The 'audit of war' had revealed, to anyone willing to see, the true extent of Britain's industrial weakness. Labour, at least early on, had distinct advantages, inheriting a coherent set of wartime controls, and basking in an unprecedented degree of political superiority both inside and outside Parliament. Intervention, perhaps on the French model, to induce the kinds of technical and managerial innovation that were needed to arrest Britain's long-term economic decline, seemed a real option. As it was, the possibilities were not even explored, largely, the argument runs, because of Labour's hazy thinking on industrial subjects and general lack of political will. In Marquand's words, which find echo in the works of historians as diverse as Miliband, Middlemas and Barnett, 'the chance for a radical reconstruction of the supply side of the economy was lost'.[76]

This looks, at first sight, to be a highly impressive case, but on closer examination much of it turns out to be assertion rather than real argument. Many historians have been interested in the Attlee Governments, but most have concentrated on welfare reforms or foreign policy, for example, at the expense of any real consideration of industrial issues. Those who do examine economic policy and performance generally adopt a macro perspective.[77] As a result, whole areas of government activity have tended to remain unexamined, largely imagined rather than established. A measure of the bias that exists here is the confusion to be found in many accounts about even the more obvious of Labour's initiatives on industry. The creation of the British Institute of Management was an important achievement of these years by any standards, yet it is largely ignored in almost all of the literature.[78] Lack of precision also clouds evaluations of Cripps's Working Parties, with one prominent authority confusing these with the very different Development Councils.[79]

In fact, a detailed and rigorous review of the evidence shows that many historians have simply got it wrong. The Attlee Governments *were* very interested in industrial modernisation and *did* develop appropriate policies to pursue this goal. There is room for legitimate argument about what this package achieved, and it seems very likely that gains were not as great as was expected. However, blame for any relative failure cannot simply be placed with Labour. In fact, as this book will show, the blunting of industrial modernisation policies occurred largely at the hands of British industrialists themselves.

It remains only to indicate how the argument that follows will unfold. The starting point is the production crisis of 1941–2, when Labour, having entered the Coalition, found itself involved in the battle to raise output for the war effort (Chapter 2). This episode, and the industrial deficiencies that it revealed, led to the whole issue of industrial efficiency being opened up in an unprecedented way. A particular focus was on the quality of British management, but towards the war's end almost every facet of industry was discussed in depth, with each of the interested parties formulating policies for the peace (Chapter 3).

Once the Labour Government was in power the opportunity and the strong incentive to devise a strategy were present, and 1945–7 saw the development of a wide range of initiatives and policies (Chapter 4). In the later years of the Government three broad areas emerged as especially important in the battle to ameliorate efficiency. Good 'human relations' at the workplace were seen as vital because of the belief that the coming of full employment meant a new era in the labour market, and because the shortage of investment meant that 'the human factor' appeared to be one of the most obvious short-run routes to increased productivity (Chapter 5). Management efficiency, raised as a problem in the early 1940s, was also regarded as crucial in this period (Chapter 6). Finally, the coming of the Anglo-American Council on Productivity promoted the whole issue of the relevance and applicability of American models of industrial organisation to Britain (Chapter 7).

Industrial efficiency is an enormous and complex issue. It is almost impossible to give an exhaustive list of the factors which may affect it. This book does not pretend to cover every aspect of the issue as it presented itself in the 1940s. Rather, the focus is on the most important areas of ideas and policies as they impacted upon manufacturing industry, importance being measured by the weight of activity but also by the influence of Labour's approaches on the evolution of the economy. To a significant extent Labour made itself into a 'party of industrial modernisation' over this period, and this represented a major shift. The conclusion (Chapter 8) therefore attempts to assess both the political and economic significance of what had happened.

Chapter 2

The production crisis, productivity, and the rise of the management question, 1941–4

In 1941–2, Britain was rocked not just by military reverses abroad but also by a production crisis at home, as deliveries of armaments and munitions consistently failed to reach what were considered reasonable targets. The Government sought to cope with this latter situation in the first instance through a range of organisational and legislative measures, geared to maximising resources in the required sectors. At the same time, there was a growing official concern with the question of productivity. It was recognised that, once the economy was fully mobilised for war production, further growth in outputs would be possible only by the rationalisation and streamlining of manufacturing processes. This chapter examines the logic that dictated a productivity focus, and then looks at how the Government responded to the challenge of stimulating intensive growth in the period to the end of 1943. A final section summarises a debate that emerged fully over the following year, concerning the future of industrial management. It asks why discussion of this variable increasingly came to dominate the whole productivity question.

During the early years of the war, those at work in Britain's factories were encouraged to believe that they were playing a crucial role in ensuring the nation's survival. As Douglas Jay expressed it on the BBC, behind 'the Battles of France, and Britain, and Greece, and Iraq', the sudden and short-lived military flare-ups, was 'The Battle for Production . . . going on all the time, by day and night'. Without victory here, the situation would indeed be bleak.[1]

Yet it was also increasingly clear that in this home front engagement things were not going well. In January 1941, 62 per cent answered with a negative when Gallup asked, 'Do you think all is being done that can be done to increase war production in this country?'[2] In July, *The Economist* bluntly concluded that war output was 'chronically insufficient'. A few weeks later, it returned to this theme, arguing that 'Notwithstanding the remarkable results which have been achieved in the face of many difficulties, production . . . is not as high as it might be. Every test reveals deficiencies which can be remedied.'[3]

By the beginning of 1942, *The Times*, too, was becoming anxious, with a widely reported leader backing 'competent judges' who assessed Britain's output of arms as 40 per cent below the amount possible. It could not be denied, the paper declared, that 'the ever broadening stream [of war production] . . . flows less strongly and widens less quickly than it could and should do'.[4]

Over the following months, this theme both dominated press discussion and acquired a sharp polemical tone, as Mass Observation succinctly reported:

> All is not well in our war-production at present. *Something* is seriously wrong somewhere. Different people point the accusing finger at different wrong points and potential strong points. The amount of pointing, especially in all types of printed matter, adds up to a veritable forest of inked fingers.[5]

Some targets for blame seemed essentially to be dictated by political prejudice. Diehards of the Right were obsessed with the supposed defects of the labour force: there was widespread 'deliberate slacking, deliberate idleness and shameless agitations for higher wages', at the very time when the 'flower of our land' had been 'mown down at two shillings a day in Crete and elsewhere through lack of arms'.[6] For the Left, Capital was the obstructive vested interest. 'All too frequently', one investigative journalist contended, 'the needs of total war and the interests of influential sections of the community do not coincide.'[7]

On the other hand, there was also a strong strand of technical criticism, which took existing patterns of ownership and control as largely given, but suggested that within them much better results could be achieved. One problem, for this lobby, was the Government's organisation of procurement. All too often, specifications were changed needlessly or orders not matched to the actual capacities of firms.[8] Yet improving this situation alone would not, it was asserted, solve the problem. Another obstruction to efficiency lay, all too often, within the firm, in out-dated attitudes and practices. The Select Committee on National Expenditure was particularly vocal in making this point, arguing in one much reported enquiry, for example, that: 'Management is one of the most important factors affecting output. The evidence shows that idling is frequently due to bad management or want of supervision.' *The Economist* concurred here, believing that the course of events in 1941–2 had 'proved' that good management was 'the scarcest of all factors of production'.[9]

The Government's eventual reaction to this welter of criticism centred, in the first instance, on organisational and administrative measures, with a new Ministry of Production, created in February 1942, being perhaps the key innovation.[10] Nevertheless, members of the Cabinet recognised that, as some of their critics were arguing, this type of action alone would not be enough. The administration's first responsibility, certainly, was to fashion a system which could mobilise resources for war production as fully and as efficiently as possible. Mistakes had been made over this in the early years of the hostilities, which were now being rectified by the various reforms enacted. Yet once this process was completed, and Britain's manufacturing industry was on a total war footing, it would still be necessary to keep on increasing output if the strategic plans of the military were to be fulfilled. Extra capacity could hardly be brought in from abroad. Nor could further resources be switched from home consumption, as civilians were already judged to have made enormous sacrifices.[11] The only hope, therefore, as Ministers gradually recognised, lay in improving productivity: more would have to be obtained from each unit employed. Cripps, the new Minister of Aircraft Production, and perhaps the keenest Cabinet advocate of industrial efficiency, described the logic behind this conclusion during a broadcast at Christmas 1942:

> We have now reached the time when the inflow of fresh labour to our aircraft industry will gradually dry up and yet we must continue to expand our production so as to expedite our victory. How are we to do it? Not by longer hours; that only leads to exhaustion and inefficiency. . . . No, we must improve our methods and cut out all waste of labour – and, let me say, of materials too.[12]

The task must increasingly be, in *The Economist*'s paraphrase of official thinking, 'to extract the last ounce from the resources already harnessed in the war factories'.[13] Accordingly, Ministers of production departments began to spend more and more time attempting to ensure that this was done.

Of course, consciousness of the productivity issue in relation to the war effort had always been present to some extent since the rearmament programme of the late 1930s, and a number of schemes to promote efficiency were already in existence. Thus, the Ministry of Labour had long encouraged the appointment of personnel officers in munitions factories, and had in fact made grants available so that suitable candidates could receive the required training in this field at various universities.[14] The same Ministry's welfare schemes – providing doctors and canteens at the works – were also designed, ultimately, to make labour more efficient.[15]

However, from mid-1942, the drive for productivity was very much transformed, in both scale and content. The watchword of efficiency now became accepted as of great importance in most production departments. At the same time, there was a growing awareness that the greatest gains would be made only if the scope of official initiative were broadened. Training schemes, such as those already established, were clearly important. But there was also a need for more direct intervention, to ensure, for example, that individual firms' production processes were as well organised as was possible. All of this added up to a significant departure in government–industry relations.

One indication of the changed atmosphere was the progress that was made with establishing Joint Production Committees (JPCs).[16] The idea of expanding local consultative machinery to advise on matters relating to production had been extensively discussed during 1941, with attitudes ranging from the enthusiastic (Communist shop stewards) to the downright hostile (many employers). Bevin was sympathetic, but the Government as a whole remained cautious, anxious to maintain consensus in the face of boardroom antipathy and trade union leadership unease. By the end of the following year, however, the situation had been almost entirely transformed. In February 1942 the Ministry of Supply approved the setting-up of JPCs in the Royal Ordnance Factories. The following month an agreement between the Engineering Employers' Federation and the unions provided for the creation of JPCs in engineering establishments with over 150 workers. Subsequently, similar arrangements were concluded in shipbuilding and iron and steel, so that by December 1942 there were over 2,000 JPCs in existence, covering plants employing some two million workers. In each case, the motivations of the different parties involved were, of course, often different: some union activists saw the JPCs as a way of increasing industrial democracy, while some employers were more impressed by their potential for containing and disarming discontent. Yet what excited the Government, and ultimately proved decisive, was the contribution that the local committees might make to improving productivity. Cripps was the most enthusiastic proponent of JPCs in the Cabinet, but his observation that 'in a happy factory where there is good co-operation there is also efficient production'[17] was broadly shared by the majority of his Ministerial colleagues.

However, if the JPCs represented the most visible side of the new official concern, equally important innovations were occurring in less publicised areas, as various Whitehall departments sought to galvanise private industry into more efficient methods. The new Ministry of Production, for example, was from the first very much concerned with promoting best practice and by the end of 1943 had constructed a network of committees, panels and agencies to achieve this end. One initiative involved the creation of an expert advisory service in each region, which could be consulted by client firms and was qualified to offer information on, amongst other things, 'production layout and method, casting, designing, planning, rate-fixing, machine loading, office organisation, inspection and general administrative and financial problems'.[18] Another scheme, the Mutual Aid by Technical Experts or MATE facility, was aimed at getting efficient firms to share their knowledge as widely as possible. Panels of experts were recruited from the larger companies and then used, like a fire-brigade, to help smaller employers in difficulty.[19] At the same time, the Ministry also reserved the right to make its own investigations where it felt that this would be helpful. A special Industrial Panel, consisting of employers and trade unionists alongside the civil servants, was created for this purpose.[20]

Meanwhile, productivity consciousness was also transforming more mundane aspects of the Ministry's operations. Typical here were a number of innovations on standardisation, such as a case involving welding equipment of 1943:

> the Directorate of Industrial Electrical Equipment of the Machine Tool Control found that one of the principal obstacles to the rapid expansion of welding – a conspicuous saver of labour – in shipbuilding and repairing and in tank production was the lack of standardisation of welding plant, components, plugs, sockets, etc. In co-operation with the Admiralty and the BSI [British Standards Institute] the Directorate worked out British Standard 1071:1943, which covers the complete range of multi-operator A.C. welding equipment from the incoming supply of current to the electrode holder. As no user can obtain new welding equipment without a purchase certificate from the Control, and as a certificate will normally be issued only for the purchase of standard equipment, the result will be that modern high-speed high-voltage welding will quickly become universal in all work for which it is appropriate.[21]

Alongside the Ministry of Production, the Ministry of Aircraft Production (MAP) was also very active over the productivity issue, particularly after Cripps had taken over control of its operations at the end of November 1942. Especially noteworthy here were the contributions made by the Production Efficiency Board (PEB) and the Technical Costs Branch (TCB).

The PEB was created by Cripps in the month of his appointment and consisted essentially of four key figures – Sir C. Bruce-Gardner (the Chairman of the Society of British Aircraft Constructors), F.E. Chappell (an Amalgamated Union of Engineering Workers [AEU] official), A.G. Shaw (one of the country's leading experts in personnel management and motion study) and Sir J. Buchanan (a secretary from within the Ministry) – plus back-up staff.[22] The Minister's idea was that the PEB should deal with production efficiency in both its capital and labour aspects. It would serve as 'a small, highly qualified advisory body to carry out investigations in the field, as distinct from the usual administrative work of the headquarters and regional staff of the Ministry'[23] and would report direct to the top.

In fact, the PEB came quite quickly to be regarded as an outstanding success. One substantial achievement was the fillip it gave to personnel management, through, for example, specially sponsored courses at universities. At the same time, the PEB fulfilled its brief to carry out various detailed investigations of its own, which led to improvements in areas such as methods of machining and salvage of scrapped work. Finally, there was also a strong effort made to popularise motion study. Shaw had worked for Metropolitan–Vickers, a pioneer in this area, and she and Cripps persuaded that organisation to lend teaching staff and premises in order to train nominees from various other aircraft factories. The result was a number of courses from 1943 onwards which did much to popularise this relatively new form of work study.

The TCB had originally been part of the Admiralty, being transferred to MAP and then greatly expanded at the beginning of the war.[24] By 1943 a considerable number of specialists were involved: 'rate-fixers, planning engineers, time and motion study experts . . . as well as 100 cost accountants and clerks'.[25] The unit's central function was to measure costs accurately in order to fix suitable contract prices, but this inevitably led to a concern with efficiency. In fact, rather as with the PEB, the TCB soon began to be called in whenever MAP or other Ministries sensed that firms were performing below an acceptable standard, in order to recommend realistic solutions. One of the principal officers involved described how the TCB operated as follows:

> The firms chosen for investigation are visited by trained rate-fixers who study the processes in the factory and spot the particular weaknesses in the system. These may be due to factors beyond the control of individual workers, such as faulty operational lay-out or uneven supply of materials, or they may be due to a poor level of output on the part of the workers, sometimes caused by bad rate-fixing. . . . In this way it is possible for the investigator to demonstrate not only to the management of a factory but to the Production Committee as well, the exact cause of the high labour cost of the work in question, and to obtain their agreement to the measures necessary to reduce this cost.[26]

How big, therefore, had the Government's machinery for improving industrial productivity become by the end of 1943? This is not an easy question to answer for a number of reasons. There is, firstly, the question of definition, of deciding which civil servants and advisers were acting primarily to an efficiency brief. The Ministry of Labour's 800 Labour Supply Inspectors were initially concerned solely with 'forwarding dilution' but, as the war progressed, some spent more and more time on the wider aspects of labour utilisation, which clearly contributed to the drive for productivity. Unfortunately it is impossible to evaluate in any more detail what this may have contributed to the overall equation.[27] At the same time, it is clear that the key agencies which were charged with pursuing productivity were sometimes actually weaker than they formally appeared. One continual problem for all of the institutions involved was how to recruit sufficient qualified staff. Industry itself had been an important source in the early years of the war but, by 1943, this option no longer existed. The end-product was that some parts of the Government apparatus often struggled to cope. It was noted of the TCB in early 1944, for example, that: 'Its studies tend to be retrospective (i.e. made after contracts have actually been placed) and are now heavily in arrears. This is due to lack of staff.'[28]

Nor, finally, can Government estimates of the forces being deployed do very much to clarify the issues at stake here. The following reply to an enquiry about the scale of MAP's activities on productivity is typical in its vagueness:

> I am afraid that we cannot give you even a guess at the full cost of the steps taken . . . to improve efficiency of firms . . . [.] . . . the costs of the specialist services represent only a fraction of the total. For what the figures are worth, you may like to know that PEB salaries . . . amount to £9,000 per annum. . . . The Technical Costs Branch costs in salaries about £240,000 per annum.[29]

Nevertheless, accepting these various qualifications, it is clear that, by late 1943, the Government-created apparatus to improve efficiency had reached quite impressive proportions. Thus, the JPC network was largely flourishing, as the figures in Table 2.1 illustrate. Moreover, the situation within Ministries had been substantially transformed. Departments reacted to the productivity drive with varying degrees of enthusiasm, but all accepted the goal of promoting efficiency, and some had shown themselves prepared to pursue it with some persistence. Nowhere was the new spirit more in evidence than at MAP. Indeed, as one civil servant noted, 'the activities of most branches' of this Ministry were aimed 'in greater or less degree . . . at improving industrial efficiency'.[30] Some idea of the scale of what was involved here can be gained from the fact that the PEB alone had advised nearly 300 factories by the end of its first year of full operation.[31]

Reviewing the progress that was made obviously gave advocates of the productivity drive considerable pleasure, but it also provoked several questions. By late 1943, it was clear that Britain would be on the winning side of the war, whether victory came sooner or later. What lessons could be drawn from the productivity policy being pursued, especially in terms of the future, post-war relationship between Government and industry?

In attempting to answer this question, civil servants recognised, first of all, that the record proved that government intervention could make a positive difference. Some experiments, of course, had failed. Thus, the Munitions Management and Labour Efficiency Committee, set up in late 1942 to 'put into effect measures for increasing the productive efficiency of the munitions industry', seemed to have been almost

Table 2.1 Joint Production Committees at establishments in engineering and allied industries, 1942–4

Date covered	*Total no. of JPCs*	*Total no. of JPCs in firms with 150+ workers*	*Total no. of workers*
Dec. 1942	2,644	2,037	1,914,000
Dec. 1943	4,427	2,843	2,676,000
June 1944	4,567	2,959	2,666,000

Source: BT 171/210 'Origin of Joint Production Committees', p. 3, enclosed with Note by G. Calder, 13/5/1946.

wholly ineffective, a consequence both of its unwieldy constitution and of its lack of influence in supply departments.[32] However, against this, many other initiatives could be justifiably regarded as considerable successes.

Comment on the JPCs, for example, had been on the whole quite positive. An AEU enquiry of 1943 noted that the smooth running of the consultative machinery was not universal, but ended with a generally very favourable conclusion: 'the committees have fully justified their existence and have proved themselves a factor of incalculable value in the war effort.'[33] *Business* journal was also enthusiastic about what had been achieved. A survey during the winter of 1942–3 led it to conclude that the JPCs were a 'success' and had 'come to stay'. In June 1943 a more detailed investigation into employer attitudes towards the committees was equally positive. *Business* now found that, though some owners of medium-sized firms continued to regard JPCs with suspicion, the vast majority of both big and small employers were a good deal more favourable. Moreover, it was generally felt that JPCs were valuable in the pursuit of productivity: when asked by the journal whether their own committee had 'contributed towards increasing efficiency and production', no less than 70 per cent of the employers questioned had answered in the affirmative.[34]

More direct kinds of intervention also seemed to have yielded important results. MAP staff kept close track of those who had attended motion study training courses and generally found that they had produced significant innovations on return to their respective factories. The increases in output per employer that resulted were variable, according to the type of job and the efficiency of previous methods, but there was usually considerable progress:

> The average increase in output of the jobs studied . . . was 140 per cent, the lowest figure being 30 per cent and the highest 800 per cent. This latter result was rather exceptional, though there were two jobs . . . which were about this figure.[35]

TCB staff, too, could point to a range of successful investigations, in which cost data had been used to break price cartels or as leverage in improving the performance of less efficient units.[36]

On top of this, it was impossible to ignore some less tangible benefits that had flowed from the overall policy. An example was the situation with personnel officers. Relatively few companies employed such staff in the 1930s, but during the war numbers increased substantially, encouraged (as has been noted) by the joint efforts of various Ministries.

By 1943, indeed, it was estimated that there were around 5,700 personnel officers working in factories with 250 or more employees – probably a fourfold increase on pre-war days. Yet the change involved here was more than just a question of numbers. There had also been appreciable improvements in the whole way in which the profession saw itself and was seen by others. As one authority put it in 1944:

> In spite of the fact that industry as a whole failed to grasp and apply these essential principles [of personnel management] in the early days of the war, there has since been a notable development both in the quality of personnel management and in the extent to which it is practised. . . . The experience of the last five years has shown that industry will emerge from the present war with a greater appreciation of the value of personnel work, and a higher level of technical application than ever before.[37]

However, if officials could be reasonably pleased with the progress that had resulted from some of the productivity initiatives, they had to recognise, as well, that there was little room for complacency. Close contact with industry had revealed a scale of inefficient practice amongst manufacturers that the civil servants found deeply shocking. Thus, many firms were found to have little idea about a rudimentary question such as how long it took for raw materials to move through their plants.[38] Even more seriously, few could produce even near accurate costings data. The scale of this problem was revealed during an investigation of 3,000 Ministry of Supply contractors in 1943–4. This concluded, amongst other things, that:

> (a) Comparatively few firms have efficient costing systems;
>
> . . .
>
> (d) Many small firms have no system at all;
> (e) There is an apathy towards costs by British manufacturers;
> (f) American controlled companies have costing systems far in advance of most British manufacturers, appear to be more cost-minded and use the information available to a greater extent.[39]

Clearly, as officials recognised, in analysing these kinds of finding some allowance had to be made for mitigating circumstances. Many firms had been asked to expand very fast in the early part of the war, using whatever resources, methods and locations were most easily to hand, and this had hardly encouraged streamlined working. Many contractors, too, remained short of key personnel because of the call-up, so that it was hardly surprising if, for example, accounting practices were somewhat deficient. However, accepting all of this, the civil servants concluded, did not explain away the problem. Day-to-day contact with industry and special enquiry alike revealed not just sub-optimal working but many instances where industrial efficiency could only be described as actually below what it was 'reasonable to expect'.[40] To officials, therefore, the conclusion had to be that employers themselves were often partly culpable: they were either oblivious to some productivity issues or too conservative to adopt any but very simple ameliorative measures.[41]

In the light of this, civil servants in production departments were increasingly persuaded that government initiatives on productivity could not end with the war. Britain's economic position would obviously be precarious in the early years of peace, with efficient manufacturing the condition of survival. Some employers might be able to meet this challenge unaided, but it appeared from wartime experience that many would simply have to be pressured into adaptation.

However, accepting this broad conclusion, there was still the question of what precisely should be done in practice. Officials recognised that their current successes were being obtained in a peculiarly favourable environment, where departments enjoyed both enhanced legal capabilities and the considerable leverage which went with their positions as sole purchasers. Yet this situation, it was generally assumed, would be hardly likely to outlive the war; indeed the pressure for a relaxation of controls, the moment that peace was declared, seemed to be growing with each new Allied victory. What needed to be decided, therefore, was how policy should be modified to cope with the likely, very different parameters of a peace-time society. What could the government do to encourage productivity growth once its special powers had disappeared?[42]

A variety of civil servants commented on this question, but discussion was most animated in the Board of Trade, the department at the heart of more general industrial reconstruction matters. Here some officials favoured solving the productivity question within the context of a much wider package of macroeconomic measures.[43] Others, however, argued that, though such an approach might no doubt yield benefits, overall success would not be achieved unless there were parallel interventions at a micro level, particularly over what was seen as the key question of management. The case put forward by this latter group and the policy initiatives that followed form the subject of the rest of this chapter.

The Board of Trade first began to examine the management question during the summer and autumn of 1943, as a response to growing government interest in a wide range of reconstruction problems.[44] Officials believed that, within firms, good management was the key to general efficiency. They observed, as well, that standards of management varied considerably: while some bigger companies had done much to introduce modern practices, the situation as regards 'the majority of small firms', in particular, remained deeply unsatisfactory. This meant, as one adviser put it, that the potential impact of any advance here would be considerable: 'there is more scope for improvement at this level than is generally realized'.[45] What appeared most necessary, officials concluded, was a government-backed body which could promote best practice and thus raise overall standards.[46]

To test the water on this proposal, the Board's Internal Reconstruction division decided that they should raise it with the Steering Committee on Post-War Employment, a high level body of senior officials which had been created by the Cabinet Committee on Reconstruction Priorities to adjudicate on a whole range of post-war economic policy questions.[47] After some deliberation, the Steering Committee agreed that the Board had made a good enough case to warrant it making further investigations.[48] The problem for officials was now to see how their ideas could be translated into practical recommendations.

In developing their strategy, the civil servants recognised that no real progress would be likely without the active support of industry. A new official body could not, in other words, just be foisted on manufacturers, but must be created with their consent.[49] In the light of this, the Board decided that its first move should be to consult in confidence with a variety of figures who were known to hold progressive views on the management question. How would they react to the idea of a 'Business Advice Bureau', set up and financed by the Government, which would involve itself not only in propaganda but also in research, and even in activities such as vetting the growing number of industrial consultants?[50]

The information uncovered by these enquiries was both encouraging and daunting. Those questioned agreed that management standards were often rather poor, particularly in smaller firms.[51] Moreover, it was generally accepted that Westminster should do something about this; that, as B.S. Rowntree put it, 'there was room for Government assistance in the development of scientific management in industry'.[52] The investigators even found a reasonable degree of support for their specific recommendations. L.J. Cadbury was not particularly keen on the

Business Advice Bureau (he wanted resources to be used on teaching management, especially in the provincial universities) but several other respondents emphasised the need for some central co-ordinating body.[53]

Against this, however, the Board had its attention drawn to a whole range of practical difficulties which stood in the way of any kind of intervention. It was clear, for example, that the trade unions would be somewhat suspicious of what was being proposed. A Ministry of Labour official noted that the term 'scientific management' would, at any rate, have to be avoided in discussions with the unions since it was 'associated with the worst faults of the industrial consultant'.[54] Moreover, the Board's business advisers warned that their own views were probably untypical, and that many employers might actually be hostile to the measures proposed. In part, this stemmed from the widespread belief that the less the Government had to do with industry the better.[55] But it was also reported that many employers held more specific reservations about the whole idea of improving the management function. Management, in this view, was an art and not a science, and so research and education were hardly appropriate. The end product was a general indifference to the whole question of amelioration, as the prominent industrial consultant L. Urwick reported:

> My own experience is that it is extraordinarily difficult to persuade even comparatively enlightened business people that scientific management is just as important to them as engineering or chemical or physical research. They always tend to regard it as a fad which they pursue in an amateurish sort of way and along cheap lines.[56]

In the light of all of this, the Board decided to widen its enquiry to encompass existing management organisations. If one could be found that was sufficiently influential, it might be boosted with government help into a new nucleus, thus avoiding the problems of a full-bodied intervention. Did any have the right potential?

The prospects here looked unpropitious. Most of the ten or so functional associations (the Institute of Production Engineers, the Institute of Labour Management, etc.) were very small (with between one and three thousand members) and so were impecunious and had limited impact.[57] Moreover, petty rivalry seemed to be endemic: as a Board informant put it, 'Each association was interested in its own particular branch of management and tended to be jealous lest other associations should encroach on its field.'[58] Finally, it was apparent that taken together, these organisations had most contact with big business, and much less with medium and small-sized firms.

Better prospects for the Board seemed to lie with three quasi-umbrella institutions: the Institute of Industrial Administration (IIA), Management Research Groups (MRG) and the British Management Council (BMC). However, on investigation it was clear that there were problems here too. The IIA appeared to be the most vigorous of the management organisations, having grown from 550 members in three branches at the beginning of the war to 1,400 members in 14 branches by 1943.[59] The aim of this body was to raise standards, principally by providing a well-developed system of examinations for its members to progress through, and this certainly had something in common with the spirit of the Board's own thinking. On the other hand, it could not be denied that the IIA was still rather small, with an income of only around £3,500 per annum. At the same time, the composition of its membership provoked unease. There was a sprinkling of directors in the organisation, which the Board liked, but not all that many functional managers of the highest grade, which it did not. Additionally, members tended to be drawn from a relatively narrow range of sectors – 'the munitions industries in the wider sense' – and, once again, the bigger firms. The Board could only conclude, therefore, that the IIA, though it was certainly a worthwhile organisation, would not be suitable in any wider role.

The MRG were a collection of 119 firms in eight sub-sections which ran regular meetings and some research on questions of mutual interest.[60] What made this aggregation attractive was its high level of activity and the fact that counted among its members were a number of notably progressive companies. Board officials were told, further, that the Federation of British Industries (FBI) looked on the MRG with great favour and often referred management queries to them. On the other hand, there were obvious problems with Group 1, the most prominent of the sections, and the one containing the biggest firms.[61] It was known that many Group 1 members had very good track records on management innovation and research, but close investigation revealed that few wanted this knowledge made public, a factor that dramatically diminished the usefulness of the organisation in any new project.[62] On top of this, the Group 1 Secretary, who had much influence through the MRG, proved at best uncompromising when approached by the Board. As one official recorded, dealing with him could be both complicated and vexing:

> The trouble is that he is inarticulate and exceedingly odd in his manner. Yet he has acquired a great and detailed knowledge of

> management affairs through his long association with . . . Group 1 firms. He is slightly mad, I think, but there is possibly a germ of sense in his madness.[63]

It appeared unlikely, therefore, that the MRG would fit easily into any government scheme.

This left the BMC. Yet here, again, there were problems. The BMC had been formed after the Sixth International Management Conference, held in London during 1935, in order to help to prepare the British contribution to the Seventh Conference, scheduled for New York three years later.[64] Subsequently, some useful work had been done, promoting education in management and attempting to reduce the overlap between the different management associations, especially in the regions. Activity had been suspended during the early years of the war, but it was now understood that Lord Leverhulme, always the key figure in the BMC, wanted some kind of relaunch. However, as with the other organisations, surface promise hid fundamental problems. Board enquiries revealed that the BMC had never been able to recruit many members from industry. There were doubts, too, about Lord Leverhulme, whom one leading BMC figure described as 'not a suitable person to develop a live co-ordinating body'.[65] Finally, potential difficulties seemed to surround the organisation's relationship with the FBI, which had apparently been far from uncomplicated. A Board official put the situation as follows:

> I gathered the impression . . . that the Council was backed in the first place by the FBI (closely associated in this matter with Management Research Group No. 1) because there was a degree of national and international dignity attached to it, but that the interests which were prepared to back it for this purpose were not enthusiastic about the genuine promotion of the management movement – in fact, I suspect they were anxious to prevent it becoming too strong, but the war conveniently intervened.[66]

Reviewing its enquiries, therefore, the Board recognised that it was facing a rather uncomfortable dilemma. Information gathered on management standards suggested that these were often abysmally poor. In fact there was a widespread ignorance of modern methods, especially in small firms, typified by the fact that there were 'scarcely any good British textbooks on industrial management'.[67] On the other hand, it was not easy to see what could be done to improve things. Progressive manufacturers and experts agreed that there was probably a good case to be made for some kind of state-supported Business Advice Bureau. Yet much of the rest of industry was indifferent or hostile to this idea, and that included the most important representative body, the FBI. One way out of this difficulty might have been to use an existing management movement organisation as a core for the Board's initiative, but investigation of this possibility had provided little encouragement. Most management institutions were too small and introverted; as one civil servant put it, 'there are many organisations but too little organisation . . . there is confusion (chaos might not be too strong) in a clamour of separate interests each striving for special recognition of its own subject or form of organisation.'[68] In addition, the one or two that might have formed a new nucleus had, on closer inspection, enough unattractive features to render each of them unsuitable.

One way out of this quandary would have been to drop the whole idea of any government-backed initiative on management, but civil servants recognised that this was not really an option, given the future economic difficulties which the country faced. The only possibility, therefore, was to try to maximise support for the Board's general ideas and hope that the details of any necessary policy could be worked out as things went along. Specifically, as G.L. Watkinson, the Under Secretary who had co-ordinated much of the enquiry on management expressed it, the baton would now have to be handed to Board allies. 'We have to get from outsiders', he concluded, 'a strongly backed request for action on these lines to which the Government can accede.'[69]

In the end, it was decided that the best way to achieve this would be through a high-powered independent committee, which could investigate the whole question of management in British industry and make recommendations to the President. Civil servants agreed that the best person to chair this body would be Sir Cecil Weir, a leading Business Member who had been very successful in the pre-war world of Scottish commerce.[70] Other names floated included R. Rootes, B.S. Rowntree, G. Marchand (Chairman of the IIA) and A. Loughlin of the TUC.[71] The suggestion of this latter figure provoked some controversy in the Board and, on reflection, it was agreed that her name should be withdrawn, since, though she was certainly well qualified to contribute, the employers' associations would not be represented and it was 'important to avoid a political tinge'.[72] In further deliberations with the President, it was agreed that a safety-first policy would be best all round, and so the final committee line-up featured two further Business Members (B.H. Peter and G. Cunliffe) alongside the chairman Weir.[73]

The Weir Committee began work on 29 December 1943, with the following terms of reference:

(a) To consider whether it is necessary to set up a central body to be responsible for improving the standard of management generally and to link the work of existing organisations specialising on particular aspects of management and, if so, what assistance Government should give.
(b) To consider the function of such a central body and the difficulties of organisation which may be encountered in the course of its establishment.
(c) To consider what steps could be taken to make advice on management problems available to small firms.[74]

Its first priority was to assess the main protagonists and to gather information, and over the following two months it met with 43 individuals and representatives, ranging from management consultants to official deputations from bodies such as the FBI.[75] These consultations covered essentially the same ground as the earlier Board enquiry and revealed a similar pattern of enthusiasm and doubt. Urwick once again backed an interventionist approach, arguing that 'the time had come to persuade the existing associations to sacrifice part of their identity in a central body'. But he warned that the Government's relationship with the new organisation would have to be carefully arranged; it might be a good idea to provide premises at nominal rent, but 'Treasury control resulting from financial aid should be very remote'.[76] Against this, a number of informants were markedly less enthusiastic. The highly rated Treasury O. & M. expert, I.J. Pitman, was not in favour of establishing a central body for management and argued that industry should sort out its own problems, using the accountancy profession in a new role.

> At the annual audit accountants could point out that other firms in the same industry were producing goods of equal quality at a lower price or with a smaller amount of labour. . . . He suggested that the trade organisations should collect information of interest to efficiency which should be available in confidence to accountants.[77]

Several of the industrialists interviewed also expressed doubts, almost always on the grounds of their dislike of any extension of government intervention. A representative small businessman thus emphasised that he 'did not agree with the idea that any central body which might be set up should *control* management, and saw great danger in this'. The answer, once again, was to leave industry to sort out the problem itself, on the basis that the 'art of management' was in any case 'a highly practical thing'.[78]

More seriously for Weir, the peak associations also made it clear that they were not really interested in what the Board was suggesting. R.B. Dunwoody, representing the Association of British Chambers of Commerce, told the Committee that 'he regarded the principle of government grants to be a dangerous one to establish, since so many organisations could claim to be of national importance'.[79] The FBI was equally negative. One of its representatives stated that 'his members felt that it had not yet been proved that there was a body of doctrine behind management as there was in technical subjects'. Sir Guy Locock, Director-General of the FBI, was more circumspect though in the end just as damning:

> Sir Guy said that the opinion of industry was that some instruction [in management] was needed, though there was a strong feeling that management was a subject that could only partly be taught, and it was felt that exchange of information between firms would greatly help in the right direction.

He added a personal belief that encouragement must come through some central body, but noted that 'the FBI were unable to give their views on this matter since it had not been fully considered'.[80]

Such attitudes were depressing and prompted Weir and the Board to do some stocktaking, to decide how best to proceed. A confidential memo revealed that 'staunch supporters' of the Board proposals were few and far between: the National Institute of Industrial Psychology, B.S. Rowntree, J. Ryan (an influential director of Metal Box who was active in MRG 1), L. Urwick, the IIA 'possibly' and the BMC 'possibly'.[81] The need was clearly to win over some of the doubters. It was therefore decided that Weir should hold a meeting of representatives of all of the interested associations in order 'to get their general co-operation on the project'. This occasion could be stage-managed, with some exhortatory speeches and an intervention from a trusted 'plant' on the floor rallying those present behind a suitably worded resolution. It was agreed that an ideal statement of intent should read:

> That this meeting would welcome the setting up of a central organisation, sponsored by the Government, to stimulate the development and adoption of good management practice in

> association with industry and with the existing organisations interested in management questions.[82]

The date fixed for this meeting was 9 February 1944, and invitations were issued accordingly. However, it was very soon obvious that things were not going to go as planned. Most of those invited to attend, including the TUC, responded positively, but this was not true of the employers' organisations. A National Union of Manufacturers representative told Weir that he would be unable to come, 'but would be interested to see a note of what had taken place'. The FBI, too, reacted negatively, with Locock informing Weir 'that he would be most interested to hear the outcome of the meeting next week' but that 'Unfortunately none of his members would be able to be present as they had another engagement'.[83]

All of this was something of a blow, but worse was to follow at the meeting. Weir himself opened the proceedings with a speech outlining the need for what he now termed 'the British Institute of Management'. He was followed by a number of generally positive contributors, including Lord Leverhulme, Marchand, Ryan, Urwick and Rowntree. Things seemed to be going well, and so Marchand and Ryan introduced the agreed resolution from the floor. However, this did not have the desired effect, because many of those present still felt uneasy about the degree of government intervention that seemed to be implicit in what was being proposed. One speaker suggested that the words 'sponsored by' be amended to read 'associated with', while another felt that the right formula here was 'initiated and supported by'. After some debate, those present accepted this second amendment, passing a resolution that read:

> this meeting would welcome the setting up of a central organisation, initiated and supported by Government, to stimulate the development and adoption of good management practice, in association with industry and with existing organisations interested in management questions.[84]

This outcome may have pleased some of the less progressive elements present, but it angered those who actually wanted to get the whole problem resolved. P. Lindsay, of Morgan Crucible, wrote to Weir complaining that the sole result of the meeting was a decision 'to put old wine into a new bottle'. He added, 'I presume the greater and much more vital question as to how industry is to be persuaded to partake of the wine, will be debated on another occasion.'[85] Harry Ward, closely associated with MRG 1, was even more critical. He recorded that the whole proceedings had been carried out 'in an air of *naïveté*', with the real problem being neither formulated nor remotely resolved. He appended a list of specific complaints:

> 1 There was no real representation of industry. . . . No FBI representative was there. . . . The relation of the new body to these organisations was not even realised.
> 2 No mention of trade and employers' associations was made . . .
> 3 The relation of the organisation to the Ministry of Labour, the Ministry most concerned, was not touched upon . . .
> 4 It was clear from Sir Cecil Weir's comments that he was not well briefed, and that he has no real appreciation of the job to be done.[86]

Weir himself saw the meeting as a partial setback, though in many ways an inevitable one. He had come to the conclusion that industry would only be converted to the measures proposed in the medium term. The first priority was therefore to win over the specialist management organisations; they had 'done useful work . . . and naturally they should be given an opportunity of contributing to the work of any new central body'. If the meeting had achieved nothing else, it had at least allowed this process to begin. The aim now, which the Board agreed with, was to write a report which would be sufficiently persuasive to convince the Treasury that the British Institute of Management deserved to be supported – an essential precondition if any further progress was to be made.[87]

The Weir Report on Industrial Management was forwarded to the President, Hugh Dalton, on 23 February 1944. It began from the premise that management was a crucially important function which had all too often been inadequately developed. Indeed 'some' large firms and 'many' of their smaller competitors were inclined to be 'self-satisfied' about the quality of their management.[88] This situation demanded both 'carefully planned propaganda' and 'a growing volume of information and advice' on modern management methods. Existing professional bodies had done good work in propagating ideas, but they were not up to what was now required, for a number of different reasons:

> The professional character of many of these bodies limits the extent of their propaganda and precludes the participation of the firms not large enough to employ highly specialised managers. Small firms, even if they were willing to subscribe to a sufficient number of the

> twenty or so specialist bodies to cover the range of their operations, would rarely employ managers qualified for membership. Further, the ability of the organisations to undertake research . . . is severely limited by lack of funds.[89]

The answer was to set up a new body supported at least partly by Government finance which 'would be the central stimulating force for raising the standards of management in the United Kingdom, and . . . the authoritative spokesman for British management at international conferences and discussions'. This, it was suggested, might be called the 'British Institute of Management' (BIM).[90]

Having justified this key proposal, Weir next went on to sketch out in detail what the new organisation might look like. The Committee felt that membership of the BIM should be open to everyone who could pay a modest fee, and not conditional on involvement in an existing functional association, as some of those bodies wanted.[91] As regards finance, Weir unsurprisingly came down in favour of government assistance. The success of the whole venture would only be likely if there were some large-scale activity very quickly, which a newly created organisation could hardly be expected to fund. Consequently, the Committee recommended that the Treasury be asked to make grant-in-aid of £75,000 for each of the BIM's first five years, with the hope that subscription income would be increasing all the time as the organisation established itself.[92]

Finally, Weir moved on to look at the wider aspects of the BIM's relationship with the Government. The Committee recognised that some kind of supervision from Whitehall would be necessary, to make sure that public money was being spent properly and that the organisation was evolving on the right lines. But beyond this, it was stressed, 'the Institute should be free to work out its own policy and programme'. A similar perspective informed Weir's recommendations on how the BIM should actually be run: the Minister responsible (probably the Lord President) would appoint the first 12-person governing Council, but in later years some of this body were to be provided by elections of the membership.[93]

In presenting this report, Weir did his best to convince Dalton that the management issue was now fully resolved. The specific recommendations in the document, he wrote, had been endorsed by 'a unanimous resolution at a very representative meeting of Management and other organisations'. In addition, it appeared that large sections of Whitehall were equally in favour. As Weir observed:

> We have discussed the matter with representatives of interested Government Departments, and while the officials whom we met made it clear that they would not commit their Ministers, it seems more than probable that our recommendations and the general lines of the report will be warmly supported.[94]

However, it was quite evident that many others of those who had been involved in the discussions did not share this view. Thus, opinion in departments of state remained quite divided, whatever Weir believed. The Board of Trade was, of course, behind the proposals, as were the Ministry of Labour and the Board of Education. But officials in the Ministry of Production made it clear that they were by no means necessarily sympathetic. A typical reaction came from N. Kipping, who felt that the BIM might easily be 'yet another management organisation', albeit 'one perhaps of higher quality than the others'. The real answer, in this view, was for the Government to 'stimulate the existing organisations to set up a Council themselves'.[95]

Outside Whitehall, too, doubt lingered on. The specialist management associations felt that their prestige was threatened, especially given Weir's insistence that membership of the BIM should be open to all and not just confined to accredited experts.[96] Moreover, it was an open secret that the FBI's position remained essentially unfriendly. After the completion of the Weir report, Sir Guy Locock had thought it advisable to seek the views of Sir George Beharrell from the Dunlop Rubber Company, who was the FBI's acknowledged expert on management matters. Beharrell's reply urged caution: he supported the resolution passed at the February meeting but wanted more details before making a further recommendation. It was essential, he added, 'to prevent the new Institute, if formed, from becoming the plaything of the so-called "efficiency experts"'. Furthermore, interference from Whitehall or Westminster must be sharply curtailed:

> I feel that the success of the proposal will depend on the limitation of Government interference. . . .
> If the Institute were to be run as a kind of Government Department I would not expect it to be very successful. It must be run by Industry and the sooner Industry could run it without Government help, the sooner would be its great success.[97]

Such advice was very similar to that provided by the MRG's Harry Ward, who had already urged FBI opposition to the Weir report on the basis that it was 'wrongly conceived and based on errors of judgement'.[98]

All of this left the Board of Trade in a rather difficult position. Dalton was convinced by much of the Weir argument, and in fact wanted his department to be the link with the BIM if it were formed. On the other hand, he recognised that, given the opposition, if a strong enough case were not made out for the new initiative, then the crucial element of government support – finance from the Treasury – would not be forthcoming. To avoid this outcome, Dalton decided that the Board's next move must be the collection of further information on the poor level of British management, with the emphasis on concrete examples. Only when this task was completed would the whole question be put to the Cabinet.[99]

To conclude, how did the productivity question stand at the beginning of 1944? As this chapter has shown, interest in productivity had first been stimulated by the production crisis of 1941–2. This had generated ameliorative measures and at the same time changed attitudes. Most importantly, it had encouraged the belief, at least in Government circles, that the key variable in relation to productivity was management. Without better management, it was believed, all other possible reforms would fail. The end-product was the train of initiatives which led, as has been shown, to the Weir proposals.

In all of this, the key players had been, of course, a small group of Ministers and civil servants. However, it was becoming obvious that others held views on the subject – sometimes strong views – and that these would almost certainly have to be taken into account during the reconversion period. The following chapter looks at what happened in the final year of the war, as outside interests began to play a more prominent part in influencing events.

Chapter 3

Debates and initiatives, 1944–5

Until 1944, public discussion of Britain's post-war industrial future was fairly muted.[1] During that year, however, and in the early months of 1945, this situation changed considerably, as many came to recognise the severity of the country's economic circumstances. All sides accepted that Britain would need to export well above the pre-war level once peace was declared, and that consequently home industry would have to become very much more efficient. But there was far less agreement when it came to proposing how exactly this latter objective should be attained. The Labour Party believed that Britain's plight was desperate – so stark that Morgan Phillips could declare before the 1945 election, 'We must modernise or perish'[2] – yet doubted if private enterprise alone was up to leading a recovery. The answer was for the state to become involved in industry and to force the adoption of up-to-date methods. The Conservatives, on the other hand, argued that capitalist entrepreneurs were, for the most part, more than fit to conduct the reconstruction process; the main danger was of Whitehall's bureaucrats stifling native initiative. In peacetime Britain, the Tories asserted, the state might be the servant of industry, but never its master. This chapter looks in more detail at these contrasting approaches; examines how they were received by others involved in the debate; and concludes by considering what the widening political divide meant for policy formation in the Coalition Government's final year.

It is appropriate to start with Labour thinking on production and production-related issues because, of all of the participants in the argument about Britain's industrial future at this time, it was Labour that more often than not made the running. The party's ardour here stemmed from a number of different factors. One influence was a growing understanding among its leaders and supporters that desired welfare reforms would not be possible in a bankrupt country. At a more prosaic level, there was, too, the hard experience of key figures such as Cripps, Bevin, Morrison and Dalton, Coalition Ministers who had seen Britain's industrial ills at first hand and in some detail. Out of these influences came a distinct and coherent set of policies, designed above all else to boost economic efficiency as soon as possible once the war had been won.

Labour approached the peace, of course, with a long-standing commitment to a range of social reforms. Yet its leaders recognised that the economic foundations on which welfare policies would be built had become distinctly shaky. There was, most obviously, much bomb damage, and a greater amount of war-related disruption. Moreover, a crippling lack of recent investment meant that even relatively untouched facilities often seemed dilapidated and wholly unsuited to efficient production, as Cripps reported in early 1945:

> Our factories are many of them completely out of date, and we are years behind in their equipment with . . . up-to-date machine tools and machinery of all kinds.[3]

It was clear, certainly, that Britain's trading pre-eminence had gone forever, even if Germany and Japan were temporarily removed as competitors. The country, to quote Cripps again, was 'no longer *the* workshop of the world, but merely one of many workshops'.[4]

This meant that, for Labour, economic and social objectives became more and more related and intertwined. Morrison could thus tell readers of the *Daily Herald* during May 1945:

> Social security and social reform and a permanent advance in the economic life of our people can only proceed with greater efficiency in industry, greater production and a greater national directive to national economic ends.[5]

Lord Latham made the point even more bluntly when he argued in the same paper that 'Socialism will only succeed if we make it pay in a greater national income'.[6]

In such circumstances, it was inevitable that for many in Labour's ranks the key questions were increasingly about how the desired measure of economic growth could best be engineered. One line of thinking here focused on various macro policies.[7] Nevertheless, it was also widely accepted that there would have to be micro interventions, too. Labour argued that this was inevitable because private enterprise was simply not up to the tasks at hand, whatever the wider framework: one could not gain, as Morrison put it, 'a quart of Socialist prosperity out of a miserable pint capitalist pot'.[8] The reasoning employed here was coloured partly by ideology, but mainly by experiences gained in conducting the war. Thus, at an abstract level, Labour believed that some important branches of industry were dominated by monopolists, who were essentially interested only in preserving their own bloated earnings.[9] Yet even if this argument were put on one side, the weight of evidence still came down against unregulated private enterprise. The war had revealed starkly, for example, that many small capitalists were indifferent to technical innovation. The simple fact, as Cripps, a veteran of over 500 wartime factory visits, constantly reiterated, was that the typical entrepreneurial outlook remained profoundly conservative, revealed most damagingly in a deep suspicion of 'so-called-new-fangled methods'.[10] Moreover, the existing type of employer would, it was felt, find it particularly hard to adapt to changes that were taking place in popular attitudes on the shop floor. Labour analysts believed that workers were now, largely because of the war, better educated and more confident than ever before. If full employment were achieved in the first years of peace, these characteristics would be greatly reinforced. There could be no going back, therefore, to the kinds of harsh industrial discipline prevalent in the 1930s, and new, more progressive methods would have to be tried. Again, it looked as if private enterprise, if left to itself, would be neither willing nor able to make such a change.[11]

In the light of these difficulties, Labour suggested that optimal reconstruction would only be achieved through, in Morrison's idea, a 'ladder of control'.[12] The party was determined to regulate some sectors directly, through nationalisation, and others very closely, using anti-monopoly legislation.[13] On the other hand, it accepted that these types of policy would only be feasible or applicable in a minority of cases – wholesale nationalisation, for example, was simply politically impossible, even if in fact really desirable.[14] Further down the ladder, therefore, Labour would have to develop strategies which, while respecting private ownership as a fact, nevertheless tried to move industry in a progressive direction. Given the wider resource position, such strategies could not mainly be about, for example, pumping in subsidies to aid re-tooling. Measures were needed which could boost efficiency as quickly as possible and as cheaply as possible. This inevitably meant some reliance on techniques that had been used in the war.

The package that Labour finally proposed included several different components.[15] One idea, which had first been proposed by Morrison in

March 1943,[16] was for a set of enquiries into various backward industries. These investigations would hopefully facilitate thinking about what Whitehall interventions would be most beneficial in each circumstance and in parallel contribute to the spreading of good practice, by identifying techniques used by the more efficient firms in each sector.[17] Secondly, Labour made it clear that it remained convinced about the merit of JPCs, and expected that they would have an important role to play in promoting productivity growth after the war.[18] The party's position on this subject rested on several foundations. Observers on the Left generally believed that JPCs had been a success in the war, achieving what was expected of them.[19] At the same time, the JPC idea fitted in with wider Labour ideals about how people should be treated, at work as much as in society. Bevin was a particular proponent of this view:

> Men will follow when they know they are getting a fair deal, and at this time in our development this means that they must be treated as equal partners and must be given the facts.[20]

On a more technical level, finally, the JPC could be seen as an institution whose time was very much just about to come. Labour observers, to repeat, believed that old forms of industrial discipline would most likely be inappropriate in the first years of peace, because of the impact of full employment. In this scenario, linking the worker to the enterprise through participation was one of the best instruments left for ensuring labour commitment. Cripps was not alone, therefore, in believing that the JPC's crucial role would be 'in stimulating the individual worker's interest in output, and thereby increasing his efficiency'.[21]

The third component in Labour's package was concerned with management. The war had, of course, focused attention on management as never before, and this was as true in the ranks of the Left as elsewhere. Amongst Labour Ministers, there was a growing awareness that managers could play a vitally important part in making or breaking an enterprise.[22] What was needed for the future was a cohort of managers who were both technically competent and attuned to (once again) what were predicted as the coming industrial relations realities. This meant that there would have to be a departure from the 'old haphazard idea that anyone with some technical knowledge could be the boss'.[23] In future, as Cripps in particular tirelessly argued, the function must be thoroughly professionalised. Anything else was unacceptable: 'there is really no more right for an unqualified person to manage a factory than for an unqualified doctor to perform an operation.'[24]

In practical terms, therefore, there would be a need for what the Weir Committee had already recommended – a strong central institute of management, backed by the government, which could build up the necessary professional and educational standards.[25]

This was a significant departure for Labour, and, within its own ranks, quite a controversial one. In the inter-war period, the party had done relatively little thinking about management, hazily assuming that the Webbs' *nouvelle couche sociale* would play its part with competence and integrity should any industry ever actually be nationalised.[26] Perhaps consequently, there remained many in Labour's ranks who continued to see management as the enemy, merely the most clearly identifiable face of the capitalist class. In part this was nurtured by trade union attitudes, gut feelings against those who gave the orders on the shop floor. But there was also a more theoretical underpinning at play here, derived from James Burnham's recently published *The Managerial Revolution*.[27] This book, with its quasi-Marxist jargon, had caused quite a stir amongst Left intellectuals, and was viewed by some as a timely warning of the totalitarian consequences which would result from allowing managers too much power. Nicholas Davenport added an extra twist to such anxieties by predicting, in the columns of the *New Statesman*, that the managerial state was most likely to develop during a period of Labour rule, because of the party's stated intention of placing large blocs of industry under nationalised, and therefore bureaucratic, control.[28]

Naturally, such propositions could only vex those of Cripps's disposition, and so there was a steady stream of counter-argument. Much of this came from the pen of Austen Albu, one of the few Labour supporters other than Cripps to have had management experience.[29] In Albu's view, the growth of the large-scale joint stock enterprise in the pre-war period had caused profound changes in the relationship between owners and managers, such that the latter had in many cases come to see themselves as independent experts, dedicated to efficiency rather than the narrow profit and loss mentality of the capitalist. The war had strengthened this trend if only because so much responsibility was now placed on management's shoulders. As a group, therefore, managers could not be seen as having inherent social and political interests. On the contrary, they could be won to Labour, given the right approach. One essential of this, for Albu, was that there would have to be a new kind of outlook in the Labour Movement. The days of purely oppositional politics were past; Labour and the unions must become involved in shaping the fate of the enterprise, and act in an intelligent and informed way, so as to complement management skills.[30]

This was a powerful case, and it gained from being both optimistic (certainly in contrast to Burnham's prognostications) and apparently congruent with what was known of recent Soviet experience.[31] Unsurprisingly, therefore, much of what was being proposed soon found its way into the official party view. Thus, 'Licinius', in *Vote Labour? Why?*, a propaganda booklet issued just before the 1945 election, could suggest that, of all of the parties, only Labour wanted the manager merely to be him/herself. Indeed socialism meant precisely 'carrying the managerial revolution to its logical conclusion'.[32]

The fullest exposition of Conservative views on the country's manufacturing prospects was the 1944 report, *Work: The Future of British Industry*, a document that had emerged, under Henry Brooke's guidance, from the Tories' Central Committee on Post-War Problems.[33] The argument presented here was based on a sober assessment of the nation's likely post-war trading position:

> When peace returns, for the first time in our history we shall find ourselves facing the prospect of an adverse balance of payments not likely to be less than £200,000,000 a year or nearly half the average annual value of our pre-war exports.[34]

In these circumstances, it followed that the government had an over-riding duty to help industry in whatever ways were possible. Much effort would have to be put into perfecting international agreements which were capable of generating prosperity. At the same time, it was also accepted that Whitehall had a part to play at home. However, this was very different from the one outlined in Labour plans.

The Conservatives began from the belief that over 'the whole broad field of industry, private enterprise generally best serves public service'.[35] Quick reconstruction and economic survival therefore depended upon giving entrepreneurs their head:

> It was private enterprise that designed and built the Spitfire and the Lancaster. The same qualities of brain, hard work and courage are what we shall need most, when the time comes to turn Britain's great productive capacity back with all speed from war production to meet the world's peacetime needs.[36]

Two observations followed from this. The first was that direct government control of industry must be avoided at all costs. Nationalisation remained deeply objectionable on ideological grounds, but its major fault was that it encouraged inefficiency. Nevertheless, and here was the second conclusion, accepting this did not mean that the state should simply be banned from the whole industrial sphere. The crucial point was that Whitehall should see itself in a supporting role, as the provider of the best possible climate in which private enterprise could thrive. There was no room for a repetition of the pre-war pattern, when the attitude of government towards industry had allegedly been 'narrowly regulative, restrictive, [and] negative'.[37]

In practical terms, therefore, the central focus of state–industry relations was to be around a new 'Ministry of Industry and Commerce', an institution 'inspired by a more positive and constructive conception of its duty to help British industry to grow healthily, make good any weaknesses, sell its goods, and provide employment'.[38] In addition, state agencies might play a part in promoting scientific research and technical education; developing and enforcing a location policy; and policing monopoly abuse (though this was not seen as a major threat). The report recognised that unity of purpose *within* firms would be important during reconstruction and it endorsed joint consultation ('The principle inherent in Joint Production Committees . . . should continue to find a place in British industry in peacetime'),[39] though it implied that Whitehall should do no more than proselytise over such matters.

Brooke's document received a good deal of attention in Conservative circles,[40] and was broadly endorsed by leading figures such as Lord Woolton, who took up the refrain that a post-war Tory government would not intervene across the board, but merely 'give such encouragement as properly felt within . . . [its] competence'.[41] Nevertheless, the tenor of the analysis was felt to be too complacent by some on the left of the party, and efforts were made to develop an alternative set of proposals. The outcome was the Tory Reform Committee's *Tools For The Next Job*, published in early 1945.[42] This document began with a much more pessimistic account of Britain's economic circumstances than had appeared in *Work*, focusing especially on the productivity gap which existed between home and US industries. Nor did it share the official document's great faith in unregulated private enterprise, suggesting that business was often slump minded and most interested in restriction.[43] The end product was a set of policy prescriptions which involved the state far more than Brooke had felt necessary.

The Reform Committee began from a belief that the country's problems were related essentially to its lack of up-to-date capital equipment and plant. The situation was so serious that it could only be resolved with some government involvement. What this meant in detail, the Committee argued, was that Whitehall officials should sit down with industry and decide upon a national programme of modernisation.

Individual firms would then be expected to decide the details of how they were going to reach the specified targets, with the necessary expenditure financed partly from the centre (through a mixture of grants and tax concessions). Meanwhile efforts would be made to secure labour's co-operation by allowing workers to participate in the formulation of the overall policy, always provided that they dropped 'arid political discussion' and instead dedicated 'their intimate knowledge of industrial practice . . . [to] the cause of expanding productivity'.[44] In this proposal, therefore, the government was to act as both facilitator and ringmaster. The Committee hoped that compulsion, though it might be necessary, would never become widespread. In the worst cases, recalcitrant firms might have to be forced to pursue national goals but, in normal circumstances, bolstering the entrepreneur's bank account and promising him or her full independence would be enough to ensure compliance.[45]

Measured against previous Conservative policies, this sounded quite radical, and so there was a measure of debate within the party as to whether it was at all acceptable. Some critics of business conservatism were clearly impressed by the proposals, and even succeeded in getting a degree of support for them from the rank and file.[46] Nevertheless, at the top of the hierarchy, attitudes remained essentially unchanged, and so Conservative leaders entered the election campaign urging measures of a much more traditional type. Typical here was an article in July 1945 by Oliver Lyttelton, which accepted that Whitehall had some role to play in promoting productivity growth, but emphasised again that the mainspring of change must be private enterprise. Above all, the Minister concluded, the government 'should not concern itself with the actual running of any industry, a function for which it has no aptitude or experience'.[47]

Thus far, it has been suggested that in the last year or so of the war, there was a growing divide between Labour and Conservative Parties on future industrial policy, with the former proposing a much greater degree of state involvement. The following paragraphs extend the argument somewhat by looking at how other institutions, interest groups and commentators reacted to this polarisation. Could one or other political party claim to represent a wider consensus, or was the cleavage inside politics replicated without?

The press, to begin with, took quite a lively interest in industrial affairs at this time,[48] though much of the comment, in line with various long-standing allegiances, simply reiterated party positions. On the Right, therefore, *The Daily Telegraph* came down strongly in favour of the Tory approach. The paper was in no doubt about the severity of Britain's economic plight, even to the extent of questioning whether the country could really afford the Beveridge reforms.[49] Nevertheless, it was equally certain that private enterprise would rise to the challenge, as long as labour behaved itself (dropping forever the restrictive practices that had been suspended for the duration of the war) and the government provided the right kind of support.[50] This latter condition was crucial, since too much interference might smother initiative. To achieve the right balance, the *Telegraph* concluded, administrators must remember the 'principal lesson' of the war: 'that Government should be the active ally of industry, not its repressive tyrant, nor the conductor of one vast State monopoly'.[51]

Against this, on the Left, the *News Chronicle* broadly supported the Labour case. There should be, it warned, no 'delusion' about the state of British industry. Nor could plans for new kinds of welfare provision 'conceivably fructify' unless exports were increased. Entrepreneurs might be able to achieve this latter objective on their own, but the prospects were not encouraging. The government must therefore hold itself ready to intervene: 'If our industries cannot themselves attain a reasonable degree of efficiency, there will be a strong public demand for State interference; and this demand Parliament will find it difficult to resist.'[52]

Amongst less partisan commentators and publications the balance of support was more complicated, though there was certainly a drift to Labour as the Allied victory approached. *The Economist* was particularly concerned by the productivity gap which had opened up between Britain and America (quoting Rostas), and editorialised at some length about possible solutions. Efficiency, it argued, should become a national priority: 'To the two existing slogans of "Full Employment" and "Social Security" there . . . needs to be added a third, "Productivity", on which the first two depend.'[53] This might or might not mean central government involvement, according to the circumstances; but Labour statements on measures to improve efficiency were 'indeed welcome' as at least pointing in the right direction.[54] *Scope*, the business journal, took a similar line, though concentrating on the narrower question of industrial management. There was, it argued, much to criticise in the way in which British firms were run, though 'a highly trained, highly professional management' would be the first essential if recovery were to be achieved. In these circumstances, Cripps's speeches on management were wholly laudable: what he had to say 'needed saying' and would bear 'repeated emphasis'.[55]

Finally, it is worth noting that the Labour case also received some backing from Edward Hulton, the influential publisher. Hulton observed that in pre-war days, it had been assumed, on the subject of growth, that the owner would be 'the driver' while the trade unionist would be 'the guard and the brakesman'. The position was now very much more complicated, because big business tended to be run by a new class of managers. At one level, this was a wholly welcome development, because managers were primarily concerned with efficiency. Yet, Hulton insisted, the situation needed to be watched closely, because it might easily degenerate, as Burnham forecast, in a totalitarian direction. Given this danger, the argument ran, there was every reason for a prominent government and trade union presence in the administration of business.[56]

Turning to industry itself, it is again evident that division rather than consensus was the most prominent characteristic in debate. Labour's plans received support from the unions, and from a number of progressive managers. On the other hand, the plans were strongly opposed by most employers, who wanted nothing less, when it came to issues such as the state's relationship with industry, than a quick return to the pre-war status quo. The reactions of each of these groups will now be elaborated on in turn.

In looking at what was going to happen once the war ended, there was a strand in union opinion that argued for what was seen as a return to basics. The unions had been drawn into all kinds of unusual arrangements because of the national emergency but, when the war was over, they would be best off returning to what they really knew, the fight for the rights of their members. Thus, the official-turned-MP Tom Fraser could argue, for example, that the management of industry was 'not the function of the Trade Union Movement':

> Trade Union leaders ought to be experts in their own industry, but their chief function must remain that of serving their members by representing their grievances to management and employers.[57]

Against this, there were others who believed that the lesson of the war was that unions should become *more* involved in industry, building on their recent admission into the corridors of power to influence decision-making over a wide range of issues beyond mere wages and conditions. G.D.H. Cole was a particularly keen proponent of this latter view, because he felt that there was no real alternative. Britain would be in economic crisis after the war, necessitating an increase in efficiency 'at a great rate'. Industry, in these circumstances, could not remain static:

> It must modernise its processes, and it will have to change the use which it attempts and is permitted to make of its labour force and the relations which exist between employers and workers.[58]

Thus, the unions would be confronted with a new set of problems, and a choice as to how they should react to them. Cole hoped that the outcome would be fresh, more flexible and imaginative union strategies. Certainly, he warned, a refusal to change would be economically damaging and politically disastrous:

> I am afraid of the Trade Unions and the more restrictive type of employer coming together in such a way as to perpetrate [restrictionism] . . . and hold the consuming public to ransom by acting jointly in defence of standard margins of profit, standard wages, standard conditions.[59]

Different parts of the union movement reacted to these arguments in different ways. Nevertheless, at leadership level there was a growing acceptance of the Cole position.[60] This meant, in terms of the industrial policy debate, that an older union rhetoric demanding public control of business on grounds of moral equity was now recast so as to reflect fully the importance of the efficiency issue. The end product was strong support for the type of policies in Labour's programme.

The most authoritative exposition of this new union thinking came in the TUC's *Interim Report on Post-War Reconstruction*, which was accepted by the Blackpool conference of 1944.[61] The authors of this document conceded that the union movement's primary purpose must be the pursuit of bread and butter issues – wages and conditions, full employment, perhaps an advance in industrial democracy – but went on to insist that action here must be accompanied by activity on broader issues. This wider focus was necessary, they argued, because real advances in everyday standards for the membership would be unlikely so long as the entire economic system remained unplanned and to some extent dominated by the whims of selfish monopolists. The need, therefore, was to reform industry in such a way as to promote expansion, which in practice meant adopting a package of measures similar (though not identical) to those proposed by Labour: nationalisation of key sectors, tripartite boards regulating those industries that were left in private hands, and JPCs.[62] Only these kind of policies would, it was claimed, be able to break the log-jam and thus guarantee popular gains:

> One of the strongest arguments for . . . forms of public control which we propose is that these changes are essential for efficient industrial

organisation and to ensure that industrial efficiency serves its proper purpose of improving the standard of life of the community.[63]

The *Interim Report* represented quite a bold departure in trade union affairs, but its adoption was clearly the reflection of a trend rather than an isolated occurrence. In fact, new thinking was surfacing over a number of issues and in a variety of places. There were, therefore, several locally produced alternative industrial plans, in which individual unions attempted to apply the approach of the TUC document to their own particular circumstances.[64] Typical of these was a National Society of Pottery Workers' reconstruction report which explicitly recognised both that growth in efficiency was crucial and that its achievement would necessitate institutional reforms which were designed to curtail the power of some individual entrepreneurs.[65] Symptomatic, too, were changes in union views on management. A significant number of ordinary members continued to see managers as the enemy or, at least, as the visible representative of the enemy. But this hostility – as in the ranks of Labour – was no longer all pervasive and had been replaced in some quarters by more open attitudes, similar to those advocated by Cripps and Albu. In this view, it was 'no part of the responsibility of management to associate itself whole-heartedly with . . . private capital'; rather managers should come over and join 'the community against vested interests'.[66] Nor was this merely a rhetorical commitment, as can be seen from the considerable growth of ASSET (the Association of Supervisory Staffs and Engineering Technicians) over the war years – from 1,786 members and 44 branches in 1939 to 11,000 members and 220 branches in 1945.[67]

It may be concluded from this brief examination that, when it came to industrial policy matters, Labour and the unions were marching for the most part broadly in step. On the other side of industry, however, the position was very different. Some managers and owners were, it is true, inclined to more liberal attitudes on issues such as state intervention and labour representation, often as a result, they claimed, of wartime experience. Yet this group remained a small (if vociferous) minority. The vast majority of business people wanted nothing more or less than a return to their pre-war prerogatives, especially to having the time and space to make a reasonable profit away from state or union interference.

Exponents of the progressive case first came to the fore with the production crisis of 1941–2. During this period, as has been shown, management was faced with problems on all sides and at the same time bombarded with criticism. These were traumatic circumstances, which provoked some people into arguing that the real problem was the system under which they worked, with all that this implied about the future arrangement of industry. One manager could assert, therefore, that there was a 'spirit of revolution . . . abroad in England', epitomised by the 'great many young men of all ages in the ranks of . . . authority' who had decided that 'the old order must go'. In future, those at the top of industry should devote themselves not to profit but rather to 'the welfare of the country and . . . its people'.[68] Such a perspective might, of course, lead management into some strange alliances, but this would be no bad thing, as another executive candidly accepted:

> If Management . . . really does feel that its primary responsibility is to the community, it is marching towards the same ultimate goals as organised labour – even, with few exceptions, as extremist labour organisations. . . . Industrially, as well as politically, internecine warfare means national suicide.[69]

This kind of histrionic comment fitted the mood of 1941–2, but gave way to more sober reflection once Britain's victory seemed assured. Two themes dominated the later analyses. One related to the practical lessons that could be learned from the great industrial push. Here, the major propositions tended to be about labour and its management. Thus, E.F.L. Brech, a colleague of Urwick's, argued in an influential article that the production front had shown that 'effectiveness in work' tended to be essentially 'a function of personnel relations', and therefore correlated 'primarily with morale'. The logical consequence of this was that firms would in future have to take human relations very much more seriously, which, amongst other things, meant democratising decision-making:

> The only way in which full regard can be paid to the contribution which employees can make to the morale of their organisation is to invite them to share in its governance.[70]

Such speculation about intra-firm relationships fitted into a wider framework of propositions about ownership and control. These, once again, revolved around doubts about the suitability of unregulated private enterprise. The war had demonstrated at a general level, the argument ran, that capitalism would not provide for social or national objectives without strong state involvement. The partnership between industry and government so recently evolved must therefore be extended to the peace, a point emphasised by the general manager of Osram to readers of *Industry Illustrated* during mid-1944:

> though I want to see private enterprise survive, I believe *noblesse oblige* is not a principle good enough to secure the harmony that we want. It is not enough to try to convince the people that private enterprise has had a change of heart and that it realises in a sort of feudal spirit its responsibilities towards its 'tenants'. I think whether we like it or not industry has got to be knit in with the State by some measure of Government control, which need not be hostile and need not be harsh, but must be something which will to some extent . . . fortify the unaided consciences of those of us who are trying to manage industry.[71]

All of this added up to a fairly moderate package, yet it was not one that the reform-minded found easy to make popular. In part, this was simply a logistical problem. Most of the leading progressive figures were associated with the fledgling management movement, and could therefore easily reach a number of like-minded enthusiasts. On the other hand, to communicate with those outside this circle remained very much more difficult. Many employers were biased against anything even remotely connected with the management movement, because they feared that the arrival of a third grouping might easily disrupt a laboriously built up network of bilateral agreements linking them to labour.[72] Moreover, the prevailing feeling in boardrooms tended to be that managers had no business dabbling in industrial politics anyway, since their only responsibility should be to their companies. Indeed, *Scope* went so far as to claim that:

> the majority of employers do not recognise the right of their managers or paid executives to exercise any independent influence on industry: they pay them (so they say) to carry out the policies of the employers.[73]

This was not an environment that encouraged the spread of liberal ideas. But what made the reformers' task considerably more difficult was the fact that even when their voices were heard, they tended to be accompanied by a barrage of counter-propaganda. Typical, here, was material emanating from the National Union of Manufacturers (NUM), an organisation supported by Austin, Dunlop and Courtaulds, as well as many other firms in lighter branches of industry.[74] The NUM's position was that private enterprise had not failed the nation, in the war or before 1939. Indeed, the suggestion of a 'decadent body . . . somehow galvanised into life by the lightning flash of war and by association with government departments' was mere propaganda. 'Most people' knew that British industry was 'thoroughly sound at heart and full of life and vigour' during the 1930s, and that this explained why it had been able to play so successful a role in a 'war of machinery and production'.[75]

The inevitable consequence of all of this was that the larger slice of business opinion remained wholly untouched by the reformers' case. Nowhere was the mainstream's conservatism more in evidence than over questions relating to reconstruction. The FBI's cautious position on post-war industrial issues had been signalled in its comprehensive report of 1942, and was now confirmed (as has been shown) in the jockeying over the Board of Trade's management initiative.[76] Outside the employers' peak organisations, the key concerns were also of a highly traditional kind. Business opinion, observers noted, was usually quite complacent about post-war markets, and often most agitated by the kind of wage drift and extension of union power that had been a feature of the last two or three years.[77] There was, certainly, no desire to experiment any further on issues such as control, and most employers, as an authoritative Ministry of Production survey found in 1945, saw little future even for the existing JPCs ('There is . . . a pretty general opinion that the workers really have very little to contribute . . . I do not think we should blink [from] the fact that unless . . . encouragement is active the Committees will tend to fade out').[78] Efficiency was sometimes mentioned as an issue – usually in terms designed to castigate government red tape – but more often than not was simply ignored. Thus, when *The Times* reviewed an FBI policy document on industry in late 1944, it was shocked to have to report: 'Searchers for a pronouncement from this authoritative source on the efficient modernisation of the mechanical apparatus of British manufacturing . . . will look here in vain.'[79]

The conclusion that emerges from this survey is that there was no real consensus at this time when it came to discussion about future industrial policy matters. Labour had arrived at a fairly definite position, which seemed broadly congruent with statements emanating from the unions and from some progressive managers, but it was faced by a highly antipathetic bloc, consisting of the Conservatives and the majority of the employers. To complete the picture, it is necessary to ask how this political division was handled inside the Coalition Government. In practical terms, this means looking at the Board of Trade, since, of all of the departments, it was the one most involved over industrial reconstruction issues. The Board, as the previous chapter has shown, had already been converted to a measure of interventionism. How did it fare with this policy during 1944–5?

Board activity over this period was of two main kinds. Some of the department's effort went into intra-government politicking: the whole business, as an official described it, of trying to make others realise

> how unsatisfactory the position was before the war, why it may be worse and not better after the war, the very great importance of increased efficiency and, above all, the futility of expecting increased efficiency unless the Government takes energetic action'.[80]

On the other hand, it was always recognised that this battle would never be won unless the Board could come up with more than just general exhortation, and so great importance was placed on drawing up a realistic programme of ameliorative measures – 'a closely integrated policy for tackling and relating all the various aspects of efficiency and development'.[81] This led officials to examine a wide range of possible options, relating to various questions of research, design, production and, as has been described, management.[82]

At first, the search for solutions appeared to proceed fairly smoothly, producing some valuable results such as the Weir Report. Nevertheless, by the beginning of 1945, it was becoming obvious that the Board had become bogged down, with all specific initiatives, as one senior participant complained, subject to 'continued delay . . . due to circumstances that we cannot control'.[83] The position over a proposed re-equipment subsidy was typical. The idea had originated in the Board and then been put to other departments, but the result was only endless prevarication, as a report of January 1945 indicated:

> Ministers decided in February [1944] that the Treasury should work out a scheme with an estimate of costs. There was some official discussion in March, April and May, but since then no progress has been made. In July, the Chancellor wrote to the President saying that he thought the proposal should be dropped. Draft reply awaits President's consideration.[84]

What had gone wrong? Clearly, part of the problem was that all civil servants at this time continued to be greatly over-worked, since too many proposals were being pushed at what was, in any case, very cumbersome reconstruction machinery. Nevertheless, it is also apparent that other, more deliberate factors were in play, notably a variety of pressures from elsewhere in Whitehall which were aimed at emasculating the Board's position. To illustrate what was going on here, it is apposite to focus once again on the management question, since, as Chapter 2 has shown, Board initiatives over this issue were from the first well developed, relatively high profile and quite controversial. What, then, had happened to the Weir proposals after their presentation to Hugh Dalton in February 1944?

The President's first move on receiving the Weir Report, it will be remembered, was to ask his civil servants to contact other departments in order to collect hard information on cases where improved management had boosted productivity. The idea behind this exercise, Dalton explained, was to augment his hand if and when it was decided that the proposals on management should go before a full Cabinet committee.[85]

The Board's enquiries were completed by the middle of July, and confirmed the picture that Weir had already painted. Some businesses were efficient, while others had been made so with government help. On the other hand, the most striking finding was just how poor general standards were. As the report summarising the replies explained, 'the general experience of the Departments' was that there existed 'great scope for improvement in all branches of management'. Moreover, the 'deficiencies in the field of management' were not confined to 'particular aspects' but extended 'through the whole'.[86]

While considering exactly how to proceed in the light of these findings, Dalton decided that he should alert his ministerial colleagues about the Board's wider perspective on the crisis facing Britain. Accordingly he put together a paper which pulled no punches in describing the urgency of the situation. One of the great dangers, he wrote, 'perhaps the main danger', was that the country would not see 'clearly and easily enough' the grave difficulties that lay ahead of home industries in the transition. There was prevalent 'a hazily optimistic assumption' that Britain could easily secure an increase in the export trade, but hard evidence to suggest that this would happen was minimal. In this scenario, an increase in productivity was plainly indispensable. As the paper concluded, 'If we achieve the American standard of efficiency, we can, on British wages, look to the future with some confidence. But if we fail, we cannot.'[87]

Dalton's analysis was presented to the War Cabinet Reconstruction Committee's Sub-Committee on Industrial Problems at the end of July, together with a note from him which underlined the 'pretty bleak' prospects before the country and the need for 'vigorous and varied' action.[88] However, despite all of his effort, most of the Ministers present were not impressed. In fact, several Conservatives went so far as to question the very basis of the President's view. Since Britain would be faced by a sellers' market after the war, they argued, much of Dalton's pessimism was misplaced. If industrialists were holding back now, this was only because they needed reassuring about the Government's intentions. Given the correct leadership, all would come right, as Lord Woolton's 'private conversations' with various entrepreneurs had shown him: 'There was no lack of enterprise in a number of industries and if an export drive were initiated by the Government there would be a ready response.'[89] The message was rammed home further a few weeks later when Dalton presented a second paper, listing possible measures which could be taken to promote exports and productivity; this was met, once again, with almost total indifference from most of his ministerial colleagues.[90]

In the light of these setbacks, the President decided that he ought to move cautiously on Weir, and that his best tactic would be to collect official views on the Report itself, in order to identify any weaknesses in the proposals, and to rally support. Opinions were, therefore, collected from all of the departments concerned. This exercise showed that there was general backing for Weir in the Admiralty and in the Ministries of Works, Labour, Supply and Education.[91] The Ministry of Aircraft Production, too, was in favour, with Cripps writing that he was 'extremely anxious' that something should be done about the report 'as soon as possible'.[92] On the other hand, Lyttelton's Ministry of Production registered its opposition. The disagreement here was not with the substantive proposal (there was 'room for a properly constituted central organisation to study the problems of management') but rather with the suggested level of government involvement. As a Ministry official explained:

> we feel that an attempt to set up an organisation of this kind under direct Government auspices would be foredoomed to failure since a Government sponsored organisation would start with so serious a handicap of suspicion and distrust that it might never succeed in making good however sensibly and conservatively it were run.

A better option, in the Ministry's view, was that there should be 'an endeavour . . . made' to establish an independent organisation on a voluntary basis, capitalising on the experience and wealth of large firms that were already involved in the management movement.[93]

Much more worryingly, the Board's enquiries also revealed that the Treasury position was far from helpful. It had always been recognised that support from this direction would be crucial, and so, when the Board put its case to the Treasury, it did so in very moderate terms. The Board noted that a management institute would not be viable if left to private enterprise, since, as Weir continued to emphasise, industry in the main had still to be convinced of its usefulness. What was needed, therefore, was government start-up money – perhaps £50,000 – which could be added to subscriptions from big firms (possibly £5,000) to get the new institution functioning. Exchequer resources should only be provided, the Board emphasised, on the understanding that they would be temporary, and that the Government expected industry to respond and quite quickly take over funding altogether.

This was a carefully argued case, but it proved inadequate to shift the Exchequer's scepticism. The Treasury's central objection was that 'the financial balance of the proposals' seemed 'wrong':

> In our view, the efficacy of the scheme very largely depends on the degree to which Industry itself is prepared to finance it. It follows that the Government's contribution should be a minor, not a major, proportion of the expenditure of the Institute; and should be conditional on funds being found from industry for whatever additional sum, on close and realistic consideration, is agreed to be the minimum necessary to make the project worth pursuing.

The Treasury was therefore prepared to provide £5,000–£10,000 per annum, and to see the Board 'active in encouraging the promotion' of the proposed institute; but it wanted industry and the management movement to make the detailed arrangements about getting the project started, and the same sources to provide the bulk of the funding.[94]

The extent and character of this opposition made it difficult to see what should be done next; in some frustration, Dalton asked Sir Charles Bruce-Gardner, one of the Board's most senior industrial advisers,[95] to review possible options. The end product was a report, delivered in mid-January 1945, which essentially came down in favour of the Ministry of Production's earlier advice. Bruce-Gardner agreed that management had often been weak during the war, though he emphasised several mitigating factors such as the very rapid expansion of production and a loss of capable men to the forces. The need for the future must be to reach medium and small-sized firms (the most inefficient), but it also had to be recognised that these would be loath to involve themselves with any government-backed body. The Board, therefore, should forget the Weir proposals (which Bruce-Gardner felt to be poorly formulated) and instead do all it could to get industry involved in helping itself, which in practice meant encouraging big, progressive firms to share their knowledge and resources.[96]

Dalton, beset by other problems at the Board,[97] told his officials that he was inclined to accept this advice. However, a last-minute intervention from Cripps led to the Ministers agreeing that they should make one final effort on behalf of Weir and should submit his proposals to the Cabinet Reconstruction Committee's Sub-Committee on Industrial Problems.[98] Accordingly, Dalton drew up a paper detailing the different possibilities over the management institute and underlining his own support for Weir.[99]

This was presented to the Sub-Committee in early March 1945 but did little to change existing attitudes. Cripps recorded his support for Dalton but ran into sustained opposition. Indeed some (un-named) adversaries among the Ministers present were now prepared to argue not only that state intervention in management matters would be pernicious but also that management was not, in any case, a science that could be perfected. The end product was an instruction to Dalton that he should explore possibilities within the following highly conservative guidelines:

> A better course than that proposed in the [Weir] Report would be to suggest to employers' associations that the Government would welcome the combination in a central body, with council, of the more valuable of the existing management organisations. . . . This would provide the advantages of a central focus for study of management problems, a library and other needed facilities. . . . There would . . . be no question of the Government providing finance.[100]

Some days later, when this outcome was discussed in the Treasury, a senior official minuted that the Weir Report's condition was now 'grave', while another added the written comment that it should 'R.I.P.'.[101]

In the light of this, it seems reasonable to conclude that the Coalition Government was as divided on productivity related issues as interests in the rest of the country. Again, the key issue concerned intervention. Labour Ministers such as Cripps and Dalton argued that the state should be used to force change, but they were continually frustrated by their Conservative colleagues, who took a more *laissez-faire* approach. The next chapter looks at what happened once this impasse was resolved with the resumption of electoral politics.

Chapter 4

Early post-war efforts, 1945–7

The election campaign in 1945 revolved around a number of issues, but Britain's industrial future was certainly at the centre of debate.[1] The electorate was confronted with a fairly clear-cut choice. Labour was pessimistic about the state of industry, and therefore stressed the need for drastic measures. Some sectors, it was true, had performed well during the war, and could be left to develop on their own. But others had 'wholly or partly failed' and would therefore need careful attention. Policy prescriptions here ranged from outright nationalisation in a minority of cases to 'constructive supervision' in the majority, the aim being always to increase efficiency.[2] The Conservative approach also stressed the need for greater productivity, but there was a much greater belief in the Tory ranks that private enterprise could rise to the challenge. The essential condition, the party argued, was that entrepreneurs should be allowed to operate freely. Controls must be dropped as quickly as possible. There could certainly be no question of long-term state involvement, as *Mr Churchill's Declaration of Policy to the Elector* emphasised:

> As against the advocates of State ownership and control, we stand for the fullest opportunity for go and push in all ranks throughout the whole nation. This quality is part of the genius of the British people, who mean to be free to use their own judgement and never intend to be State serfs, nor always to wait for official orders before they can act.[3]

Given this division in approach, it was inevitable that Labour's final triumph on 17 July would provoke intense speculation amongst the owners of industry. Was Britain now headed down an entirely new industrial road, featuring wholesale nationalisation and coercion? In the business press, some stressed Labour's realism and essential moderation. The party had a distinctive approach, and it would deal with industrialists gently but firmly. However, there would be no rush to impose ideology for its own sake; the 'wiser heads in the party' were 'keeping policy in line with the brittle facts'.[4] Yet such soothing opinion did little to calm nerves in the boardroom. The *Financial Times* noted that the new government's arrival was causing 'apprehension' across 'a wide area of private enterprise'.[5] A journalist writing for *Business* was also struck by the fear and hostility that existed in some quarters, noting that 'our investors and business leaders' could now be divided into three categories:

1 The Defeatists, who are living partly on capital, clamouring for higher dividends, and exclaiming 'Après nous le déluge!'.
2 The Die-hards, determined to fight to the last ditch for the return of the 'good old' order of society.
3 The Progressives, who, with faith in the country's future, are striving to reach a compromise with the new spirit of our times.[6]

Within the incoming government, the lead role in promoting industrial policy was immediately given to Cripps, appointed President of the Board of Trade. Cripps had, of course, guided MAP's initiatives on productivity during the war and was certainly the Minister most clearly identified in the public's mind with industrial modernisation, being described, for example, by one periodical as 'a fanatic for business efficiency'.[7] Moreover, the Board of Trade's general remit gave plenty of scope for innovation: it had responsibility for about 70 manufacturing industries outside of engineering, which covered nearly half of the factory workers in the country.[8]

Cripps certainly recognised that he faced a challenge and immediately set out to brief his department on Labour's policy objectives. The new administration would have to play a more interventionist role: 'It is the policy of the Labour Government to take a much closer interest in the performance of British Industry than has been done hitherto.' No Board industries were to be nationalised, so this meant effective supervision. The aim had always to be improved functioning: as Cripps emphasised, 'We must in every possible way, staff, buildings, machinery, management, research and design, make our industries as comparatively efficient as possible.'[9] Specifically, the immediate focus was to be on setting up Working Parties, reactivating the idea of a central management institution and ensuring the continuation and broadening of MAP's efficiency advisory service.

In initial discussion at the Board on Working Parties, it was agreed that a small number should be set up as quickly as possible, in order to provoke a quick improvement in actual industrial practice and at the same time provide a factual basis for determining longer term policy. Cripps was in favour of a common format – equal number of employers and workers under an independent chairperson – and it was agreed that an initial batch of target industries might include pottery, wool, footwear, furniture and hosiery, all sectors that would be vital in providing exports. Consultation with both the FBI and the TUC revealed that neither body was immediately hostile, though Board officials recognised that they would have to move carefully if any kind of consensus was to be maintained.[10]

In discussing the immediate aspects of this policy, Cripps became aware that he needed to be thinking about where tripartite investigations might lead in the longer term, and he therefore asked his officials to inform him about previous Board thinking on this theme. This inquiry revealed that a group of civil servants had been working on an Enabling Bill for Coalition Ministers, under which there was provision for Industrial Boards (on the lines of the Cotton Board) to assist in the co-operative development of, for example, research. But the big problem here had been the attitude of industry itself: when a circular soliciting views on the idea had been sent to over 100 employers' associations in late 1944, only about a dozen were in any way positive, with the majority not even bothering to reply. Moreover, the FBI had clearly indicated that it was against this type of legislation.[11]

This latter point reinforced Cripps's perceptions about the conservatism of much of British industry, but he indicated that if Labour was going to set up some kind of permanent machinery in various sectors, it would not be of the kind envisaged in previous Board proposals. Labour, he emphasised, did not agree with 'so called "self-government" for industry' and wanted much more democratic structures. Officials were therefore instructed to do some further thinking on the whole subject, 'bringing the workers fully into the picture'. Indeed, Cripps's determination on this point was so strong that he was not even willing to consider any qualifications. Thus, when Raymond Streat of the Cotton Board urged him to be more flexible, he would not relent, leaving Streat to record in his diary: 'He seemed to be quite set on his tripartite conception and nothing I could say moved him.'[12]

The Board's recommendations on Working Parties were put to the Lord President's Committee on 27 August, exactly one month after

Labour's election triumph. Cripps based his case on the perception that 'a high degree of industrial efficiency' was 'a national interest of the first importance'. In the light of this, he argued that a useful starting point would be investigations into various trades, with the object of generating 'agreed and considered' statements about how practice might be improved. These enquiries should be conducted by joint teams and should focus only on 'major questions', so that they would be completed very quickly. Cripps repeated the list of industries that he felt were suitable for treatment (all 'highly important from the point of view of consumer needs' and perhaps 'export significance'), adding that he now favoured handling cotton in a similar fashion. The President also included some indication of his thinking on longer term policy, suggesting the establishment in each industry of 'a permanent advisory body which would be the channel through which the Government would keep in touch with the progress of the efficiency plan'. These bodies would be tripartite and advisory, like the Working Parties. Compulsory action might be necessary in extreme cases, but it would be for the government, and the government alone, to exercise such powers.[13]

Much of this was quickly endorsed by Cripps's colleagues, but there was one area of disagreement. Cripps had argued, to repeat, that Working Parties should be made up of equal numbers of trade unionists and employers, under an independent chairperson. However, other Ministers were doubtful of this formula, suggesting that, with only one outsider present, the two sides of industry might collude against considering any radical recommendations. The Working Parties should therefore be made up entirely of impartial members or at least with independents predominating. Cripps's reply to this was that he did not want sectors to feel that the government was 'imposing schemes of reorganisation on them without full knowledge of the conditions in the industries'. Consequently, there could be no question of excluding those from the various trades involved. Nevertheless, the President agreed that an augmented independent presence would be acceptable, and it was decided that the final formula should involve each of the three constituencies in equal proportion.[14]

With his ministerial colleagues behind him, Cripps next turned to the task of convincing industry about the merits of the Working Party idea. He had, as mentioned, received indications of co-operation from the FBI and TUC but, while the unions continued to support the new initiative, it was quite clear that employers were far more hesitant. The President's statement about the future of the cotton industry on 13 August, which promised no nationalisation if industry co-operated in modernisation, was designed to calm nerves and according to the *Financial Times* had something of the required effect.[15] Yet it was quite evident that apprehension and even hostility still remained.

Thus, opinion in the upper reaches of the FBI turned out to be rather mixed. In discussions during August, Sir Clive Baillieu (President of the FBI) argued that Cripps was not to be feared. He had gained the impression from talking to the Minister 'that the great bulk of industry . . . would continue to be run by private enterprise'. Moreover, even in relation to Working Parties, there was no suggestion that the government wanted to impose solutions, only stimulate industry to provide its own. As Baillieu concluded, Cripps's 'primary purpose as regards these industries was to make private enterprise work more efficiently'. However, others were more suspicious. There was, for example, a feeling that the Working Parties would interfere with management's right to manage and would boost the trade unions. Worse, the new bodies might be the first stop on the road to nationalisation. In this situation, the majority concluded, the FBI should move with stealth. There were dangers in outright opposition on 'purely political grounds' both because it might alienate public support and because it might provoke the government into stronger action. The right strategy must involve two prongs. On the one hand, the FBI must use the 'first class opposition' to put the public case for unrestricted private enterprise. On the other, it should engage in a campaign of discreet lobbying to influence those at the Board. As Beharrell insisted, every effort should be made 'to see that His Majesty's Government was carried out in accordance with what appeared to industry to be the wisest policy'.[16]

In the industries where Working Parties were scheduled to be implemented, opinions also varied. Private contacts which the Board had with the hosiery manufacturers suggested that, though they disliked being classified with the cotton industry (a notorious bastion of inefficiency) and being given only equal representation with the trade unions, majority opinion was 'not unfavourable' to the idea of the enquiry itself.[17] Against this, the cotton employers continued to emphasise their opposition to the whole Working Party idea. According to *The Times Trade and Engineering*, there was 'a strong feeling . . . [that it] was not desirable and . . . would not serve any useful purpose'.[18] Similar views held sway in the Potteries. Thus, the Stoke *Evening Sentinel* warned that the Working Party plan was 'insidious and sinister' and added: 'This is not nationalization, which purports to pay "fair compensation" for what it takes. It is pure and unadulterated confiscation. It is political brigandage.'[19] Moreover, familiar fears surfaced when a Board emissary met the Pottery Manufacturers' Federation. The employers claimed that they had nothing against an enquiry, but rejected Cripps's format. They argued that the suggested body had been deliberately designed to keep them in a permanent minority position. More seriously, it seemed to push the industry ever nearer state control:

> The manufacturers . . . feared that as a result of the recommendations of the Working Party they would be committed to a permanent Board or Council which would, through the Government, impose unwelcome and undesirable interferences with the business of individual firms.[20]

Given these attitudes, Cripps concluded that he ought to proceed with caution and diplomacy. He recognised, first, that as his advisers argued, the choice of chairpersons to lead the Working Parties might be crucial in determining employer attitudes[21] and took care to ensure that the high profile appointment for cotton – Sir George Schuster[22] – was a figure who would be acceptable to the Manchester employers.[23] At the same time, Cripps made something of a concession over the question of how the employers' representatives on the Working Parties would be chosen, agreeing not to nominate as he saw fit but rather to accept the recommendations of manufacturer bodies, provided that at least one half of those put forward were under 45 years of age (a stipulation that would, it was hoped, curtail the influence of the older and more reactionary).[24] Finally, the President was also prepared to provide more direct reassurance, going out of his way to visit key manufacturing centres of the industries in question and to talk to those involved. In each case, Cripps emphasised that he did not aim to replace private enterprise and that the Working Parties were only temporary institutions. His speech at Stoke was typical:

> Sir Stafford . . . told them that his plan did not mean nationalisation, and that he did not want to 'boss' the industry. He said that the Working Party was a device which had been used during the war and indicated that it would be dissolved when its work was accomplished.[25]

These tactics seemed to bring results, so that by early autumn the Board felt that it could detect a definite softening in employers' attitudes.[26] Thus, when Cripps came to announce the first five Working Parties (covering boots and shoes, cotton, furniture, hosiery and pottery),[27] in mid-October, he prefaced his remarks by stating that he had received 'the most cordial co-operation from both sides of industry'.[28] Nevertheless, it was quite clear that industry did not see itself as a willing convert to the Minister's views. Indeed, some manufacturers believed that it was they, and not Cripps, who had emerged with most from the first round of negotiations. A leading figure in the Hosiery Manufacturers' Association made this point clearly, and also revealed the extent of the inter-industry collusion that had been going on, when he told his members in private:

> Many of the fears that we had in mind have been dispelled by the assurances which we have received and I think it is true to say that they are far removed from our original conceptions of the Board of Trade's intentions. We have worked closely with other industries and this approach has been fully justified and has contributed effectively towards removing some features of the original proposals to which we should have taken strong exception.[29]

The decision to revive the idea of a central management institution attracted rather less controversy than had occurred with the Working Parties. Cripps was, of course, a long-term supporter of professionalising management and so, on taking office, he immediately wrote to Dalton, the new Chancellor, arguing for the creation of an Institute of Management 'as soon as possible'. The new initiative would be crucial, Cripps declared; 'an essential weapon of attack upon inefficiency in Industry'. The only outstanding decision concerned finance: while the Weir recommendation of £75,000 p.a. for five years seemed 'excessive', it might be necessary to provide a £150,000 start-up loan and then £25,000 p.a. to 1950.[30]

Dalton's response to this estimate was caution. He knew by experience that 'a lot of the bodies, individual and corporate, now active in this field' were 'very second rate' and agreed that Weir's figure was far too high. At the same time, he was also under pressure from some of his officials, who still believed that 'the Institute must be of industrial, not of Whitehall, paternity'.[31] Nevertheless, in the end Dalton, too, felt that a fresh start was necessary and agreed to provide £150,000 over five years on the understanding that the Institute would then be self-financing.[32]

Cripps's final initiative was the creation of the Production Efficiency Service (PES). The President had, of course, supervised MAP's Production Efficiency Board and Technical Costs Branch during the war and he felt that 'the reception by industry of these services was co-operative, and the results were valuable'.[33] It was an obvious step, therefore, to create a consultancy service in peacetime. Cripps's first move, once again, was to consult the TUC and FBI about their reactions to such a plan.

The TUC recognised that the position had changed somewhat with the ending of hostilities, because improvements in efficiency would now 'in many cases, tend to increase private profits'. However, the country's perilous economic situation was such that a PES would be acceptable so long as it kept any joint consultation machinery informed of its activities and did not concern itself with piece rates or time studies.[34] The FBI's position was equally hedged in by conditions. Some employers were worried that firms might be pressured into accepting consultancy and stressed that the scheme would only be successful if it were voluntary ('It would be resented if it were supervisory or with a concealed baton'). Others argued that the whole scheme was misplaced: it would swallow up qualified experts who were already doing a good job in industry and perhaps sustain inefficient outfits that really deserved to die. The outcome was a resolution that expressed somewhat conditional support. The FBI was to recommend that employers co-operate with the Board over the PES, provided that the scheme was 'voluntary and advisory'. At the same time, the President would be reminded of the staffing problem and the 'danger of keeping the hopelessly inefficient alive'.[35]

These reactions were hardly unexpected and did little to deter Cripps. He had always intended that the initiative should be built on consent and stressed to his colleagues that 'the first incisions into any industry' must be 'through firms who would volunteer'. However, the President had already been contacted by many undertakings wanting assistance, and so felt that this was hardly a problem. In fact, the only point raised in relation to the President's idea when he presented it to the Lord President's Committee concerned the charges that the PES should levy, but Cripps's emphasis on the important role that the service might play convinced the Ministers that it must in fact be free.[36]

Much of Cripps's early work at the Board was, therefore, about creating institutional structures. However, the President was also aware that his policies needed to be explained to the public at large, and so a part of his first few months at the job was spent in what was really public relations work. Typical of this was a keynote speech, widely reported in the press, to the Lancashire and Cheshire Federation of Trades Councils at Blackpool on 9 September. Cripps began his address on this occasion by reminding his audience of the 'extreme difficulties that confronted the nation'. 'They were not', he emphasised, 'on the eve of entering Utopia.' Britain had fought a war which had effectively 'destroyed' its economy. The country might borrow its way out of its immediate predicament, but it was necessary to look further ahead than that and to opt for 'the much harder but more honest and self-reliant way of working out our own salvation'.

On the basis of this sobering assessment, Cripps went on to outline what was required in practice. He emphasised that British industry was often very backward. Inefficiency, in turn, had led to a poor industrial relations climate. The end product was a 'vicious circle' of decline. What was needed, therefore, was for someone to break the circle, and this meant government action ('it was for the Government to see that it was broken, and broken quickly'). Cripps wanted the Board to be the agent that helped private industry to modernise. It was in these terms that his specific initiatives – the Working Parties, the management institute, the Production Efficiency Service – could be justified. However, there was no question of coercion or of taking advice only from manufacturers. The government wanted to proceed on a tripartite basis and hoped that 'a great and important part would be played by trade unionists'.[37]

This was a moderate and conciliatory message, and it gained from the fact that it was so obviously fully compatible with wider government policy. Thus, all Ministers were convinced that enhanced production was absolutely essential if there were to be any advance to socialism.[38] Moreover, there was also agreement with Cripps's key conception that the government should be 'a helping partner' to industry. Labour certainly wanted to nationalise some sectors, but it recognised that ownership in most of manufacturing would remain undisturbed. There could be no quarrel with private enterprise, only with, in Morrison's phrase, 'private unenterprise'.[39] The need was to get all parts of each industry to work as efficiently as the best in their industry.

By October 1945, therefore, Labour had arrived at a definite set of policies in relation to what it wanted from industry and had made its objectives widely known. Neutral commentators remarked upon the administration's clear intent, with *Industry Illustrated*, for example, observing:

> There can be no question of the present Government's serious determination to make British Industry the most efficient instrument possible for restoring the country to an early condition of solvency.[40]

The next part of this chapter will look at how these intentions fared over the period to the end of 1947, looking in turn at the Working Parties, the management institution and the PES.

The first batch of Working Parties, to repeat, were created in mid-October 1945 and, in the wake of this launch, Cripps had immediately to decide how the whole scheme might in future develop. He had originally envisaged a rolling programme, telling the *Daily Herald*: 'We propose month by month to pick out new ones [i.e. new sectors suitable for the working party treatment] until we have been through all the major industries . . . not dealt with by other Departments.'[41] Yet he was now advised by some of his senior officials that such an agenda might be politically unwise.

Civil service caution was founded upon the perception that the Working Party idea was provoking rather mixed comment in media and interest group circles. *The Economist* and the *Financial Times* generally welcomed Cripps's innovation, though each felt that the enquiries should have been given more of a co-ordinated focus (as the *Economist* put it, the Working Parties had been sent off 'into the wilderness of industrial policy without any course to steer or any compass to assist them in holding to it'). *Industry Illustrated*, too, was broadly favourable, though rebuking the President for not including managers as a part of his conception.[42] Yet there was also a bloc which argued that the whole scheme should be terminated. Thus, *The Daily Telegraph* talked of 'committees of outsiders thrust upon industry from above', a theme embroidered further by the *Statist*, which warned:

> There is a strong possibility that working parties will in fact degenerate into groups of busybodies whose interference in the domestic affairs of industry will merely make for reduced efficiency and wholesale resentment.[43]

More worrying still was the open hostility being shown by the National Union of Manufacturers. This organisation's position was founded upon general and specific logics. On the one hand, the Union did not accept Labour's basic premise that industry was often very backward: after all, Britain had 'put up a magnificent show during the war', and it could do so again in the post-war years 'if our people are allowed to get on with the job'. Anyway, the Working Party idea as currently conceived was a poor one because it put the employers in 'the position of a criticized minority'. In fact, the Union predicted that the new bodies would degenerate into 'factions of sectional interest' – 'far too much like the ugly things which reared their heads on the Continent and which we have defeated with so much suffering and loss'.[44]

Given this variable comment, the civil servants concluded that Cripps would be wise to proceed with some care. The President could not ignore his critics; moreover, on the best reading, he could assume only that he had received 'acquiescence, not full support, from industry'. The sensible course, as the Board's Permanent Secretary, Sir John Woods, carefully outlined, was to institute a pause:

> Personally . . . I should prefer, before being publicly committed to particular enquiries in a second batch, to have seen a report or two and to have got the public reactions to those reports. This, it is true, might involve a delay of as much as two or three months. But this would not necessarily be an excessive premium to pay against the risks.[45]

Cripps obviously considered this advice closely, but in the end decided to persevere with his original conception of the programme. As he explained, five industries did not provide a large enough sample on which to build a long-term industrial policy. Equally, there could be adverse political reactions from the Government's own supporters if there were any delay in setting up further Working Parties. The only option, the President decided, was to press on down the road that was already being followed.[46]

Over the following few months, therefore, there was a considerable expansion in the dimensions of the programme, with Working Parties being established in a further twelve industries – carpets, china clay, heavy clothing, light clothing, rubber-proofed clothing, cutlery, glassware, jewellery and silverware, jute, lace, linoleum and wool.[47] This meant that by April 1946 the Working Party apparatus had reached quite impressive proportions. The new institutions covered industries employing over one million workers, a third of those in manufacturing industries other than metals and chemicals or a sixth of all Britain's factory population.[48] Moreover, Cripps had been able to draw in some fairly impressive names as chairs or independent panellists, including General Sir Ronald Forbes Adam (Adjutant General to the Forces), C.R. Morris (Head of King Edward's School, Birmingham), N. Pevsner (the architectural historian) and L.S. Sutherland (Principal of Lady Margaret Hall, Oxford).[49] However, none of this stilled the critics, and much antagonistic discussion of the Working Party idea continued inside and outside Parliament. Churchill was quoted as saying that Cripps was 'putting Socialist nominees' on to Working Parties, an unsubstantiated allegation but one that received much press coverage.[50] Lord Woolton told the *Sunday Times* that the President was almost daily acting 'the schoolmaster to industry', lecturing it on 'the need for improving efficiency and management'. He concluded with a broadside at the whole Labour stance:

> The truth is the Government has taken on more than it can do; the business of Government is to lay down the broad principles for the well-being and good conduct of a country. When it attempts to determine the detail of operations it is taking on a task for which it has neither competent staff nor the quick machinery that detailed commercial decisions demand. The great trade drive of Britain is being stifled at its birth.[51]

The first two Working Party reports were published at the end of May 1946. The document on pottery appeared first and contained thirty specific recommendations.[52] The Working Party began from the view that the existing employers were still vibrant enough to solve the problems that they faced: 'The present state of the . . . industry is not wholly satisfactory, but it has retained sufficient strength and enterprise to set itself on its feet without intervention by the Government in the operation of free competition.'[53] Nevertheless, a number of reforms were urgently required, and these the Working Party proceeded to identify. There should, it argued, be strict enforcement of the Factory Acts, statutory minimum wages and a much simpler remunerations structure, so as to improve the conditions of labour. Secondly, there was a clear need to modernise the manufacturing process in many establishments, in particular by introducing flow-production methods and reducing the number of lines on offer. Furthermore, most ancillary functions in the industry were inadequate: all firms should improve their research and art and design activities, and systemise their costings techniques. Finally, the Working Party turned to considering how these changes could be encouraged. Manufacturers had in the past, it was recognised, been involved in a degree of collusion and this would now have to be discouraged by public scrutiny of financial data. The specific recommendation here was summarised as follows:

> Because of the existence of voluntary price agreements in the industry all firms should be required to supply the Government with regular information about their profits and, as soon as a costing system can be worked out, their costs of production.[54]

In addition, the Working Party felt that there was a need for a 'standing Pottery Advisory Board', constituted, once again, on a tripartite basis under an independent chairperson. Such a body would, it was argued, be able to follow up points raised in the course of the existing enquiry; 'initiate and pursue investigations to further the efficiency of the industry'; and 'communicate to the Government matters that the industry [wished] . . . to put before it'.[55]

The Working Party report on cotton was a much longer and more complex document, running to 278 pages and 34 recommendations.[56] It was also notably marked by a division of opinion: while Schuster, one employer and all of the trade unionists were fully behind the main report, three independents (led by John Jewkes of Manchester University) and three manufacturers accepted only a proportion of its recommendations and had added a 21-page 'Memorandum of Dissent'.[57]

The 28 points on which all agreed covered a number of different subjects. There was a need, it was stressed, for a comprehensive survey of existing plant and an independent enquiry into the textile machinery industry. Furthermore, many ancillary functions, as with pottery, needed improvement. Firms must introduce better and uniform methods of costing, and enhanced training schemes to improve the quality of their managements. Market research activity, too, needed to be expanded and focused around a newly created central marketing company, owned co-operatively. Moreover, some effort was required to make the industry more attractive to labour, with the minimum condition here being an immediate review of wage arrangements. Finally, all on the Working Party were also convinced that little progress on these specific recommendations would be made without some central body to chase them up. Accordingly, again as with pottery, there was backing for a new tripartite body, 'The Cotton Council', with specific responsibilities over, for example, the plant surveys, market research and training.[58]

Where opinion divided was over the issue of what to do with the industry's spare and out-dated capacity. Schuster and his allied signatories of the main report believed in a substantial degree of rationalisation, which was to be achieved using compulsory powers. Their recommendations therefore outlined schemes for amalgamation, the scrapping of redundant machinery and the provision of re-equipment subsidies. Jewkes's group, on the other hand, were completely against this kind of interventionist policy and felt that the free market should be left to ensure that the industry would reach an optimum size. Unwanted combination could only introduce the abuses attendant upon an oligopolistic market structure.[59] As the trade union members of the Working Party sourly observed, this boiled down to a pair of long-standing *laissez-faire* propositions:

> *Firstly*: 'You must trust each employer to know what is best for his own business and leave him to settle his course without any suggestion of fitting in to a common plan.'
>
> *Secondly*: 'If you want to get more production, the chief way to do that is not to improve mechanical equipment, but to get more out of the workers.'[60]

Because these were the first two Working Party reports to appear, their publication generated much attention in the newspapers and periodicals. Both *The Times* and *The Economist* gave considerable space to the pottery document, praising its thoroughness. Each felt that the report was unlikely to prove contentious (indeed *The Economist* went so far as to call it 'anodyne').[61] Others were quick to emphasise the enquiry's apparent backing for private enterprise. The NUM *Journal* found the report 'refreshing' because it was 'a complete vindication' of the existing owners – it pointed to 'deficiencies, but not inefficiencies'.[62] The *Financial Times* made a similar point. The Working Party had done 'a businesslike job' and its recommendations were 'without detectable political bias'. Employers could collectively feel much reassured: 'Despite proverbs about single swallows, the fear that working parties necessarily foreshadowed radical Government interference in the affairs of non-nationalised industries should be slightly allayed by the first report to be published.'[63] The cotton report provoked even more comment. All were agreed that the enquiry had been worthwhile, with a correspondent in *Industry Illustrated* calling the report truly important and 'justifying the Working Party mechanism in no uncertain manner'.[64] Perhaps surprisingly, there was also a measure of consensus against the Jewkes approach. *The Economist*, it is true, believed both cases on the issue of intervention to be not proven, and regretted the lack of agreement.[65] However, the *New Statesman*, *Manchester Guardian* and the *Spectator* were roundly critical of the 'Memorandum of Dissent', with the latter going so far as to characterise it as a 'sentimental search for some Victorian elysium'.[66]

In Government circles, most attention focused inevitably on the cotton report. Cripps had had to interrupt his Board duties and go on a mission to India, but he was kept fully informed of the position that was developing. His officials were upset by the dissent in the report, fearing that it would encourage 'the recalcitrants' in the industry and hide what had been agreed.[67] As they informed Cripps, the situation was now very delicate:

> The employers, fortified by the independent members, have taken a stand in opposition to Schuster that probably goes beyond their real feelings. A wrong move now might harden the opposition into a continuing policy of non co-operation. Operatives naturally enough have moved in the opposite direction. . . . Stage is therefore set for a period of clash and antagonism, employers saying 'Hands off the industry', operatives saying 'Nationalize', moderate elements on both sides being submerged. The industry cannot afford the time for sterile and embittering controversy.[68]

This left Cripps with very little room for manoeuvre, and he therefore decided to buy time. The Government, it was announced, would wish 'before final decisions were reached, to have the opportunity of discussing some important aspects of the proposals with bodies representing employers and operatives in the industry'. Meanwhile, immediate action would be taken where there was no controversy, for example over the planned enquiries into existing plant and textile machinery supply. At the same time, recognition would be given to the Working Party's recommendation about a new tripartite body by asking the existing Cotton Board to take on new functions.[69] Here, Cripps was able to provide further reassurance, since he had managed to convince Sir Raymond Streat, widely respected on both sides of industry, to become both chairman of the Cotton Board and of any successor body.[70]

With these immediate points settled, Cripps turned to consider what he should do about the Working Party strategy in general. All at the Board were agreed that as many people as possible should read the reports, and so each was issued at very modest price (the pottery document cost 1s 3d, the cotton document 3s 6d). There was general recognition, too, that many of the recommendations needed to be followed up and so the Board formed a small but high-powered 'Working Squad' to monitor what was being done on each specific point and to encourage progress.[71] More generally, the Government had to decide whether any new legislation would be required, now that both Working Parties had come out in favour of a centralised board with a degree of power. On this issue, however, Cripps turned out to be fairly determined. He had resolved that 'a short four or five clause Bill empowering the Board of Trade to set up Industrial Boards etc.' would be included at the beginning of the next parliamentary session, in November 1946. All that now remained was to consult the peak organisations on their views about this, since the President 'agreed on the importance of carrying the FBI, etc.' with the Board's thinking.[72]

The FBI had played a waiting game during the early months of 1946 but, with the publication of the first two reports, its leadership recognised that the time was now right to come up with a definite policy statement. The FBI had, of course, always believed in trade associations administering trade interests, and it was obviously necessary to think closely about whether the suggested tripartite bodies would jeopardise what was really a rather fundamental principle. Accordingly, representatives from 13 Working Party industries were called together and questioned about their views on the enquiries and future developments. This consultation revealed that six groups of employers were favourable about the Working Parties and the rest lukewarm. More significantly, opinion about the next step was also divided. Some, including those from the furniture, glassware and pottery industries, argued that permanent tripartite bodies were desirable. They would carry weight in negotiations with the government and allow trade union officials to be educated about the real problems of doing business. Moreover, there was need for an 'entirely different outlook if nationalisation was to be avoided', and so the new institutions should be accepted for pragmatic reasons if no other. Against this, there were others present who could see no good in going down this road. The worry in this camp was about boosting the authority of the unions and allowing government officials a foot in the door. In addition, there was a gut feeling that the existing owners knew best and should not be hamstrung:

> He deprecated the idea of handing over the responsibility for an industry to an outside body on the grounds that it was in the national interest that it should be done when in fact all the experience and knowledge of the industry were in the hands of those who, in the past, had built up the business of which the industry consisted.

These were feelings that, at any rate, found favour with those from boots and shoes, linoleum and heavy clothing.[73]

In this situation, the FBI leadership had little alternative but to set up a committee to examine the whole question further, and this started meeting in mid-July.[74] By mid-September, it was agreed that another meeting with Working Party representatives would be opportune, and the different groups were once again called in to face the leadership. However, the intervening months had hardly healed the division of opinion. No one was in favour of a single model of tripartite body, applicable in all situations, and all agreed on the need for keeping the government's influence in whatever transpired to the absolute minimum. But there was, as before, disagreement about whether any kind of new body was necessary. Some again repeated warnings about the unions and argued that the existing trade associations would be perfectly able to organise initiatives, such as boosting research, which the Working Parties had suggested be devolved on to the tripartite boards. Others felt that to do nothing would be politically inept. A member of the Hosiery Working Party underlined the case for tactical concessions:

> The hosiery industry had found it impossible to resist the setting up of a Working Party but the dice were somewhat heavily loaded against the employer members. Unless they were prepared to make certain concessions in regard to a continuing body, they would have been looked upon as completely reactionary, a view which the public would have been taught to share. If the employers had stood out against a continuing body, the . . . majority of the Working Party would have favoured a very different kind of continuing body than . . . was now recommended. . . . By conceding a continuing body, the employers had been able to secure that it was relatively innocuous, and possessed no statutory powers.[75]

The consequence of this was that when the FBI finally came to deliver its verdict to Cripps in early October, expediency seemed very much in evidence. Baillieu stressed to the President that his organisation continued to believe that trade associations should remain the fundamental institutions in representing the needs of industry to government. They were, he insisted, 'over a large area of industry, adequate for the purpose' and, in consultation with the Board, could 'carry through any developments which . . . [were] needed to meet the present and future situations'. However, he admitted that other solutions might on occasion be justified, particularly in cases where the trade association was weak. There might be need in some situations for advisory councils, though these should never have executive powers: 'I was asked to underline the fact that these bodies should be advisory and not executive. Any executive action that is needed should be left to the established organisations in the industry.' There might be cause even, in a 'very small number of cases', to go further and create a 'Statutory Supervisory Board with executive powers'. But, Baillieu warned, pursuing this latter course would be impossible unless the employers in question had already sanctioned it. Implementation without consent would render impotent whatever was created.[76]

This declaration left Cripps in a rather difficult position. Board opinion did not rate trade associations highly. They had, after all, done little in the past to aid modernisation. Furthermore, their essential character did not encourage the belief that they could be transformed into engines of progress. As one Board official noted on reviewing the FBI's policy:

> The emphasis on Trade Associations completely ignores the extent to which they are governed and their activities limited by trade politics and personalities, and the influence of large firms. So long as their officials are directly dependent on voluntary contributions for their salaries and on this or that manufacturer's backing for their chances of advancement, I do not see how one can hope to get very far with real co-operative enterprise.[77]

Yet Cripps was also aware that simply ignoring the employers' opinions might provoke significant political difficulties.

Some factors did, it is true, seem to encourage persistence with the existing strategy. Press coverage of the FBI position was in some important cases rather critical.[78] All of the next batch of Working Party reports – covering boots and shoes, hosiery, furniture and heavy clothing[79] – once again recommended some form of continuing tripartite body. Moreover, there was now increasing pressure from the TUC not to back down. From the trade union point of view, the Working Party reports were by no means perfect, but they did at least seem to represent an advance.[80] On the other hand, the FBI policy was understood to be nothing more than an attempt to scare the government into submission.[81] Cripps must therefore stand firm: as the TUC emphasised to him, he should prepare legislation which would allow the creation of what were now being talked of as Development Councils with statutory powers, regardless of whether those in an industry felt that such a body was desirable or not. If necessary, 'various methods of persuasion' should be used to bring the employers into line.[82]

However, it was also clear that the employers were becoming more hostile the nearer the Minister came to introducing legislation. Pressure was being exerted at two levels. One line of attack involved attempting to influence the Board about the final shape of the Bill, by, for example, insisting on a clause ensuring that a Development Council could never be imposed.[83] More generally, employers' organisations continued to argue that legislation was quite superfluous, since Working Party recommendations could be carried out by current institutions. A Board official recorded in early 1947:

> It looks as if the BEC are working with the FBI in their opposition to the Bill. The idea is . . . to show that many of the functions proposed for Development Councils are unnecessary because they are being or could be performed by existing joint machinery . . . [or] Trade Associations; therefore there is no place for Development Councils at all and the Bill should be dropped.[84]

In fact, some groups of manufacturers in Working Party industries had taken this tactic a stage further by setting up allegedly joint organisations to deal with, for example, the recommended expansion in research.[85] What made all of this even more serious, as Cripps had to recognise, was the fact that because employers were spending so much time and effort on trying to thwart legislation, progress with implementing the technical changes that were highlighted in the enquiries remained in most cases very slow.[86]

This was clearly a rather disheartening scenario, but Cripps decided in the end that the best course of action was to proceed as planned, and during February 1947 the Industrial Organisation Bill was presented to the Commons. In introducing this legislation, Cripps returned to many of the themes that had marked Labour policy since the end of the war. The Working Party reports, he noted, showed once again that much of British industry needed to be modernised. Big firms were often very efficient, but smaller units required help in improving their standards. The state needed to play a part here because industry's performance was a national question. Moreover, no other institution or set of institutions could do what was necessary. Trade associations were certainly not acceptable substitutes:

> Trade associations are, essentially, bodies representing employers only, just as trade unions represent employees only. For the purposes which we have in view, and which the working parties had in view, it is essential . . . that both employers and employees . . . be represented. . . . It is, therefore, out of the question for anyone with an up-to-date realisation of the development of relationships in industry to imagine that any body could be acceptable for such a purpose, unless it included both employers and employees.[87]

The legislation was designed to 'provide methods for enabling private enterprise industries to bring themselves up to date'.[88] But it was framed so that new initiatives would be introduced with the agreement of all sides and not, as in the past, at the whim of employers.

Turning to the details of the Bill, Cripps noted that what he proposed was enabling legislation, since proceeding by introducing specific statutes for each industry would only mean disabling delay. The new Bill allowed for the government to be able to create Development Councils after consulting with everyone in an industry. The new bodies would be charged with increasing efficiency and improving the service which the industry could render to the community. Each was to be made up of members drawn from three constituencies – employers, employees and independents. Much of the work to be done would be essentially advisory. Nevertheless, the Development Councils were to have some statutory powers, so that, for example, they could maintain a register of persons carrying out business in the industry and raise levies to cover their expenses. Parliamentary control would be ensured because the House was to vote on each specific order for setting up a Council. Moreover, the Councils themselves would have to present annual reports to the Minister responsible.[89]

The Conservatives' reaction to Cripps's proposal was not favourable. Lyttelton explained that his party, too, wanted British industry to be efficient but did not believe that this was the way to go about ensuring progress. The Conservatives were anxious about the form of the legislation – they felt an enabling bill gave too much power to the Ministers – and the new bureaucracy that it might help to create. Most of all, they opposed the basic assumption involved, that the government had a direct role to play in modernising industry. As Lyttelton saw it,

> The fundamental question is whether we abandon the voluntary method of negotiation, and undermine the voluntary organisations which exist in this field, in favour of State machinery such as the development councils.[90]

For Conservatives, therefore, the issue was at bottom about preserving employers' rights to determine their own futures. Mr Sidney Shephard, MP for Newark and a hosiery manufacturer, made this point very clearly. After calling the Bill 'thoroughly bad and mischievous', and arguing that it would not increase productivity, he went on to note that it would 'perpetuate permanent control':

> I was always a little suspicious that this was what would happen. When the President . . . set up his working parties, I thought that there was a little more in it than mere efficiency of industry. I thought he was after closer control over industry, and I think we all realise that by this Bill he has achieved his object.[91]

Given such feelings, it was not unexpected to find the Conservatives opposing the Bill on its second reading and harrying it through the committee stage. During the final reading, their tactics changed somewhat, with the focus now on the introduction of modifying amendments. The most important of these was presented by Lyttelton and involved restricting the Minister's right to form a Development Council: he was not to be allowed to make an order if 'a large majority of the persons carrying on business in the industry, representing the greater part of the production in that industry, and a large majority of the workers in that industry' were opposed to it. This quite clearly struck at the heart of the Bill, and was thus unacceptable to Labour. Cripps had always stressed that orders would be issued only after consultation, but he was not prepared to drop the right to proceed as he saw fit if circumstances demanded it. What could be achieved, after all, if the least progressive elements in the industry were actually in the majority?[92] With such opposition brushed aside, the Bill now became law.[93]

Nevertheless, even with legislative backing, the Board still found that making progress over this issue was extremely difficult. Cripps faced problems in obtaining adequate numbers of trained staff to prepare Development Council legislation,[94] but his biggest obstacle remained the attitude of the employers. The Board agreed that its best chance of success would be to pass orders for only one or two sectors at first, in order to put pressure on the more recalcitrant,[95] but it was soon clear that even this rather modest objective would be rather difficult to see through. Some groups of manufacturers (for instance, those in pottery) simply refused any kind of co-operation, insisting that their industries did not need the new institution.[96] Others continued with the tactic of developing apparently alternative forums for activities such as research, in the hope that this would undermine any kind of case that the Board was putting together.[97] By the end of 1947, therefore, the situation remained essentially deadlocked. The TUC was reportedly becoming restive, fearing that the Board might finally retreat from its original purpose.[98] Yet the Board recognised that it had little room for manoeuvre. As one official explained, 'in one industry after another' the civil servants were meeting 'the same opposition from the Employers' Associations'. Moreover, to those officials involved it was quite clear that the resistance was being co-ordinated and that, in fact, 'the FBI were behind it'.[99] All that the Board could do, it seemed, as Harold Wilson replaced Cripps in the President's job, during the autumn of 1947, was to pledge that it would 'have a go' again at 'particular industries'.[100]

What of the other two Board initiatives? Taking the question of the management institute, first, it will be remembered that Cripps and the Cabinet had quite quickly agreed after the 1945 General Election that the Weir recommendations should go ahead on the basis of a £150,000 five-year grant. Soon after this decision, Cripps determined that his next move must be to consolidate support amongst industrialists. He felt that an influential committee was needed in order to examine exactly how Weir should be implemented. To head this committee, Cripps turned to Sir Clive Baillieu, President of the FBI.[101] Baillieu accepted, and in ensuing discussions it was decided that his committee should be composed of as many leading businessmen as possible, in order to diminish the scope for the kind of wrangling – with management consultants, management associations and small business interests – that had been evident to some extent in previous discussions.[102] In the end, 15 of the 23 appointments came directly from the world of big business (they included the Deputy Chairman of ICI, the General Manager of Barclay's Bank, the Chairman of Courtaulds and the Vice-Chairman of Morris Motors), while several others were indirectly connected in that they held high office in various employers' associations.[103]

The Baillieu Committee reported in early March 1946. It accepted that the need for a central institute was 'urgent'[104] and then went on, as requested, to outline what the new institution should look like. Since, as Baillieu emphasised, the suggested British Institute of Management (BIM) was not to replace existing management bodies, one of its prime responsibilities would obviously concern co-ordination. But the BIM was also to have wider duties, especially in relation to research, education and propaganda.[105] Moreover, it would, as a professional body, be able to offer an appropriate system of qualifications.[106] However, the Committee did not want this latter function to mean that the BIM should only service an élite, and it underlined the fact that the membership base must be as wide as possible, encompassing the management associations, industrial and commercial firms, trade associations and trade unions, and interested individuals.[107] Finally, on finance, it was agreed that the Cripps/Dalton formula was the right one, though a rider was added that if the BIM were still not self-financing in year six but if it had proved its worth, 'Government aid on a moderate scale for a further period would be warranted in the national interest'.[108]

Cripps generally welcomed these recommendations and took them to the Lord President's Committee, where they were accepted with very little comment.[109] Outside the government, much of the interested periodical press was equally positive. Favourable editorials appeared in *Industrial Welfare* and the *Engineer*, while *Industry Illustrated* was enthusiastic enough to claim:

> The plan is far and away the most shapely and robust so far produced. . . . It has a positive air about it, it is sponsored by a very determined member of the Government and above all it has substantial Treasury backing.

'The establishment of this new body', the journal predicted, would 'give an immense stimulus to scientific management'.[110]

However, elsewhere old prejudices remained potent. N. Kipping (now Director-General of the FBI) warned Cripps that the Baillieu Report, whatever the composition of the Committee, was a 'compromise'. In the management field, he reiterated, there was a profound cleavage between the 'operative side and the Institutional side', with the former viewing the latter as 'of little value'. Baillieu's conclusions were seen by the institutions as on balance against their interests, and so Cripps could expect considerable opposition from this direction. Furthermore, Kipping added, it was by no means certain, again in spite of the way in which the Baillieu Committee had been put together, that industry would in fact provide the required support, and so the government should be prepared to have to continue funding after the fifth year. Kipping ended by advising that Cripps should stand firm but that he could not expect an easy next few months as far as this project was concerned.[111]

More worrying from the Board's point of view was lobbying that continued to emanate from the secretariat of the old Management Research Group 1, now renamed the Industrial Management Research Association (IMRA). This involved a series of 'confidential reports', circulated to members and to non-members such as the TUC, and reaching as far as the USA, which ridiculed the Baillieu recommendations and condemned the 'quackery' that would arise from them.[112] What made this particularly serious was the fact that IMRA was known to have close links with the FBI. Not all FBI leaders agreed with the kind of criticism being offered – indeed one went so far as to call it 'ridiculous'[113] – but it remained unarguable that the IMRA line had found considerable support amongst many of that organisation's major industrial subscribers.[114]

The upshot of all of this was that when the Board came to begin implementation of Baillieu's scheme, it found it extremely difficult to make much progress. The first task was to form the BIM's ruling

Council, but the Board was hindered here by a lack of willing volunteers.[115] In the end, Cripps had to settle for a group that was essentially a permutation of long-term Board contacts: a few consultants alongside such veterans of state–industry deliberations as Baillieu, Kipping, Schuster, Streat and the new Industrial and Commercial Finance Corporation Chairman, Piercy.[116] This was clearly a set-back, and it reflected a wider sense of drift, commented on by *Industry Illustrated* in July 1947:

> What has happened to the much-vaunted proposals for a central Institute of Management? It is now over 15 months since the President . . . made his statement in the House . . . accepting the recommendations of the Baillieu Committee, and it is more than 6 months since the appointment . . . of the Council. . . . The only sign of life that has since appeared was a recent advertisement for a Chief Executive.[117]

Indeed, even when a Chief Executive was finally appointed in the autumn of that year, the nomination did little to raise spirits. The man picked to do the job, the Hon. Leo Russell, no doubt had many fine qualities – being an ex-Etonian, veteran of Montgomery's staff and then Assistant Secretary at the Board of Trade and gentleman farmer[118] – but he could hardly be presented as the obvious choice to galvanise a new management institution, since he had not even applied for the job. The BIM, like the Working Parties, seemed to have become bogged down in intrigue.

Cripps's third area of interest, the PES, by contrast developed fairly smoothly. The service was launched in March 1946 and had built up its establishment to nearly thirty by April of the following year.[119] The approach taken remained strongly influenced by human relations. The PES, *Industry Illustrated* reported, could give 'technical assistance in connection with any production difficulty' but, as its Director F.E. Chappell remarked, technical efficiency alone would not necessarily produce the desired results. There must be 'special attention . . . accorded the human problem'.[120] This was clearly a message which some firms were interested to hear, and so the PES found itself almost continually busy, handling, for example, 121 major and 254 minor enquiries over its first eight months of operation. The type of work undertaken varied enormously:

> At one end of the scale the function of the Service has been to steer a problem that has been worrying . . . [a] firm into the appropriate

> Department channel; at the other end one or more officers have sometimes been involved in days or weeks on the factory floor.[121]

This was hardly sufficient to transform the economy, as a later FBI assessment recorded; but it did nevertheless represent clearly 'useful activity'.[122]

Cripps would, therefore, look back on his years at the Board of Trade with some frustration. The President had been able to raise the productivity issue in front of many different audiences but he had found it much more difficult to create dynamic institutions with which to tackle Britain's real problems. Indeed, two out of his three initiatives were proceeding only very slowly, opposed at every turn by various groups of employers. Had other Labour Ministers been able to make any better progress on the productivity issue?

This is not an easy question to answer because all of the non-Board of Trade strategies to improve efficiency were essentially small scale and therefore not subject to much publicity. Nevertheless, it is clear that other departments were not without their successes. Thus, for example, the Ministry of Labour was continuing to gain some notable results with its Training Within Industry (TWI) programmes. TWI, which originated in the USA, was aimed at supervisors and involved showing them how to be better communicators. The advantage of the scheme was that it could be completed very quickly, since it usually involved only five two-hour training sessions. Moreover, TWI seemed to bring results. Thus, almost as soon as the Ministry of Labour had set up its TWI facilities at the end of the war, the technique was being described as 'arousing . . . extraordinary enthusiasm amongst managers'. Soon thousands of supervisors were being shown TWI each month, and in fact as many as 100,000 may have been schooled in the method by the end of 1947.[123] Like the PES, TWI did not transform Britain's productivity position, yet neither can its impact be described as negligible.

This largely concludes the discussion of Labour's policies on productivity in the first two post-war years. But it would be wrong to conclude this chapter without drawing attention to a fresh emphasis that was increasingly evident in the Government's approach to productivity as the period drew to a close. Labour's initial programme, to repeat, had mainly been concerned with creating new institutions in order to raise standards. As the months of 1947 passed, however, there was growing recognition that such an approach alone might well be inadequate. It was all very well to open up the production process and to educate managers, supervisors and workers as to how things could be done better, but all of this effort would be wasted unless there was some mechanism to ensure that such people would want to work in the improved ways. What the Government needed, the argument ran, was more knowledge about motivation and incentives and a set of policies to match. This change of approach is explored in all of its dimensions during the course of the following chapter.

Chapter 5

Human relations and productivity, 1947–51

Much of the change in emphasis about the productivity issue that became evident during 1947 stemmed from, and was shaped by, the growing influence of the 'human relations' approach to industry and its management. The term 'human relations' embraced a number of different perspectives and was in some ways nebulous, but its central thrust hinged upon an admonition that the workers needed to be treated as more than just a factor of production, especially if real gains in efficiency were to be made.[1] This chapter looks in detail at why the 'human relations' approach surfaced in 1947, and then examines how it shaped government policy over the ensuing years. Particular emphasis is placed on two official initiatives – the Committee on Industrial Productivity (CIP) and the relaunching of Joint Production Committees – though some attention will also be given to the question of incentives, seen by some contemporaries as very much a related issue.

The turn to 'human relations' as a key to the productivity question occurred for a number of reasons. One general factor that encouraged the change was the fact that many people were increasingly inclined to talk of productivity in general as if *labour* productivity were its only component. This stress on the workers' efficiency was partly conditioned by wartime experience, when manpower planning had been so important. However, it was also encouraged by current economic circumstances: everybody recognised, after all, that in the post-war world, with resources constrained, growth must depend to some extent on how well the existing workforce did its job. What made the idea of labour productivity all the more appealing was the fact that it seemed to be fairly easily quantifiable, as Rostas's work for the Board of Trade apparently demonstrated.[2]

More specifically, the growing popularity of a 'human relations' perspective was also linked to a particular perception of what was going on in the workplace. Most on the Left believed that labour discipline had traditionally been enforced by the fear of unemployment. Moreover, it had long been predicted that once this 'stick' was removed, workers would respond positively, intensifying effort as a mark of gratitude for 'their' government's wider reforms. Unfortunately, however, there was little real evidence that this was actually happening. In fact, reports from the production front seemed often to suggest that apathy rather than a new zeal was the most common condition.

Of course, some of this comment could be dismissed as Right-wing exaggeration, but there were enough authoritative observations on this theme to indicate that it was not all the product of uninformed prejudice. Some credence had to be given to a *Times Review of Industry* report in April 1947, for example, which described 'many managements' as feeling that 'the actual effort put forward by the individual worker' was 'less than . . . before the war'. Nor was it possible to ignore a *Nature* editorial on incentives which concluded: 'while fear is happily disappearing as a goad to work, no positive enthusiasm is taking its place'. Indeed, Government Ministers could hardly fail to be aware that there was some substance here, since their exhortatory 'Work or Want' campaign in the spring of 1947 had achieved so little that it was openly being described as disastrous.[3]

For many on the Left, therefore, the important questions about production were increasingly to do with topics such as motivation. The general consensus was that 'capitalist discipline' had broken down; workers were, in other words, no longer afraid of their bosses' power, largely because unemployment had ceased to exist. In this situation, as G.D.H. Cole explained, there was 'no adequate feeling in the factories in favour of reaching the highest possible level of efficiency'; indeed, there could well be reasons why workers might be becoming more attached to a type of 'unconscious, or half conscious, restriction'. What Labour needed to do, therefore, was to encourage the growth of a new understanding, which would provide those on the shopfloor with self-discipline. For Cole, this meant talking to the workers directly: the administration must give 'clear indications' to workers that it wanted not just their 'acquiescence' but also their 'positive collaboration in organising to achieve the required result'.[4]

Inevitably, Ministers reacted to these promptings in somewhat different ways. Cripps had long been an enthusiast for involving the worker, though others were certainly less positive on this score. Nevertheless, during 1947 there was growing agreement in all quarters that, as one periodical put it, the 'peculiar circumstances' that affected productivity in Britain related 'as much to human relations as to technical efficiency'.[5] In these circumstances, it was inevitable that the Government should begin considering what it could do to ameliorate the situation.

One decision was to launch a formal investigation into the whole question of the human factor. The origins of this development lay with a committee that Morrison had formed in early 1947. The Advisory Council on Scientific Policy, under Sir Henry Tizard, was charged with finding the 'most appropriate form of research effort to assist the maximum increase in . . . national productivity during, say, the next ten years, including research in natural and social sciences'. The Tizard Committee, as it was popularly known, was not considered to have been very successful in general, but it had come up with one significant finding, that the human factor was extremely important. Indeed, a sub-committee of the main Committee had gone so far as to argue:

> Current fundamental research in physical and biological sciences is unlikely . . . to have any material short term effect on increasing productivity. . . . The blunt fact . . . is that the problem is essentially psychological in the short term.[6]

Clearly such a conclusion fitted the mood of late 1947 and so Ministers began discussing what it meant in practical terms. Officials reported that quite a number of organisations were already working on aspects of human relations – the Tavistock Institute, the National Institute of Industrial Psychology, etc. – but their efforts tended to be uncoordinated. In these circumstances, Ministers agreed that their best option would be to form 'a good steering body', a central organisation, to be named the Committee on Industrial Productivity, with several offshoots examining specific questions. Crucial amongst the latter would be a panel on human factors, which might be headed by Sir George Schuster.[7]

Schuster was in agreement with this proposal, and, as the year ended, approached both the FBI and the TUC to gain their co-operation. The TUC was generally acquiescent, though the General Secretary, V. Tewson, emphasised that he did not want all of the emphasis in the new enquiry to be on labour. Nor should public statements on what was intended lend themselves 'to misrepresentations, such as that the workers were to be psychoanalysed'.[8] The FBI, on the other hand, was more cautious. It was not prepared to obstruct Schuster in public, but behind the scenes remained highly suspicious. The FBI's leadership felt that it should have been consulted at an earlier stage and did not really like the whole idea anyway. An enquiry might perhaps be useful, but there were great dangers, particularly with the subject Schuster was tackling, 'of doing harm', particularly if 'theorists' became too involved.[9]

Given this climate of suspicion, those involved in an official capacity clearly felt that it was their duty to 'talk up' the whole project and so, during 1948, both Tizard (by now in charge of the whole CIP exercise) and Schuster were to be heard singing its praises. The former felt that he was directing a 'survey on survival'. Britain must catch up with best overseas practice, or perish: 'We've got to do it quickly, too. . . . I've set a time limit of two years. If we haven't got results in that time we shall have failed.' Schuster made much the same kind of point, arguing that something must be done 'to bring the laggards into line': 'You will be starting a new era if you can get British industry to depart from its old traditional methods of secretive individualism and join in co-operative effort.'[10]

This was a powerful message, and it at first seemed to bring results. Thus, Schuster's panel was quickly operational and boasting a prestigious membership, including L. Russell from the BIM, J. Tanner and E.P. Harries from the TUC, and representatives from the National Institute of Industrial Psychology, the Medical Research Council and the Tavistock Institute.[11] This, in turn, allowed a quick start with actual investigations, the majority being joint ventures directed by the panel and carried out by teams of experts drawn from existing organisations.[12] Within a relatively short time, therefore, enquiry was being undertaken on such diverse subjects as work load and machine control (involving the Cambridge Psychological Laboratory); morale (involving the Medical Research Council's Industrial Psychology Research Unit); and human relations within particular settings (for example, the Glacier Metal Company project run by the Tavistock Institute).[13]

This was an impressive performance but, in the end, it proved difficult to sustain. Schuster's relationship with bodies such as the Medical Research Council remained less than easy, complicated by administrative and funding problems.[14] Moreover, the condition of the wider CIP organisation continued to be unsatisfactory, undermined by, amongst other things, a rapid turnover of personnel.[15] In fact, Tizard's first report was given an almost universally poor reception, with *Industry* concluding that it did 'not inspire confidence'.[16] The final blow to the whole initiative came as a result of the success of the Anglo-American Council on Productivity: as that body blossomed, the CIP was left requesting its own liquidation, convinced that the work that it had started could best be finished by others.[17] The CIP had bequeathed a legacy of detailed studies and had reinforced some general points about productivity. It could not be said, however, to have galvanised either the public or the two sides of industry.

The second major development on human relations came with the relaunching of Joint Production Committees. The initial impetus here came from the TUC, and reflected that organisation's perception of the role that JPCs had played during the war period. The committees' contribution had been 'uneven', but there was 'little doubt that when they were worked with enthusiasm by both management and labour they produced excellent results'.[18] This appreciation was the basis for an approach to the employers that together they should recommend to the National Joint Advisory Council (NJAC) – the major 'peak' tripartite body for industrial relations – that it should encourage the relaunch of JPCs. At the NJAC such a policy was agreed in the following terms:

> The NJAC approved the principle of the setting up of joint consultation machinery, where it does not at present already exist, for the regular exchange of views between employers and workers on production questions provided it was clearly understood that:
> (a) The machinery would be purely voluntary and advisory in character;
> (b) It would not deal with the terms and conditions of employment;
> (c) It would be up to each industry to decide the appropriate form of machinery.[19]

In advocating this policy, S. Bagnall from the TUC argued that 'JPCs were fundamental if the workers were to be made to feel that the state of the nation was their personal concern'.[20] As this suggests, the TUC had come to put a great deal of weight on JPCs.

In part, this resulted from the TUC's general support for the Government's campaign to increase output. The organisation's commitment here was demonstrated in a number of ways. For example, in response to the production crisis in 1946, the TUC called a conference to encourage trade union executives to pursue the production drive; in 1947 it agreed to the partial reintroduction of labour direction under the Control of Engagements Order.[21] Thus, the TUC was willing to go a long way with the Government's production policies. At the same time, the TUC saw JPCs giving rein to the workers' perceived desire to be involved in production issues, as they were thought to have been in wartime. There were worries about the scope that JPCs might give to 'disruptive' behaviour by Communist shop stewards but, by and large, the TUC nailed its colours firmly to the mast of extending the joint committees. Successive Congresses in the late 1940s saw calls for JPCs to be made compulsory, a demand that was accepted by many unions and by Labour Party Conferences.[22]

Employers' views on JPCs were mixed. Even whilst accepting the TUC proposal for their expansion, Sir Alexander Ramsay of the FBI played down their role: 'While agreeing that JPCs were valuable [he] could not agree that they were fundamental and that their general adoption would solve the problem of the productivity of labour.'[23] This scepticism was grounded on a number of worries about what JPCs would do.

First, employers were concerned to prevent the emphasis on JPCs directing attention away from their own view that the constraints on productivity were primarily excessive taxation, too many controls and other features of government policy. This was the agenda of issues which they emphasised when asked what could be done to raise output and productivity.[24] Second, employers were worried that JPCs would tend to trespass on areas of managerial prerogative, hence the emphasis on their purely advisory character. Employers bridled at the productionist rhetoric of some of the unions, believing that JPCs were seen in some quarters as the thin end of the wedge of workers' control.[25]

Nevertheless, many employers' organisations in this period took up the urging of the NJAC to come to agreements on JPC machinery with the relevant unions. By 1949, employers and unions in ten industries (including engineering, iron and steel, shipbuilding and woollens) had recommended JPCs with a model constitution, while in another sixteen industries (including chemicals, furniture and tobacco) recommendations without a model constitution had been made.[26] By and large, employers' national bodies were willing to endorse the extension of joint consultation.

But this support was subject to clear conditions. These included the three that were listed in the original NJAC agreement, noted above. In addition, employers were very concerned to keep JPCs as purely factory-level bodies, and resisted any wider role for them. In particular, they rejected the idea that JPCs might be involved in inter-plant visits, or might form part of local or regional networks. Hence employers opposed the idea that Regional Boards for Industry should do any more than encourage JPCs where a national agreement on their role already existed. They were wholly hostile to the view that JPCs might become part of an official system transcending the gates of the factory. This was commonly expressed by saying that joint consultation was a purely 'domestic' matter, and certainly *not* part of the national planning machinery.[27]

At the level of the peak associations the picture is one of support for JPCs, albeit qualified in a number of respects amongst the employers. This common support was accompanied by an agreement on both sides that JPCs should not deal with issues of wages and conditions. Hence productivity questions were to be clearly demarcated from those relating to wages and conditions. In many ways this was a strange position: clearly many productivity-related issues (most obviously payments systems and work reorganisation) impinged on wages and conditions. However, this dichotomy was shaped by deeply entrenched attitudes and practices. Most importantly, it reflected the strength of voluntarism in industrial relations: the belief that wages and conditions should be negotiated by a process of free collective bargaining between employers and organised workers. On the union side, support for such a view wavered only briefly under the Attlee Governments, when some (mostly on the Left) argued that the logical corollary to the planned economy that they desired was wage planning. But this position never won majority support, and quickly disappeared when the Government pursued its incomes policy from 1948 and most of the Left swung round to support free collective bargaining. This later view, too, was endorsed by employers.[28]

Support for voluntarism meant that unions and employers together continually sought to limit the role of Government in the productivity drive, because of the recognition that such activity would always be likely to impinge on the sphere of voluntary union–employer agreement. Thus, for example, both sides resisted the idea of local conferences of employers and unions addressed by politicians on productivity issues, because, it was suggested, they would cut across the established pattern of industrial relations.[29]

On the employers' side, the separation of issues posed a difficult problem because the British Employers' Confederation (BEC) dealt with wages, and the FBI with production questions. This split was reproduced at a higher level, since the National Joint Advisory Council (where the BEC represented employers) dealt with issues related to collective bargaining, while the National Production Advisory Council for Industry (NPACI) addressed issues related to production (with the FBI representing employers). Both the BEC and the FBI were adamant in maintaining these distinct channels, but JPCs posed a dilemma. On the one hand, their establishment was clearly seen by Government as a production question while, on the other, both employer bodies wanted to keep them within the framework of collective agreements. The FBI accepted that this latter consideration meant that JPCs should come under the BEC and the NJAC. In consequence, FBI discussions of productivity explicitly excluded labour-related issues as being the preserve of the BEC.[30]

The TUC *de facto* accepted this division. Whilst keen to promote JPCs as a production and productivity issue (indeed, the key to that issue), it was equally concerned to maintain the tradition of voluntary collective agreements. This posture could have eccentric results, as, for example, when the TUC accepted motion study as helpful to improved production but resisted time study as impinging on wage issues.[31] More generally, the issue of JPCs illustrated the tension between a strong and continuing commitment to voluntary collective bargaining and a commitment to seeking improvements in productivity.

This tension was also very much present in the Government's approach to JPCs. The initial impetus for their revival came from Cripps and others who were concerned with increasing output and efficiency in the short run. To this end the production Ministries tried to use all available possibilities for the encouragement of the committees. In particular they attempted to utilise the Regional Boards for Industry for this purpose, aided by initiatives from within some of those Boards. However, the NJAC only accepted this role for Regional Boards subject to strict conditions, especially the existence of a prior national agreement relating to the relevant industry.[32]

In part this employer resistance stemmed from antagonism to any governmental intervention in what employers (and, to a degree, unions) regarded as their domestic matters. Thus, both sides were unenthusiastic about alternative proposals for the Ministry of Labour rather than Regional Boards to encourage JPCs; the employers, for example, refused to supply the Ministry with the names of the firms where joint consultation had not been established. But there was acceptance that if regional agencies were to have any role in this area, it should be the Regional Industrial Relations Officers of the Ministry of Labour who should be involved, rather than the Regional Boards associated with the production Ministries.[33]

The Ministry of Labour's approach to JPCs was increasingly diverging from that of the production Ministries. By the beginning of 1949 this position was quite explicit, a memorandum from the Ministry arguing that the establishment of joint consultation machinery 'should be regarded as a principal long-term industrial relations objective, and not simply a short-term objective in the interests of increased productivity'.[34]

As part of his enthusiasm for JPCs Cripps encouraged the Ministry of Labour to find a senior official to spearhead the policy of encouragement. In 1948 the Ministry concurred and appointed Lloyd Roberts from ICI, whose background was in personnel management. In effect the Ministry took the opportunity to involve someone who would encourage their view of JPCs and discourage the 'productionist' approach of Cripps. Lloyd Roberts argued that employers' hesitancy in establishing JPCs was encouraged by the fact that the campaign was 'primarily sponsored by the Chancellor of the Exchequer of whose views and intentions as to the future control of industry they have some suspicion'. He felt that:

> It would have a beneficial effect on this aspect if gradually the Ministry of Labour came to be recognised as the sponsoring Ministry, and if, simultaneously, the emphasis in the campaign were put on the industrial relations value of joint consultation rather than on its contribution to increased productivity as a direct objective.[35]

The Ministry of Labour's strategy was to emphasise joint consultation as a matter of good industrial relations, to be established by negotiation, and to be pursued (gently) by means of the Ministry's own Personnel Management Advisory Service. This approach was not unproblematic, as the BEC sometimes regarded the Ministry's personnel management role as an attempt to 'teach employers their business'. Nevertheless, from 1948 onwards, the long-term industrial relations aspects of JPCs tended to dominate over the production aspects. One indication of this was the way in which the 1949 Ministry of Labour document on Joint Consultation ended up being incorporated within the Ministry's 1953 *Handbook on Industrial Relations* in a chapter entitled 'Personnel Management and Joint Consultation'.[36]

Cripps resisted this downgrading of joint consultation in relation to immediate productivity objectives. But his position in this context was weak. On the one hand, as noted above, the Ministry of Labour's view fitted more readily with the positions of the employers' organisations and the TUC about voluntarism and the sanctity of collective agreements. On the other hand, Cripps's own attachment to the Tavistock view of joint consultation as being about building a consensus in the workplace ruled out any idea of imposing JPCs on unwilling employers. With this option ruled out, the Ministry of Labour's slow-but-sure approach was greatly strengthened.[37]

In sum, JPCs became a major issue in 1947 because both senior Ministers in the Government and the TUC saw them as tying together the immediately compelling issue of achieving more output and the feeling that a new deal for the workers in the factories was both desirable and necessary under conditions of full employment. In the initial enthusiasm, human relations appeared to link these two things in a manner that was politically congenial to the Government. But human relations notions which were taken seriously were an ambiguous basis for a campaign on JPCs which had the intention of rapidly raising productivity. In fact, human relations doctrine, along with the structure of British industrial relations, facilitated the incorporation of the committees into a quite different project, where they would be but a small addition to the armoury of good industrial relations practice, encouraged (but no more) by a Ministry of Labour determined to maintain the voluntarist basis of those relations.

How did all of this impact on another traditional Left-wing aim, the achievement of industrial democracy? Industrial democracy was certainly an important element in the political rhetoric of the Labour Government. In the 1945 Manifesto, *Let Us Face the Future*, the issue was not mentioned, but by the time of the 1950 Labour statement of principles, *Labour and the New Society*, 'democracy in the workplace' was said to be central to the creation of a 'live democracy'.[38] What was the relation between Labour's notions of industrial democracy and the policy emphasis on joint consultation?

The institutional implications of industrial democracy had, of course, long been argued about within the Labour Party, especially in the context of proposals for nationalisation. In the early 1930s the crucial battles were fought out in relation to Morrison's concept of the public corporation in which management would be appointed on the basis of expertise rather than interest representation. Advocates of workers' control fought this approach, but were decisively defeated.[39]

These discussions were re-opened in the late 1940s as the process of nationalisation took place, but the Ministerial commitment to the Morrison model never wavered; although trade unionists sat on nationalised industry boards (and the Central Electricity Board was chaired by Lord Citrine, ex-General Secretary of the TUC), they were explicitly there as experts *not* worker representatives. Coupled to this was the fact that joint consultation systems were enshrined in most of the nationalisation statutes. As purely consultative mechanisms with a limited agenda some of these seem to have had a degree of success.[40]

Policy on the nationalised industries showed how the concept of industrial democracy became almost synonymous with joint consultation and its human relations logic under the Attlee Government. Certainly, official policy statements reflected this conflation. For example, *Labour Believes in Britain* included a section on 'Democracy in Industry' which read:

> Industrial Democracy is advancing. Increasingly, the government consults with industry and industry puts its own difficulties before the Government. Development Councils, Joint Production Committees, Pit Committees and Works Councils are growing in importance in our industrial life. But these are only a beginning. More has to be done. The worker is still too often treated as a mere cog in the machine. Management must therefore be willing to bring workpeople into fuller consultation. And the worker must be ready to shoulder responsibility as well as claim rights.[41]

Labour did regard industrial democracy as very important in this period. For example, when the National Executive set out priorities for research in October 1946, the second item (after 'criteria for nationalisation') was 'economic democracy'. This was, however, defined as an 'examination of methods whereby workers can take a constructive part in the formulation of industrial policy and be induced to feel that they are working for the good of the community'. The Research Department document which followed, whilst suggesting a need for more experimentation in forms of industrial democracy, concluded: 'meanwhile we shall push ahead with the instrument the Labour Movement has now chosen for the participation by every worker in industrial democracy – joint consultation at all levels'.[42]

This position was not without its opponents. As already noted, the late 1940s saw unsuccessful pressures to reopen discussion about the workers' role in the management of the public corporation. This was linked to a wider debate on the meaning of industrial democracy and joint consultation. For example, the Union of Post Office Workers (UPW), long an advocate of workers' control, proposed a system of joint management for the Post Office, based on 50 per cent union representation on a managing board. The debate over this brought out some of the difficulties of those who wanted industrial democracy to mean something rather more than joint consultation. Perhaps most interestingly, G.D.H. Cole, long Labour's most important advocate of radical forms of such democracy, accepted the UPW view that joint consultation was different from joint management. But he also argued that the UPW scheme was about trade union control, rather than 'real' workers' control, which made it undesirable.[43]

More equivocally, even Cole was willing to see joint consultation as embodying 'the spirit of democracy', and as something to be pursued independently of whether managers were elected or worked in public or private sectors. For him, joint consultation was a basic element in the social application of democracy; and some measure of joint consultation was therefore 'an economic corollary to the admission of democratic rights for everybody on the political plane'. This argument of Cole's reflected both his rather pessimistic assessment of the current strength of belief in workers' control within the labour movement, and, more broadly, the lack of a coherent doctrine of such control in the new circumstances of the 1940s.[44] In this he was typical. Though there was a pervasive undercurrent of discontent about the collapse of industrial democracy into joint consultation, this discontent did not cohere into a significant theoretical argument or political force. Joint consultation and its human relations underpinnings therefore faced no significant opposition within Labour ranks over this period, and in fact tended to 'crowd out' any alternative vision of what industrial democracy might mean.

How, therefore, did the campaign to establish JPCs progress in this period? There is no doubt that some success was achieved, in the simple sense that many such committees were formed during the late 1940s and early 1950s. As noted above, by 1949 a significant proportion of industries had national agreements which encouraged JPCs or other forms of joint consultation, and the evidence, though imperfect, suggests that many firms responded to this encouragement.

The latest extant enquiry on the whole subject was conducted by the BEC in the middle of 1950. This suggested that most large industries had discussed and found agreement on joint consultation and that, within those industries where agreement had been reached, over 50 per cent of firms had instituted mechanisms for such consultation. Whilst this particular survey had no figures on the point, it recognised that the existence of JPCs was highly correlated with size. Slightly earlier data suggested that, on 'rough estimates', in firms with over 1,000 workers, 75 per cent had JPCs; in those with 500–1,000 workers, 50 per cent had JPCs; and in those with 150–250 workers, 30–40 per cent had JPCs.[45]

Evidence on the industrial distribution of JPCs is also imperfect, but some material survives. A survey covering a representative sample of 600 firms in 1949 found that JPCs were most prevalent in engineering

Table 5.1 Firms with Joint Production Committee machinery, 1949 sample

Sector	*Joint Production Committee* In practice	Never operated	Discontinued
Engineering	216	12	7
Shipbuilding	3	5	1
Iron and steel	11	5	0
Other heavy industry	36	28	4
Textiles	15	8	1
Building	3	7	6
Clothing	31	9	0
Food and tobacco	24	8	0
Printing	13	0	0
Other	87	38	20
Overall %	73	20	7

Source: W. Robson-Brown and N.A. Howell-Everson, *Industrial Democracy at Work: A Factual Survey* (London, 1950), pp. 7–9.

(see Table 5.1). This was perhaps unsurprising. Wartime JPCs had been concentrated in this industry, and the employers and unions in engineering had been the first to agree to revive them in 1947. Another estimate suggested that JPCs covered 782,000 out of a possible 1.25m workers in the industry. On the other hand, some sectors almost entirely lacked JPCs – perhaps most notably cotton, where they were favoured by neither employers nor unions.[46] Elsewhere, finally, though both sides were willing, progress was delayed because of disagreement on the terms on which the bodies would function. Especially controversial was the issue of whether all of the workers' representatives should be union members. This led to a long wrangle in the chemical industry, eventually settled on the employers' terms.[47]

Whilst substantial progress was made with the creation of JPCs, from the point of view of Ministers this occurred too slowly. Who was to blame here? Unsurprisingly, perhaps, each side criticised the other. Trade union leaders pointed out that insistence on the participation of non-unionists inhibited expansion, while there were also general complaints about employer resistance. Nevertheless, union leaders, too, recognised that rank and file workers often lacked enthusiasm for JPCs. Employers' organisations bemoaned the apathy of local union officials and rank and file workers, though it is clear that their own members were often quite hostile as well.[48]

The Ministry of Labour's opinion was that both of these views reflected an element of the truth. As Lloyd Roberts noted:

> My general conclusion is that the basic reason for the slow progress being made in establishing joint consultation machinery is the apathy of the general body of workers and district and local trade union officials, an apathy of which employers are quite willing to take advantage.

These attitudes were explained in the following terms:

> Some employers still feel that joint consultation has a political aspect and is the thin end of the wedge, leading to joint management or workers' control. Probably there are not many workers who understand the principle of joint consultation. If they are militant they may regard it as a step toward further control; if they are of a more average type, they may regard the idea with suspicion as a means of earning profits for the employer. In other cases both employers and workers confuse joint consultation with ordinary wage negotiating machinery.[49]

Independent sources, whilst bringing out regional and sectoral variations, also suggest that, broadly speaking, enthusiasm for joint consultation was inversely related to status in the hierarchy on either side of industry (though with the TUC always more enthusiastic than the BEC), so that national agreements were much easier to reach than those at factory level. If JPCs were established this usually arose from management rather than worker/union initiative.[50]

The BEC survey of 1950 also analysed the level at which employers and unions had agreed to implement joint consultation. The evidence from this confirms that almost all of the arrangements were for factory level bodies, perhaps with national councils as well. Most clearly excluded regional or district machinery. The only agreement relating to the regional level was in building, where a major stimulus to this kind of organisation seems to have been material shortages. This was coupled to an absence of agreement on site committees, which the BEC strongly resisted. Furthermore, district agreements were entirely absent except in the very special cases of farming and ports.[51]

What did the JPCs do? Here evidence is even more sparse and difficult to interpret. A large-scale survey by the National Institute of

Industrial Psychology found, like other studies, that welfare issues occupied a large part of the deliberations ('all tea and toilets' was a popular, dismissive view), though this survey also noted that such an emphasis was disliked by the workers' representatives on JPCs, who were critical of rank and file concerns.[52]

This focus did not seem to draw objections from the employers. They did not like JPCs degenerating into 'complaints committees', but a more common problem from their point of view occurred when the forums became mere platforms for the political propaganda of subversive elements. This latter situation worried Ministers as well, though there is no way of telling whether it was ever really prevalent.[53]

Perhaps more significant was the complaint by employers that workers and unions tended to try to get the JPCs to encroach on the sphere of collective bargaining. This fits in with some independent evidence, which reported workers as viewing the joint consultation forum as a suitable medium for negotiating benefits.[54] That employers (and union leaders) so strongly resisted this cannot have helped to offset the very rank and file apathy that was so frequently diagnosed.

Did JPCs succeed? The BEC survey of 1950 found a generally favourable response from employers, though presumably those who had established the committees were predisposed to see their benefits. The nature of those benefits was impressive – 'In the main replies indicate that the Committees have been of general utility' – with some firms reporting a better team spirit, a fall in absenteeism and an improved flow

Table 5.2 Management assessments of Joint Production Committees in 216 engineering firms, 1950

		Verdict	
Issue	*Favourable*	*No Effect*	*Unfavourable*
Output	129	87	–
Morale	183	33	–
Discipline	131	85	–
Absenteeism	117	99	–
Turnover/personnel	72	144	–
Reduced friction	196	20	–

Source: W. Robson-Brown and N.A. Howell-Everson, *Industrial Democracy at Work: A Factual Survey* (London, 1950), p. 42.

of information to the workers.[55] A survey of 216 JPCs in engineering examined management assessments of their effect; the results are shown in Table 5.2.

These figures certainly suggest a positive outcome from JPCs, though the emphasis on morale-raising effects perhaps gives some substance to the Ministry of Labour view that the committees had their greatest impact as an element of improved personnel management. Certainly, by 1950 the Ministry believed that:

> A noteworthy feature is that a number of firms are now displaying interest in joint consultation not as an aim in itself but as one of the techniques of modern personnel management and therefore helpful in attracting and retaining the better type of employee.[56]

Looking at the question of assessment in a wider context, it is clear that against the history of claims for industrial democracy and workers' control, the joint consultation movement in Britain in the 1940s was really a fairly conservative programme. Compared to the claims of guild socialists in the early years of the century, or to the Bullock proposals of the 1970s, this was a mild policy. Similarly, in comparison with what happened in, for example, France and Germany during the 1940s, the JPCs hardly appear radical. In France, a 1945 decree established *Comités d'entreprise* as compulsory in enterprises with more than 100 workers, with a remit which covered both welfare and production issues (though, as in Britain, they were to be essentially consultative, and fenced off from questions of wages and conditions). In Germany, the British Government pushed through even more radical measures, establishing a system of co-determination, with a parity of workers' representatives on company supervisory boards and a sub-structure of compulsory works councils.[57]

In Britain, however, the doctrine of human relations acted as a blockage to such radicalism. It ruled out compulsion as inappropriate, because the machinery of joint consultation was not an end in itself but essentially the representation and reinforcement of a pre-existing consensus in the workplace. In fact, the Ministry of Labour went so far as to refuse to collect systematic data about the existence of JPCs on the grounds that the 'criteria of success in joint consultation lies in the degree to which it assists in the development of a sense of co-operation and mutual responsibility, rather than in the mere existence of works committees'.[58]

Perhaps even more significantly, such a doctrine cut across notions of industrial democracy in any strong sense of the word 'democracy'.

Radical solutions here must always to some degree challenge managerial/employer legitimacy, in that they stake a claim for workers as by right having a say in running enterprises. Such rights can be grounded in different ways. They may be based on the Marxist labour theory of value (as in much syndicalism and guild socialism), or on a notion of democratic rights as in political democracy (the Bullock Report's position). But, however argued, they always dispute the unfettered right to manage. By contrast, human relations doctrine and its institutional representation through forms of joint consultation explicitly endorsed the right to manage, albeit in a particular way. As one of its leading ideologues in the 1940s and 1950s expressed this, the fundamental problem was 'how to combine authority and participation – leadership and co-operation'. And this was at bottom a problem for *management.* Such a view was accepted quite explicitly, too, by the TUC:

> Joint consultation machinery is essentially advisory as distinct from executive in its scope. In the last resort, and after full discussions with their employees, the responsibility for policy decisions must rest on the Boards concerned. The limitation, which is inherent in the policy of Congress, must be recognised and accepted and joint consultation machinery must not be expected to give executive power to worker representatives.[59]

Trade union acceptance of this doctrine was not, of course, just a question of 'ideology'. It was founded on the well-entrenched practices of adversarial collective bargaining, which had become the *raison d'être* of British trade unions. There could not be any blurring of the lines of responsibility between the rights and duties of workers and those of employers. This had long been the major basis of union objections to any form of industrial democracy, and it remained well entrenched into the 1940s (and beyond).[60]

The impact of human relations and joint consultation have, therefore, to be seen in the context of the absence of fundamental change in the structure of industrial relations during the Attlee period. Whilst some traditional features of those relations were suspended over these years – for example, by the continuation of compulsory arbitration, bans on strikes and the pursuit of an incomes policy (albeit non-statutory) – little was permanently altered.[61] As noted above, 'wage planning' was never accepted, and the attempt continued to maintain a sharp distinction between wage bargaining and productivity issues.

In the long run this latter distinction was probably fatal to joint consultation. As Alan Flanders wrote:

> The strict separation of joint consultation from collective bargaining is difficult to maintain in practice, certainly within individual establishments. Moreover the attempt to do so invariably destroys the workers' interest in it. The really successful experiments in joint consultation appear to have developed in firms where the close connection between the subject matter of consultation and negotiation has been recognised, and the same or similar committees have been used for both purposes.[62]

Flanders's diagnosis is supported by what happened in the 1950s. Despite continued enthusiasm for joint consultation under the Conservative Governments after 1951 the evidence is reasonably clear that the machinery involved suffered a serious decline during that decade. By 1957 a Ministry of Labour official felt 'chastened' by a survey which suggested that less than one third of firms with 250 or more workers had mechanisms of joint consultation. The cause of this decline had much to do with the growth of shop stewards as a potent force at workplace level. With an alternative focus for shopfloor trade unionism, joint consultation simply withered away.[63]

As noted above, in the 1940s joint consultation had been pressed from 'on high', the TUC being notably more committed than local officials or the rank and file. The shop steward movement had been weakened by demobilisation and conversion to civilian production at the end of the war, and there is some evidence that where stewards survived as a force in the late 1940s this inhibited the growth of joint consultation, though undoubtedly some shop stewards did try to use the consultative machinery.[64]

The attempted severance of wage issues from joint consultation not only affected the enthusiasm of the workers for the latter but also narrowed the range of productivity issues which consultation could encourage. Perhaps most importantly, it curtailed the possibility of using wage incentives as a means of obtaining higher production and productivity.

As has been shown, much of the emphasis on human relations derived from the view that, in the absence of the 'stick' of unemployment, high production and productivity would require the 'carrot' of better treatment for the worker in the factory. Such an approach could be endorsed from a managerial perspective, and also remained compatible with the Leftist belief concerning the intrinsic desirability of better treatment for the workers; in fact, in the 1940s there was a substantial *rapprochement* between these two views. But this did not answer questions about the other obvious 'carrot', higher pay by wage incentives.

For some on the Left, wage incentives were inappropriate in the new post-war regime: raising production and productivity was to be seen as a social duty, not something fuelled by individual payments. However, such a view was always confined to a small minority. Ian Mikardo voiced the typical attitude of both the political and union wings of the Labour Movement in 1947 when he attacked 'extremists' who believed either social duty or wage incentives would alone encourage better output.[65]

Mikardo went on to argue that traditional piece rate systems had been discredited by their arbitrary, complicated and often regressive character. He also tried to bridge the gap between 'human relations' and wage incentives by arguing that piece rates often affected output not because they directly raised incomes, but rather because they set the workers a clear task and informed them how well or badly they had achieved it. His attempted 'middle-road' thus included favouring small group incentives as against those that were individually oriented.[66] Whilst Labour's ideologues and management experts conducted a long debate about material versus moral incentives,[67] in practice the extension of incentive schemes seems to have met with little resistance. For example, discussion about the issue between employers and the TUC at the NJAC found both sides resisting a direct role for the Ministry of Labour in propagandising such schemes, but only on the grounds that these things should be done by collective agreement without government interference, not because of any hesitancy about principle.[68]

The Government's direct role in wage payment systems was therefore rather limited by employer and union hostility. However, the problem also came up in other areas of official policy. For example, during the wage freeze of 1948–50 it was accepted that wage increases linked to such incentive schemes would be exempt from control.[69] At the same time, the Government remained sensitive to the claims that high income tax rates acted as a deterrent to effort, and various ideas were floated on this, including the exemption of overtime pay in some industries from income tax (though such breeches in the general character of the income tax rules were successfully resisted, not least by the Inland Revenue).[70] Finally, the Government also worried that the rationing and the general shortage of consumer goods was a disincentive to effort, though here its hands were substantially tied by the macroeconomic imperative to divert the bulk of resources into exports and investment.[71]

Ministry of Labour figures suggest that payment by results did increase in this period. Calculations for 1951 demonstrated that 28 per cent of adult males and 32 per cent of all workers were paid in this way, compared with 18 and 25 per cent respectively in 1938. In some industries, too, there was evidence of a concurrent, significant shift in union attitudes towards piecework.[72] But this change largely took place on a separate track from the issue of joint consultation. This separation of discussion about incentive issues and the joint consultation machinery gave an air of unreality to the proceedings of the latter. Here was an area where workers were most likely to be highly interested in the implications of raising productivity, yet it could not be discussed in the consultative mechanism.

A similar point can be made about restrictive labour practices. In Chapter 8 we argue that the importance of these practices in inhibiting productivity growth has been exaggerated in much recent literature, without warrant from contemporary evidence. But whatever the importance of restrictive practices, they, like wage incentives, had to be primarily addressed in the context of wage bargaining, separated off from most of the debate about productivity. Typically, it was the BEC which produced a report on these practices, whilst the FBI's discussions of productivity explicitly ignored them.[73] Thus, coupling the productivity drive so strongly to human relations was far from an unqualified success. It highlighted certain themes – consultation, works information, the role of the foreman – whilst tending to sideline others, such as the array of issues under the heading of 'Americanisation' that is discussed in Chapter 7. That the drive was pursued in the context of a largely unreformed industrial relations system also raised tensions, by excluding certain pertinent issues from the debate on productivity. Moreover, whilst not wishing to over-emphasise one facet of the problem, it is surely plausible to say that a more radical policy to raise productivity could have been pursued if wage issues had not been regarded as 'off limits'.

Finally, it should be noted that emphasis on human relations also caused tensions within Labour's ideology and politics. The attractions of human relations to certain Labour positions at this time is surely clear. It provided the basis of a *rapprochement* with 'progressive' managerial circles in a context where Labour gave a high priority both to consensus and co-operation in general and to its links with progressive middle-class opinion in particular. Thus, for example, a Labour Party document on industrial democracy of this period cited G.S. Walpole's *Management and Men*, a classic 'progressive management' text, as embodying exactly the right approach to social relations in the factory.[74]

Yet this posture was problematic for Labour. Human relations ideology was based on a 'unitary' notion of the enterprise, as the (potential) site for the pursuit of common purposes between workers and owners. No doubt more sophisticated versions of the doctrine could accept the inescapability of *some* conflict of interest in the enterprise, but the basic thrust was clear.[75] Yet this emphasis on co-operation and consensus in the factory co-existed with an undiminished commitment to an adversarial form of wage bargaining. In the immediate post-war period, with the trade unions willing to go a very long way to accommodate government policy, this tension remained containable. But with the revival of shop-floor trade unionism in the 1950s, the 1940s 'package' proved to be an unsustainable basis upon which Labour could even consider building a new politics of the enterprise.

Chapter 6

The management question again, 1947–51

A central part of Labour's approach to the productivity issue was an almost entirely new concern with management. As shown in the previous chapters, during the later years of the war and after there was a widespread belief that British management was inefficient and that something must be done to remedy this. Prominent in the attempts at reform were leading Labour figures such as Dalton and Cripps. These Ministers were central to the Attlee Government's decision to create the British Institute of Management, and this is highly significant as a symbol of Labour's new relationship with management.

But there were other important features of that relationship. Not all government activity on management was channelled through the BIM. In the late 1940s there were a range of other institutional expressions of concern, such as the Personnel Management Advisory Service and the Urwick Committee on Management Education. A desire for reform was also expressed in the context of the newly nationalised industries which posed almost unprecedented management problems. Outside government, the unions, too, were called upon to play a part in management improvement. But above and beyond these specific initiatives was a general process of reflection on the status and meaning of management and Labour's relation to it. Was there a 'managerial revolution', it was asked, and, if so, what were its implications for Labour's traditional view of the economy and how it should be reformed?

This chapter looks at the institutional aspects of Labour's concern with management in the late 1940s and reflects on the content of that 'managerialism', before finally considering the wider ideological significance of Labour's evolving conception of management.

The BIM was officially inaugurated by Cripps, supported by Harold Wilson (President of the Board of Trade) and the leaders of the FBI and

TUC, on 21 April 1948. The leading management journal welcomed the new body as an 'impressive climax to 30 years' struggle – a consummation beyond the dreams of the inglorious pioneers who laboured throughout those discouraging decades'. Further, the 'lavish material support guaranteed by the Government' was 'the measure of its assurance of success'. The whole story added up to a great personal triumph for one man: 'Sir Stafford Cripps determined that his sponsored Institute should materialise, and his single-mindedness has sustained the project right up to the inaugural meeting'.[1]

Over the next few years, the Director of the BIM, L. Russell, attempted to turn these early expectations into real gains. Much energy was expended early on, as might be expected, in the task of finding the new organisation a home, and providing it with suitable staff and facilities. At the same time, there were constant efforts to attract members, both via canvasses of individuals and corporations and via negotiated agreements with existing management bodies (most notably the Institute of Industrial Administration). A third kind of activity involved propaganda work in the outside community, which encompassed, amongst other things, a publications programme, a series of major conferences and an attempt to set up a network of Local Management Associations (LMAs) aimed at involving the grass roots.[2]

All of the different aspects of the BIM's work were interdependent, but to many in the organisation the propaganda function was the most important. In part, this stemmed from a general perception that management standards in Britain were often quite poor. However, there was also the unavoidable fact that few managers had enrolled in any kind of professional organisation during the recent past. One estimate was that there were probably between 200,000 and 400,000 'persons exercising management responsibilities' in the country, but only 20,000 in the existing management bodies.[3] In these circumstances, successful propaganda became almost a condition of survival.

The approach that the BIM took to its public work revolved around two aspects of current 'progressive' management thinking. There was some insistence, firstly, on the importance of human relations, an emphasis that harmonised with wider Government thinking. Managers were not to 'disregard the hopes and ideals' that were stirring 'the hearts and minds of the common people'. They must recognise that a 'new dawn' had occurred, and that old-style punitive incentives to work were redundant. Management, in this perspective, needed to be about building consent and involving the workforce. The first Chairman of the BIM, Sir Charles Renold, could thus argue that the key variable in firms was morale, and that this must be carefully cultivated. As he explained, there were three conditions for success:

1 The purpose of the firm must be felt to be worth while.
2 Everybody engaged must feel that he belongs.
3 And the show must be well run.[4]

At the same time, the BIM was interested in improving all of the more technical aspects of industry – the everyday business of purchasing, manufacturing, selling, costing and accounting. The major objectives here, in every case, needed to be professional standards and modern methods; traditional 'rule of thumb' saws must be quickly jettisoned. Good management, in this conception, meant proficiency in a defined range of skills. As BIM officials emphasised, the principles to follow were the same whether the organisation was a small family firm or a huge nationalised industry.[5]

Not surprisingly, the BIM was more successful in some aspects of its work than in others. Russell found that establishing an adequate headquarters organisation was more difficult than expected (his chosen building, for example, turned out to have dry rot) but, by the early 1950s, many of the initial problems had been resolved and the BIM was operating from specially adapted premises, with a large staff and relatively good facilities (such as a library of some 7,000 items). Additionally, the Institute's track record on propaganda continued to impress. At least one management conference was held by the BIM every year from 1948 onwards, with each attracting at least 400 delegates. The publications which were produced, too, were very popular: the Institute offered 50 or 60 titles during these years, and was selling or distributing a quarter of a million copies from this list annually.[6]

By contrast, other BIM activities were clearly less successful. Progress with establishing the LMAs was slow, with only four being created by 1951. Moreover, the continuing membership campaign proceeded very much as the more gloomy had forecast. There were some notable breakthroughs, as when the deal with the Institute of Industrial Administration (really a successful take-over) yielded 5,700 members at one blow, or when talks with various unions resulted in eleven (including the NUM and the NUR) taking out subscriptions. But, in general, the situation was sticky; despite considerable effort, by mid-1951 only 959 corporate subscribers, 548 individual subscribers and 80 library subscribers had been added to the 541 founder members.[7]

One of the functions of the BIM was to bring together the wide range of previously existing management bodies and to provide an agency for education in management. But whilst the BIM focused on the education of the practising manager, there was also the question of management qualifications for those at the beginning of their career. Here, the perceived need was to bring together and codify the great range of qualifications available in the field of management, mostly offered in technical colleges. To this end the Government had established a Committee on Education for Management in 1946, chaired by the well-known managerial ideologue, L.F. Urwick. The Report of this committee was published in 1947.[8]

Urwick apparently had little difficulty in securing widespread support for his view of management education.[9] The Ministry of Education regarded him as the leading expert on the issue, for example writing to him in mid-1945 for a booklist on management topics. Most of the existing bodies which issued qualifications in management accepted his approach, with some resistance from the Institute of Mechanical Engineers, which felt that his proposals were too generalist in character to cover all of the ground required for their engineers.[10]

Certainly, Urwick's proposals were notable for their belief in general management or what he called 'scientific management'. For him, scientific management was pioneered by F.W. Taylor (and H. Fayol), but what he regarded as the mark of scientific management was not a Tayloristic emphasis on work practices so much as a *method*. That method was 'scientific' in an inductivist sense, and was applicable to the management of any kind of body. In a work of this period Urwick approvingly cited Taylor's *Principles of Scientific Management* as follows:

> scientific management, in its essence, consists of a certain philosophy, which results in a combination of the four underlying principles of management.
>
> 1 The development of a true science.
> 2 The scientific selection of the workman.
> 3 His scientific education and development.
> 4 Intimate friendly co-operation between the management and the men.[11]

Thus, Urwick's 'scientific management' was not incompatible with a human relations approach even though this was not his central concern. But, just as important, it led to an understanding of management as primarily to do with general principles of organisation. In Urwick's view, the key to the efficient functioning of large-scale organisations was the specialisation of functions, the separation of conception and execution and therefore the centrality of the 'science of administration'.[12]

This approach generated syllabuses for management education which were strategic and universalistic in character. They drew strongly on the Harvard Business School tradition of management as something understandable and teachable, separately from consideration of any particular production process. This was a perspective quite distinct from the American industrial engineering tradition, which focused attention precisely on the specifics of managing different types of production operations, and which might be considered a more legitimate descendent of Taylor's 'workshop management' orientation.[13]

Hence, for Urwick, management could (and should) be taught separately from a technical expertise which was specific to any one industry. This was an interpretation which he urged, for example, in a letter to the Institute of Electrical Engineers, during the discussions of his Report in 1946/7. It was a view, too, which largely informed the detailed syllabuses that resulted from the Urwick Committee's work, though, as P. Armstrong suggests, 'whilst the shell of Urwick's syllabus embodies his formal and abstract view of management, the scheme as a whole was compromised in its fine print with a much more productivist view'.[14]

Urwick's notions of appropriate forms of management education are important but not because of the widespread pursuit of the syllabuses that he provided. Though 100 colleges offered the Certificate course and 62 the Diploma, the numbers of awards over the first fifteen years of the scheme's existence were only 810 and 640 respectively.[15] At one level this was another 'great British failure' in management education. Nevertheless, it is important to note the way in which this approach was able to dominate the field with little resistance, and none from Government. Urwick's views did not conflict with any alternative doctrine of management. Moreover, as noted, they were fully compatible with the human relations approach which the Government treated as axiomatic. Indeed, both orientations were similar in their attention to universal principles of management practice which in turn could draw upon an emerging social science expertise, rather than upon an industrial engineering approach with its quite different levels of generality and forms of knowledge. As we shall see below, in discussing the nationalised industries, these two approaches could be combined to provide a distinctly 'Labourist' view of management.

Apart from the BIM and the Urwick Committee, Labour's concern with management was also expressed through agencies such as the Personnel Management Advisory Service (PMAS), which was set up by the Ministry of Labour.[16] This acted initially to encourage the appointment of personnel managers as specialised functionaries within firms. Their role was clearly seen as linked, once again, to the human relations approach regarding management. The PMAS focused on three dimensions of that approach – joint consultation, works information and Training Within Industry. Joint consultation, as discussed in Chapter 5, was at the heart of the human relations ideology, and was propagated by the PMAS as part of good industrial relations rather than directly linked to the productivity drive. Works information was seen as a corollary to joint consultation. The idea here rested upon the belief, so characteristic of this period, that conflict at work was largely the result of ignorance and misunderstanding. At factory level, therefore, one objective should be to provide useful information, news and views about the state of the national economy and individual companies in a simplified and digestible form, which would be disseminated to raise consciousness of production and productivity issues and thus to encourage positive participation in joint consultation.[17] Training Within Industry (discussed in Chapter 4) was aimed at supervisors, especially in their 'personnel management' role, as the front line of contact between managers and workers. The TWI programme provided a total of 30 hours' factory-based instruction, divided into sections on job instruction, job relations and job methods.[18]

How far all of this made much difference to the practices of British management is inherently difficult to judge. There was a feeling in official circles that it was a strategy which in some respects was already failing by the late 1940s. The classic 'personnel management approach' of appointing specialised personnel managers was limited by the lack of trained people to fill such jobs and by the resistance of firms worried about their overheads. Interestingly, it was also seen as constrained by the human relations emphasis on good supervision as part of line management, a view rather different from that which proposed 'personnel' as a separate, staff function.[19]

The nationalisation (or socialisation, as it was officially called) of industry in Britain under the Attlee administration opened up a new agenda on many issues. It has commonly been asserted that the wave of nationalisations in this period rested on little detailed preparation, though much of this seems exaggerated.[20] But as regards the management of these new bodies the claim does seem close to the truth. As

Austen Albu later noted, during the major debates over the form of nationalisation in the 1930s, there was a 'striking absence' of debate about how these new institutions would be managed below board level.[21]

The debates of the 1930s had effectively decided that, to amplify a point touched on earlier, Labour's preferred form of nationalisation would be the public corporation, with a Board appointed on an 'expert' rather than 'representative' basis. This line had defeated those who wished to see a direct role for workers in management of nationalised enterprises. Though the issue was raised again in the late 1940s the Morrisonian position was strictly maintained by the Labour leadership – both in the Government and the TUC.[22]

However, opposition to any notions of workers' control was accompanied by much emphasis on joint consultation as a desirable feature for nationalised industries and, in most of the industries, provision for such consultation was written into the nationalisation statute. The precise meaning of joint consultation was nevertheless obscure, and there was much debate in the late 1940s about the degree of 'Workers' Assistance in Management' that was appropriate. The major arena for these discussions was the Socialisation of Industries Committee, chaired by Herbert Morrison.[23]

The first stimulus for examining this issue was a memorandum by Morrison which emphasised the need for a forum of management, technicians and workers to discuss the 'organisation and running' of nationalised industries. He wanted such consultation to take place at local, regional and national levels. It would, he argued, 'bring the Board face to face with the problems which were concerning the workpeople and could give the workers an opportunity of presenting their ideas and grievances at first hand to the Board'.[24]

Part of Morrison's aim in raising this point was undoubtedly his desire to try to pre-empt more radical proposals for worker involvement. At a later date he was to make this explicit when he argued that if 'the arrangements were not satisfactory, there would undoubtedly be a demand for some form of direct participation by workers or trade unions in management', and such a development was, for him certainly, an ever present danger. He detected in the National Coal Board (NCB), for example, 'some signs of a tendency to overmuch consultation with the NUM on matters of management'.[25] But it would perhaps be too cynical to dismiss all talk of 'workers' assistance' as a manoeuvre designed to dish any claims for more radical forms of industrial democracy. Ministers did believe that the place of the worker in socialised industries should be different from that in the private sector, even if they were vague on what this meant, and they also hoped that this change would bring about a significant improvement in productivity.

Much of the discussion of 'workers' assistance' focused on the question of whether consultation should take place using existing channels or through new machinery specifically devised for the purpose. Morrison and the official committee which he appointed to consider the matter looked favourably on the idea of separate machinery, with the Minister suggesting that a single structure tended 'to mix up questions of wages with questions of organisation' and seeing a case for different people being involved over different issues.[26]

As so often, change in this direction was resisted strongly by the Ministry of Labour, which feared any diminution in the authority of the trade unions, always felt to be a possibility with new or specialist machinery. Such a line was sustained, seemingly successfully, throughout the Attlee government period.[27]

As the official committee considered the merits of the various arguments, the members demonstrated how discussion of the workers' role in the nationalised sector was to be dominated by the rhetoric of human relations, very much as in the private sector (dealt with in Chapter 5). As the committee saw it, the objective of consultation was 'to create within the organisation the particular kind of atmosphere or climate which will make the workers happy in their jobs'. So intangible an objective was unlikely to be produced 'merely by any institutional feature, such as a system of statutory committees'. Crucial to creating a suitable climate would be proper personnel management and works information.[28]

At the same time the committee stressed that matters of management, and the precise role for workers in it, were for the Boards of the nationalised industries to deal with. This was a constant refrain in these discussions, which was accepted by all of the Ministers involved as a principle (though Morrison in particular saw the doctrine of Board independence and responsibility as compatible with a degree of ministerial prodding).[29]

This approach was, however, very much a weapon against more radical proposals. For example, when a group of managerial 'progressives', including Urwick, Wilfred Brown of Glacier Metals and George Dickson of the London Regional Board for Industry, urged the formation of advisory councils of managers, workers and consumers, emphasising the case for the involvement of workers on human relations grounds, Morrison was willing only to concede that existing managements were 'unduly cautious and conservatively minded in their approach to the problems of enlisting the assistance of the staff'. There was, he emphasised, no call for new measures: 'He doubted whether any corporate identity could be created out of the rather divergent interests of the workers, management and consumers' and 'whether any advisory council should be raised to a degree of responsibility which would derogate from the responsibility of the executive board.'[30]

This argument rumbled on throughout the Labour Government's period in office. Any proposals for increasing the workers' role which appeared to threaten the responsibility of the nationalised Boards were firmly rejected – such as happened with the schemes put forward by the National Union of Railwaymen, consistent opponents of the Morrisonian method of organisation, and the Union of Post Office Workers.[31]

On the other hand, Ministers remained highly conscious that the existing forms of management in the nationalised industries were failing to generate the kind of enthusiasm and support from workers which had once been envisaged. In 1950 Morrison circulated to his colleagues a report about a London conference of employees in nationalised industries, which, he contended, showed 'a most disturbing situation'. He worried that a 'continuance of large-scale misunderstanding and discontent among the employees of the socialised industries' might have 'the most serious consequences for their efficiency and for the success of policy of socialisation'. Certainly the evidence cited at this conference bore out the report's statement that in many cases no attempt was being made on the part of managements to inform employees of what they were doing or why.[32]

The fears voiced by Morrison seem to have been shared by his ministerial colleagues, and so a sub-committee was established to look at the issue of 'Relations with Workers in Socialised Industries'. This accepted that these relations were not good. Whilst active discontent was unusual, passive unenthusiasm was widespread:

> there is a widespread sense of frustration coupled with disappointment at the results of socialisation. Sometimes labour relations are good by any standards, but even where this is so there is rarely, if ever, any positive enthusiasm for the new order of things.

The Committee linked these attitudes to a number of features which marked the socialised industries – the continuation in office of the old private sector management, over-large 'perks' for managers, excessive bureaucracy, and a 'lack of concern for efficiency on the part of management'. It then raised again the issue of separate mechanisms for joint consultation, suggesting that, in single structures, the salience of wage issues tended to mean that 'consultation about wider questions of policy and management will take a subordinate place'. The Committee also criticised the unions for falling short of expectations in 'educating officers and members in their responsibilities under public ownership'. But despite these quite tough comments, nothing practical seems to have resulted before the Government fell.[33]

The search for improved human relations in nationalised industries led up some eccentric paths. None was more bizarre, but also perhaps symptomatic of a strand in Labour's politics, than the burst of activity which followed a memorandum from Attlee to Morrison at the end of 1948. In this the Prime Minister recounted a discussion which he had had with General Slim in which both agreed that there was a parallel between good officers in the army and good leadership in industry. The lesson to be learnt, according to Attlee, was clear:

> There is need in industry of the kind of spirit and leadership which obtains in a good regiment, an *esprit de corps* not only of the regiment but of the company, and the platoon. I am sure that this is necessary in, for instance, the coal industry, where you want the *esprit de corps* of the pit.[34]

However, Ministers resisted Attlee's idea that General Slim might have any role in spreading the word in civilian life, 'because the impression might be given that the Government thought that the military spirit should be introduced into industry'. Nevertheless, Attlee's memorandum led to a new round of activity on human relations, with the Minister of Labour suggesting an enquiry into what was occurring in the nationalised sector. This was resisted by the Chairmen of the Boards, but the Ministry of Labour pursued the matter informally, most notably convening a conference on the issue.[35]

The focus of this conference was on good 'leadership', this being the perceived message of Attlee's original memorandum. The occasion was chaired by Lloyd Roberts from the Ministry of Labour, and the central concern, as so often in discussions of this kind, was with the role of supervisors and junior management, seen as in the 'front line' of the human relations offensive:

> The inquiry was prompted by the belief that the development of harmonious relations between managers and workers can be materially influenced by the appointment to managerial and

> supervisory positions of those who, in addition to the necessary technical and intellectual qualifications, possess or will develop those intangible qualities which indicate a capacity for leadership.

The conference also discussed some (unnamed) private sector models of supervisory training, which mainly differed from those in public industries because of their stress on the need for 'human relations' skills rather than simple technical proficiency.[36]

All of this indicates the ways in which 'human relations' ideas were floated as relevant to the nationalised sector, just as Chapter 5 showed how, as a result of the productivity drive, they became so prominent in discussions about the private sector. Allowing for the different circumstances of ownership, was the discussion of management in the public sector simply the mirror of that in the private? On the evidence of the deliberations of the Socialisation of Industries Committee, the answer is clearly that it was not. Whilst human relations did to some extent dominate the agenda for discussion on management in the socialised industries there was an alternative theme also present, which focused on the degree of centralisation or decentralisation that was appropriate in both the main administrative pattern used in the socialised industries, and the associated management structures.

This issue first arose in relation to the coal industry, which soon after its nationalisation was deemed to have adopted an overly centralised structure. In a memorandum of late 1947 Hugh Gaitskell, the Minister of Fuel and Power, stressed that the history of the industry was one of fragmentation, and that a big problem for the efficient management of the sector was the lack of managers with experience of running a large-scale organisation. (He backed this up with the assertion that the one exception to this was coal selling, which had been centralised under the Coal Mines Reorganisation Act 1930, and which, he said, was by no accident the most efficient part of the Coal Board.) This criticism was linked to the argument that the make-up of the Board was wrong, consisting largely of functional heads rather than directors with general responsibilities. Such a situation, Gaitskell argued, led to an imprecise chain of command on general management issues.[37]

This analysis seems to have been widely shared. Morrison, in particular, supported Gaitskell's views, which led him to a search for appropriate models of decentralised large-scale firms. He proposed a working party which, amongst other things, should look at how ICI and General Motors (GM) ran themselves. He himself circulated extensive extracts from P.F. Drucker's book on *Big Business* (1947) which was largely concerned with GM, presenting it as an 'essay in federalism' which offered the important message that the operational units of the company were 'run much like the units in a planned economy'.[38]

The proposed working party came to grief because of opposition from the Board Chairmen to any outside scrutiny of their efficiency (see below). But Morrison continued to pursue the issue, for example circulating a Treasury O. & M. discussion of 'Examples of Industrial Organisation', which focused on centralisation and decentralisation, with appropriate instances along with organisational charts. Morrison linked this material to a general argument that one of the main problems facing any large socialised industry was 'the determination of the right degree of decentralisation to adopt'. He was sensitive to the usual economies of scale arguments for centralisation, but again pointed to GM and ICI as examples of how efficient big companies decentralised.[39]

In the event, such discussions seem to have had little immediate effect, above all because of the continuing saga about government 'interference' in the activities of the nationalised industries. Morrison was keen on setting up an efficiency unit which would scrutinise the Boards' activities. One reason for this proposal was to pre-empt the idea of Parliamentary Select Committees on the nationalised industries, which Morrison opposed as likely to 'take up a great deal of the time of the senior officers of the boards', an attempt at compromise which failed to persuade the Board Chairmen.[40]

But this was not Morrison's only consideration. He seems to have been genuinely concerned to evolve appropriate forms of organisation for the new giant enterprises that he was so instrumental in bringing into existence. He recognised that harmonious human relations were not enough, arguing that 'while good will between both sides of industry was extremely important, there was a danger that it might be over stressed to the detriment of efficient management and increased productivity'; and, on another occasion, that 'Education and indoctrination will not be good enough, nor committees; radical changes in organisation, methods of work, and management methods may sometimes be necessary'.[41]

What is surely striking about Morrison's position is the extent to which the model from the private sector for managing large-scale organisations was treated as unproblematic. No one seems to have asked whether publicly owned industries should be run like General Motors or ICI or what this implied about the purposes of nationalisation. Morrison himself does not appear to have felt called upon to defend the parallel.

The decentralisation issue seems to have emerged as the main 'managerial' problem that was specifically related to nationalisation in this period.[42] In part this occurred because of its compatibility with the stress on human relations. Austen Albu, for example, argued that there was now a 'universal understanding of the difficulty of maintaining initiative, responsibility, communication of ideas and morale in large-scale undertakings of every kind'. This, in turn, meant that there was a need for greater decentralisation in the nationalised industries, a conclusion which, as for Morrison, pointed to ICI as the best example of decentralised management under a centralised Board.[43]

This menu of management possibilities for the nationalised industries was obviously rather limited. In practice the management systems which emerged in those industries tended to reflect arguments about collective bargaining and capital finance as much as any notion of internal organisational efficiency. However, there was some tendency to greater decentralisation with successive nationalisations, from the highly centralised Coal Board to the regional organisation of gas. But overall it is obvious that, apart from the platitudes on human relations and a rather one-dimensional notion of centralisation, Labour never really got to intellectual grips with management in the public sector during this period. On the other hand, the parallels drawn with the private sector were linked to emerging trends in Labour's thinking about company organisation and management, a topic which will be considered in the final section of this chapter.

Turning to the question of the unions and management, it is clear from Chapter 5, that the TUC and most union leaderships strongly supported the Government's productivity drive. This support raised the issue of what attitude was to be taken to management. Here, two rather different emphases co-existed. On the one hand, there was the persistent union claim for a greater share in management, meaning greater consultation from the shopfloor to the national level rather than any idea of joint management or radical forms of industrial democracy. On the other hand, there was the tendency to regard management as a technical practice, as an expert function on a par with other professional competencies. In this context management was something to be learned and thus something that, if mastered, might strengthen the unions' claim to a greater say in the running of industry. The latter position served to give an ideologically congenial gloss to the campaign by the TUC in particular to encourage union members to learn management techniques.

Both of these arguments were apparent, for example, in the report of the TUC to the special conference of union executives in September

1948. The aim here was to encourage unions to do more to take advantage of existing management training facilities. Whilst the immediate context was that of raising productivity, education in management technique, it was argued, also arose 'for the unions as a question of long term policy, mainly from the standpoint of the workers' claim to fuller participation in the control of industry'.[44]

The TUC's support for training in these latter terms was further emphasised in the document *Trade Unions and Management*, produced after the 1949 Congress. Much of this was taken up with descriptions of the kinds of techniques that unions should be interested in learning. These were seen as encompassing job evaluation, time and motion study, and work measurement. But the underlying message emphasised the longer term objective. Jack Tanner of the Amalgamated Engineering Union, for example, argued that there 'must be a development in the attitude of trade unionists to industrial management'. Management 'should be no longer regarded as a "mystery" and it was essential that . . . unions should learn its techniques and the elements of production engineering'. This kind of lesson was very much supported by E.P. Harries, in charge of the TUC's Production Department. He saw a major part of the task of that department as educating 'all sectors of the T.U. movement in the problem of management', adding that this was a crucially necessary development at workshop as well as headquarters levels.[45]

In some ways such an attitude towards management is unsurprising, given the general union commitment to production and productivity, though it is in marked contrast to the attitude typically taken prior to the war. But what is perhaps more interesting is the precise way in which this new attitude to management was advocated. *Trade Unions and Management* produced two reasons why the unions should change their approach. One emphasised individual advancement: there was a common assumption at this time that in the long run, at least in the nationalised industries, the *normal* route to an administrative job would be by training competent trade unionists in management. The other was that such knowledge would allow unions to 'react knowledgeably to simpler proposals'.[46]

This reactive posture, which characterised most of the TUC's pronouncements on management, needs to be compared with what may be called a 'radical productionism', where learning about management was seen as allowing unions 'to participate directly in achieving productive efficiency'. This contrast should not be overdrawn. There were undoubtedly shades of opinion on the issue of the degree to which training trade unionists in management involved the idea that existing managers were inefficient. But some trade unionists did certainly take a highly critical line, even though they were in a minority against the TUC view, which was that such a challenge to the legitimacy of management could cut across the industrial co-operation and consensus that it wished to establish.[47]

The position on this of one union, the Association of Supervisory Staff and Engineering Technicians (ASSET), is of especial interest. ASSET's role was central partly because, at least on occasions, it opted to take a 'radical productionist' line. But, in addition, ASSET was the union for (junior) managers and supervisors, and so was integral to the attempt to forge a new link between labour and management. Moreover, Labour's two key ideologues on management, Austen Albu and Ian Mikardo, were prominent ASSET members.

'Radical productionism' did not become a consistent ASSET position, but it was powerfully expressed on occasions and this was especially so during the economic crises of 1947 and 1949. In the latter case, for example, an editorial in the union's journal argued that: 'Inside ASSET we have many, many managers who are fighting bitterly to establish industrial democracy; are waging a ceaseless war against directors' policy that creates inefficiency and discontent.' The union also provided Mikardo (the union's parliamentary spokesman) with a platform to expound similar views.[48]

Mikardo was partly successful in getting this kind of radical view of management into the economic policies of the Left in the Labour Party. Both of the best known manifestos of the Labour Left in this period, *Keep Left* and *Keeping Left*, essentially accepted the kind of case that ASSET was promoting. The first of these, for example, attacked the BIM as too conservative in its approach to management reform: 'Its constitution and powers are circumscribed in order not to offend the existing institutions and the existing firms of consultants – a major example of that tenderness to vested interests to which we have already referred.' *Keeping Left* linked its proposal for the extension of economic planning in the name of greater efficiency to the argument that this action by the Government 'would entitle it to ask the unions to institute a mass scheme of education in management for their officers, shop stewards and other representatives, and would thus canalise the energies of the unions into a new progressive full employment function'.[49]

Mikardo was therefore something of a link over 'radical productionism' between ASSET and the Left of the Labour Party. This position, whilst noted, is not sufficiently emphasised in most treatments of the Labour Left. In fact, one of the striking features of the period is the extent to which the Left in this area mirrored the priorities of the Labour leadership. The Left, too, put increased output and higher productivity at the centre of its agenda – it just advocated more radical means than the leadership to achieve these ends. This sharply divided the Parliamentary Left from the Communists, who after 1947 rejected their earlier 'radical productionism' in favour of a posture stressing the defence of working-class standards against 'heightened exploitation'.[50]

Nevertheless, the appeal of this 'radical productionist' position should not be exaggerated. ASSET itself was an ambiguous body. Whilst there seems to have been little active resistance to Mikardo's role as spokesman for the union, its own 'managerialism' was more complex than a simple endorsement of standard contemporary Left positions. The idea of a training in management as preparation for advancement up the industrial career hierarchy was clearly popular in ASSET, and this obviously tended to produce a rather different perspective on the legitimacy of existing industrial organisation. But more important was the way in which ASSET could also be drawn into the dominant consensual approach to industrial issues.

The issue of the journal *ASSET* for July 1947 carried a front page message from Herbert Morrison. He wrote:

> I wish ASSET luck in its work and hope that by spreading and extending its membership this vast miscellaneous body of the middle class, which is composed of the technical, supervisory and the managerial classes, will become ever more competent to make an increasing contribution to the economic and social well-being of the community.

Underlying this mellifluous message lay a rather different kind of managerialism than that espoused by Mikardo. The point of organising managers into a union was not to spearhead the exposure of existing inefficiencies, but to draw managers into the great arch of co-operative endeavour across classes in the cause of higher productivity.[51]

Morrison's outlook echoed that of Austen Albu in 1942. The latter had suggested then how Labour needed to approach management:

> If the Trade Union movement were to make a constructive approach to them, proposing collaboration for positive social purposes, many of them could be persuaded that the real interests, both of themselves and of the nation, lie in an association with the political and industrial organisations of the Labour movement.

And this in turn was reminiscent of ideas put forward very clearly in Sidney Webb's undeservedly neglected work of 1917.[52] Such a view of management was embedded in a much broader view of changes in British society. The possibility of a Labour alliance with management was commonly seen not as an act of political will, but as resting on a fundamental change in the function of management in the modern corporation. In short, it depended upon the idea of a managerial revolution.

As has been already noted, the book titled *The Managerial Revolution*, written by James Burnham, had appeared in Britain in 1942. Burnham had argued that the world was already a long way down a path which would lead to managers becoming everywhere the ruling class (in a context of state-owned property). His analysis was couched in Marxist terms, and he saw this new ruling class as co-existing with different political arrangements, totalitarian initially, possibly democratic later, but always maintaining effective power.[53]

This work was a frequent reference point for the Left in the later 1940s. Broadly speaking, Labour writers, especially but not exclusively those on the Right of the party, tended increasingly to accept the central thesis about the shifting locus of power in society, a process which may perhaps be seen as culminating in the *New Fabian Essays* of 1952 and Crosland's *Future of Socialism* of 1956.[54]

The idea of a shift in the locus of power rested in turn on the idea of the separation of ownership and control in the modern corporation. This alleged separation became a commonplace in much Labour discussion of the late 1940s and early 1950s. It implied both that the 'old' idea linking political centrality to the ownership of the means of production was outdated, and also, perhaps more important in the current context, that managers were no longer 'agents of capital'. Rather, they were (actual or potential) experts in administration and human relations, a 'third estate' in the realm, with no inherent reason for being anti-Labour.[55]

Such propositions were hardly new in the 1940s, but they were becoming much more important as Labour, from its position as the party of government, had to grapple both intellectually and politically with management. Faced with issues about running newly nationalised industries, Labour was forced to take a view on how far this process of management would differ from that in the private sector. As suggested above, discussions on managing the nationalised industries implicitly suggested the difference was small. This was made explicit by Albu, once more, who argued that the real division in relation to producer units was not that between the publicly and privately owned but that between the owner-controlled and the professionally controlled, the latter making up the bulk of the private sector.[56]

Similarly, faced with the need to deal with the 80 per cent of the economy remaining unnationalised, Labour was forced to take a view on the character of the private sector. It is important not to oversimplify the substance of that view but Brady, a critic of the managerial revolution thesis, seems to have broadly got it right when he linked it to the perception of management as a neutral expertise: 'Here the thesis of Burnham's *Managerial Revolution* seems to have been taken over by Labour spokesmen and theoreticians, lock, stock and barrel' he wrote; 'In effect for the syndicalist idea has been substituted a Labour version of the Burnham thesis of management by disinterested professional experts.'[57] Indeed the whole enthusiasm for the BIM can be seen as based on this understanding of management. The central function of the BIM, therefore, was to generate and deploy 'expertise' through the economy, not least amongst trade unionists.

On the basis of such a view of management's role, Labour seemed willing to offer management their place in the sun of British politics. And there is evidence that politically this posture had some success. Cripps, the leader and symbol of Labour's new managerialism, was a popular figure with significant sections of management. But there is also good evidence of subsequent disillusionment, based on the fact that despite the foundation of the BIM and Labour's undoubted enthusiasm for managers as (potential) key agents in the productivity campaign, the stratum never really felt itself to have been accepted.

In October 1945 *Industry Illustrated* noted that the 'present government' was concerning itself with industrial management to a degree that was a 'novelty in this country' but then went on to lament the fact that official policies, especially on the Working Parties, had not broken away 'from the rather jejune doctrinaire assumptions about employer cum trade union partnerships'. There could be no doubt, the journal continued, 'that in the last analysis industry is run by the managers, who must still be there to lead the productive team, whether the political climate is a socialistic or a capitalistic one'. Later the same year the seriousness of the Government's intent about efficiency was noted, but there was also criticism of Labour for having ignored the professional manager in its new reforms. As the journal's editor put it: 'One would have thought this government would have been the most ready to recognise and appreciate Industry's *tiers état*.'[58]

In fact, throughout the Labour Government's period in office, most of the economic bodies that it established were resolutely tripartite and involved employers, unions and government (though in some cases 'experts' substituted for government as the third element). This pattern was true of such bodies as the Working Parties, the National Production Advisory Council for Industry, the Economic Planning Board, the Anglo-American Council on Productivity and most smaller scale committees. The BIM was denied its place in these forums, despite its claims, and support from MPs such as Mikardo.

The issue of management's role in such bodies does not seem to have been raised at Cabinet level, but discussions amongst senior civil servants give the flavour of the thinking behind this position. The most explicit reference here occurred in the context of debate about whether or not the BIM should send representatives to the Committee on Industrial Productivity. The BIM couched its claim for such representation by asserting that it had an analogous position to the TUC and FBI. The civil service response is worth quoting in full:

> In the first place, the analogy is false, since the B.I.M. is not a political union of managers and does not claim to represent the personal interests of managers in the way in which the F.B.I. or T.U.C. represent their members.
>
> In the second place, if the BIM claims were admitted it could only open the door to its being pressed on other occasions and for other bodies as various as NPACI, Regional Boards for Industry and Development Councils. In fact every two-sided body might well become triangular in future, and the role of the independent or Government member to ensure that the work got done with maximum reconciliation of the employers and trade unionists would tend to disappear in the claim of the non-elected manager to speak in effect for the public interest in efficiency. This would be the 'managerial revolution' with a vengeance.[59]

This view seems to have prevailed. In this instance and occasionally elsewhere the BIM *was* granted a small representation, but explicitly on the basis of its expertise, not as an interest group.

Undoubtedly, all of this ultimately rested on a sensible appreciation of political realities. Partly as a consequence of government encouragement, by the late 1940s the BEC, FBI and TUC had become significant power-brokers, and bodies jealous of their prerogative as presenters of industrial opinion to government. This governmental role given to 'the two sides of industry' both reflected and reinforced the adversarial system of industrial relations in Britain. It was a system in which organised management remained at best a bit player. As Stalin might have said, how many divisions had the BIM? But it chimed in very poorly both with the rhetoric of the managerial revolution and with Labour's attempted *rapprochement* with management in the name of production and productivity.

In conclusion, it is apparent that Labour was forced to think hard about management in the late 1940s, perhaps especially in relation to the nationalised sector. Much (but not all) of the Labour Movement was persuaded to accept that management was neutral, an embodiment of expertise, which both could and should be an ally of Labour. The expertise in question must involve a large dollop of human relations, but was to remain administrative in character and largely separate from knowledge about any particular production process. The figure of the manager was, at least potentially, both progressive and professional.

This intellectual alliance with the manager rested in turn on a conception of the large joint stock company as an increasingly benign agency, unless monopolistic or with a history of particularly bad industrial relations or investment policies. Hence the broad movement to 'consolidationism' in Labour's policies both reflected and reinforced a particular view of management and its role in the private corporation.

Such a position was not without its contradictions. If big private and nationalised companies were so similar, and ICI a plausible model for the nationalised industries, why was it so often considered for investigation by the Monopolies Commission or as a prime target for nationalisation?[60] If managers' knowledge was so important why were their counsels usually to be excluded from the major places where economic policy was discussed?

Labour could, of course, have gone down a different route and attempted a path of 'radical productionism', allying itself more strongly with 'progressive' management against employers. But whatever else might be said about such a strategy, it would have necessitated a very radical break with the party's emergent understanding of the private sector. Whereas, before 1945, relatively little had been generated on this subject, by 1951 the situation was very different. The simple fact was that Labour had been forced to come to terms with industry because of national considerations, which meant recognising and dealing with employers' associations alongside the TUC. Such a relationship effectively precluded carrying the theory of the managerial revolution into political practice.

Chapter 7

The 'Americanisation' of productivity, 1948–51

Periodically in the twentieth century British firms and governments, conscious of the economy's relative decline, have turned to the USA for a model of how things might be done better.[1] The late 1940s was one such period. As on previous occasions, looking across the Atlantic for ideas to improve efficiency and productivity was conditioned by a range of short-term factors, and these also shaped what was seen as relevant in the US model. This chapter focuses on the causes and effects of the Labour Government's attempts to encourage British industry to adopt features of American production techniques, especially but not only via the Anglo-American Council on Productivity (AACP).

It should be emphasised that this was by no means the only aspect of 'Americanisation' in the period. Private sector companies without any government role were, albeit to a largely unknown degree, attempting to borrow from US practice. As Clark notes: 'American influences in Britain were continuous from the 1890s onwards and their presence went through successions of peaks and troughs. British firms did track American developments and create fragile and particularistic channels of learning about products, processes and work organisations.'[2]

Another source of American impact on British industry was US multi-national investment in Britain. Whilst the main initiative here was of course private, it was facilitated by a general policy of encouragement from British governments, including those of Attlee. In 1949, the Cabinet Economic Policy Committee reasserted that position, ordering that US direct investment proposals be encouraged 'provided that they contribute either (a) to our dollar viability by dollar saving or dollar earning, or (b) to our general economic recovery by supplying US techniques, know-how, patented processes'.[3]

The content of 'Americanisation' was always ambiguous, and its precise meaning in the debates and initiatives of the late 1940s is considered later. But one notable feature of Americanisation in other countries at this time was strikingly absent from Britain – vigorous anti-trust policies. In the defeated enemy countries of Germany and Japan anti-monopoly and anti-cartel measures were central, at least initially, to Americanisation. By contrast, in Britain anti-monopoly policy was a very damp squib, notwithstanding the passing of the Monopolies and Restrictive Practices Act 1948. As Helen Mercer shows, the Act's impact was reduced to very little largely because the Board of Trade, which both filtered applications to the Monopolies Commission and adjudicated upon its reports, was effectively influenced by business interests.[4]

The creation of the AACP in 1948 reflected the convergence of both the British and American administrations' concern with productivity. The origin of the British Government's involvement has been dealt with in earlier chapters. For the American side the creation of the AACP was closely linked to the general policy of economic aid to Western Europe under the Marshall Aid programme. Marshall Aid's overall objectives and effects have been much debated,[5] but in the present context the most important point to note is that, as well as giving immediate aid in order (allegedly) to stave off economic collapse and Communism, it embodied a 'politics of productivity'. This rested in part on the belief that increases in productivity had ameliorated social conflict in the USA itself, which in turn led to the idea that the long-run stability of Western Europe could be secured if growth and productivity were to be encouraged by US policy. Thus, Marshall Aid became to some extent about exporting American techniques of production in order to secure the perceived benefits of an American-style social peace.[6]

In this broad context the specific idea for the AACP emerged from a meeting between Stafford Cripps and Paul Hoffman (head of the European Co-operation Administration) in the summer of 1948. The note of this discussion is quite revealing about the attitudes which the British Government held at this time:

> The Chancellor said that he recognised the great interest which the Americans took in productivity. He had himself taken a lead in this matter over the last three years and it was indeed vital for the U.K.
>
> He therefore welcomed the suggestions that the US should help us in this matter; but it was vital, if the conservative outlook of both employers and labour was to be broken down, that any arrangements should be made by industry itself and not imposed upon industry by action of the two Governments.[7]

Cripps's reaction was conditioned not only by his prior interest in productivity but also by his recognition of US sensitivities about how far European countries were making their own efforts at economic expansion and adjustment and not just relying on Marshall Aid to bale them out. Thus, whilst the AACP was never a formal condition for the receipt of Marshall Aid, it was based on a recognition by the British Government that the giving of Marshall Aid was a contentious issue in the USA, so that it would be foolish not to respond to US initiatives which might ease its political passage in Congress.[8]

Cripps was clearly also very sensitive to the politics of the proposal in Britain. He secured the support of the official representatives of the employers and unions, but both bodies interpreted the matter in the light of their own concerns. The FBI had already been alerted to the very unfavourable view being taken in the USA about British industry's performance. The head of the US Department of Labour Productivity Division, L. Silberman, had visited Britain in early 1948 and, 'although very friendly', had 'formed a devastatingly adverse view of British productivity' which compared 'even worse with American than he had been led to expect'. The FBI's response was therefore to welcome the AACP as an opportunity for correcting 'ill-informed or self-interested' criticisms of British industry by Americans, and, at the same time, reducing the Labour Government's role in the productivity issue by placing 'the whole of this question firmly in the hands of industry itself'.[9]

Similarly, the TUC had its own views as to why the AACP should be supported. At the General Council meeting when the proposal was approved, Jack Tanner of the AEU argued that 'criticism has been levelled by certain Americans on semi-official visits to this country not against British workers but against managements, and he thought it would not be harmful for American industrialists to realise the difficulties which British industry was facing'. Like the FBI, the TUC had earlier been hesitant about the Government's proposals for a renewed productivity drive in the autumn of 1948, involving direct official contact with workers and employers via local and national conferences. Both bodies to a certain extent wanted to keep government at arm's length, away from 'their' members, and saw the AACP as means of achieving this.[10]

Endorsement by the peak associations of capital and labour did not mean unanimous support for the AACP. A letter from Hornsey Trades Council to the TUC reflected an extreme version of what was, perhaps, a widespread view on the Left: 'The introduction of American methods such as the Taft–Hartley anti-T.U. bill, the use of tear gas against strikers, lynching and the Ku Klux Klan, will not increase productivity.'[11]

The AACP proposal in fact touched a raw nerve of anti-American sentiment, evident across the political spectrum.[12] In announcing the idea Cripps went out of his way to stress the agreement given by the FBI and the TUC, and emphasised that the AACP was proposed 'not on the basis of our industries being inferior to those of other countries', but because 'an exchange of experience and knowledge of production would be of great benefit to this country'.[13]

Given this endorsement, if not enthusiasm, the AACP was established in 1948 as a bipartite body, with representatives from the BEC as well as the FBI, the TUC and employer and union representatives from the USA, but no government members. It was intended that the organisation's life would be coterminous with Marshall Aid, that is, ending in June 1952. In the early stages the AACP established a five-part programme of work for itself: (i) plant visits and exchange of information on production techniques; (ii) an enquiry into maintenance of productive plant and power; (iii) productivity measurement; (iv) an examination of specialisation in industrial production; and (v) the collection of economic information. The last four of these objectives spawned committees, all of which reported rather inconclusively in 1949. This reinforced the dominance of team visits to America as the AACP's main activity (in fact the only one for which it is usually remembered). By the end of its existence the Council had arranged 49 team visits in specific industries, and 17 on specialist subjects (for example, management education). Three visits of US teams to the UK were also organised.[14]

The role of the AACP in the productivity drive of the late 1940s must be partly seen in the context of the agenda set by its major participants, the peak associations. Certain areas, notably restrictive practices (by both firms and labour), were ruled out as specific objects of enquiry by the British participants, despite the Americans' view that these were likely to be important in explaining Anglo-American differences in productivity. Such questions were simultaneously said to be a 'purely British matter', to be fairly unimportant and, in any case, to be welcomed where they existed by both employers and unions in Britain because they encouraged 'stability through organisation'.[15] Parallel to this kind of exclusion was a pact not to consider anything to do with labour relations: 'all agreed that there was to be no interference with the normal negotiating machinery and procedure of industry'.[16] However, none of these issues could be effectively excluded from the team reports, a point considered later.

More positively, both the employers and unions had various ideas as to what they thought the AACP should focus attention upon. The FBI, in setting out its 'fundamental considerations' in agreeing to the AACP, emphasised three points. It argued that:

(a) lowest cost should be the criteria of efficiency rather than production per man hour;
(b) greater efficiency was constantly barred by restrictions on capital developments;
(c) the big problem in efficiency is bottlenecks in materials and supplies.[17]

The first point related to the FBI view that production per man hour comparisons with the USA were, despite their popularity, unfair and inappropriate because they did not reflect the higher capital intensity of US production and thus distorted the overall efficiency differences. This was a highly important issue for the whole productivity drive and will be considered several times in the following pages. It clearly links to the second point, the belief of the FBI that, under Labour, investment had become the 'residual legatee' of resources rather than the first call. The Government's view was that, contrary to this assertion, it was giving a high priority to investment, but that, especially because of the need to divert resources into exports, there was a limit to what might be achieved on this front, and in any event much more could and should be done to raise output with *existing* capital equipment. The last point was a staple complaint of the FBI in this period, linked to the belief that controls were excessive and should be removed more rapidly. Thus, from the FBI point of view, the AACP was largely a forum for pressing a pre-existing and well-known agenda of issues which it saw as crucial for productivity.[18]

However, there was also recognition that by involving unions the AACP could function to raise questions in a rather different way than the normal diet of FBI representations to the Government. An FBI draft report on the AACP in 1950 argued that productivity was basically an issue of 'men and machines'. Given that machinery was largely outside the AACP remit, the focus should be on men. In this context it was argued that the Council could 'influence the psychological approach and affect the climate of opinion':

> Productivity consciousness is a long step towards the realisation of

> high productivity. It is in helping to promote this that the Council believe that its work has been and is of the greatest potential value.[19]

There is a clear parallel between the FBI and TUC approaches to the AACP. On the one hand they both wanted to use it to press their own hobby-horses; for example, in the case of the TUC, the importance of Joint Production Committees. Equally, both were convinced that in the long run higher investment was the crucial element in raising productivity. But the TUC, like the FBI in its more reflective moods, accepted that in the short run the level of capital equipment had to be taken as given. What, therefore, was left? With restrictive practices and industrial relations ruled out, the TUC, like the FBI, tended to end up with a rather vacuous psychologism. Thus, Tanner from the AEU argued that: 'if we are going to get any immediate results it does mean improved and increased co-operation between management and work people'. Naesmith from the cotton weavers saw this co-operation as being something to be spread from the peak associations to the shopfloor: 'The issue with us is how to get the people in the mills and factories and the workshops themselves lined up on the need for change and the way in which the changes should go.'[20]

The sectoral teams sent from Britain to the USA all consisted of representatives of both employers and employees, with the latter supposed to include supervisors, technicians and those from 'workshop level', including operatives and shop stewards. In practice, the composition of the teams was a persistent bone of contention. Early in 1949 Harries at the TUC wrote that the whole idea of team visits was 'going badly' because some trade associations were insisting on sending non-trade unionists.[21]

It was subsequently agreed that the procedure would be for the AACP to invite employers' associations to ask firms if they wished to nominate people for the teams; that they would be requested to do this in collaboration with trade unions; and that they would also be questioned as to whether the unions agreed to the nominations. This looks like, and seems to have functioned as, a rather uneasy compromise between the supposedly bipartisan character of the AACP and the fact that much of the non-dollar cost of the visits was borne by employers. The composition of the teams was also affected by the Americans screening-out communists on security grounds.[22]

Only one detailed account of a team visit seems to have survived. This is a case study relating to the making of the Cotton Spinning Report, by P.H. Cook of the Tavistock Institute. In this instance the worker members were nominated by the unions, and the eventual report was strongly endorsed by the employee side. Cook saw the team's efforts as making a 'serious and important contribution to its industry' and emphasised the importance of good communications within the team for its perceived success – a very Tavistock point of view.[23]

Like all of the other teams, that on cotton spinning was sent around factories in Britain before it went to the USA. This 'briefing tour' involved visiting 17 companies over a fortnight, before a six-week tour of the USA which covered 35 plants. On the team's return, 29 meetings were held to publicise its report and findings, and the average attendance at these was said to be in excess of 100 people.[24]

This pattern was similar to that for most of the teams, though whether all were quite so easily co-operative is unclear. Cotton spinning was perhaps atypical in the collaborative character of its industrial relations, though in most cases the 'screening' process seems to have ensured a minimum of discord amongst team members. Controversy arose most explicitly in cases where the unions felt that team membership had been 'fixed' by employers in order to secure a report favourable to themselves. For example, the Foundry Workers' Union protested ineffectively about the composition of the Steel Founding Team. When the team's report was published the union produced its own counter-report, which earned it a dressing-down from the General Council of the TUC on the grounds that '[the union] had obviously sought to influence shop stewards to take an antagonistic view of the Report'.[25]

What message did the majority of team reports carry about the sources of Britain's low productivity compared with the USA? With 66 reports on diverse industries, and the politically charged nature of the issue, it is not perhaps surprising that different authors have drawn rather different conclusions on this subject. For example, Broadberry and Crafts have tended to emphasise the overmanning and restrictive practices that were 'revealed' by the reports.[26] Carew, by contrast, stressed the general social-psychological approach of the reports, with their belief that the particular character of American labour was vital. Coupled to this, for Carew, was an emphasis on the need for 'scientific management' as in the American model. In this account, therefore, the most important aspect of the AACP was its 'ideological challenge to basic labour movement values'.[27]

Though having very different views about the accuracy of the AACP diagnosis of Britain's productivity problems, both Broadberry and Crafts and Carew tend to focus attention on issues concerning labour. Is this a fair portrait of the reports? It must be conceded at once that the reports did contain a great deal of rhetoric about the alleged differences in labour attitudes and industrial relations between the USA and Britain. This derived partly from the 'lowest common denominator' kind of approach of the FBI and TUC to the AACP, and was no doubt encouraged by the bipartisan nature of the teams.

Much of this material was by its very nature ill-focused and lent itself to vacuous generalisation. As a contemporary critic noted:

> The teams, it seems, have found the real secret of high productivity; it lies not in machinery, not in factory layout – in short not primarily in technical improvements, but in the American Way of Life. If only the American Way (the reports suggest) could be transferred to Britain, how hardworking, how comfortable everyone would be.

This approach perhaps reached its nadir in the Grey-Iron Founding Report, which remarked upon the observed great energy of New Yorkers, and noted: 'Several members of the Team were infected by this energising atmosphere and enjoyed a greater capacity for activity and less need for sleep than was customary for them in Britain.'[28]

Rather little detail was given about industrial relations in the team reports. Whilst much is said about the technical aspects of production, the allegedly 'central' issue of workers' attitudes and behaviour is ill-supported by evidence. Oddly enough, the only report to have comparative figures on industrial relations showed more days lost by strikes in the USA than the UK.[29] This may, of course, partly reflect the desire of the employers and TUC to keep restrictive practices and the specifics of industrial relations off the AACP agenda.

A detailed contemporary study compared the assertions of the AACP reports with evidence from American industrial relations literature to see how far US practices were as presented in the team reports. The overall conclusion was that the American worker appeared much less different from the British worker than the AACP suggested: 'We can see, then, that the Productivity teams, excellent though they were on the technical aspect of production, gave a misleading picture of the American worker and his trade union.' The study went on to speculate how this misrepresentation might have arisen, given the union involvement in the teams. It noted the short time spent in the USA, the desire that some had to 'shake-up' British labour, the selective nature of the firm visits within the USA (with four out of five firms approached by the AACP withholding co-operation) and the psychology of intensive visits in a collaborative team framework.[30]

In part, therefore, the AACP can rightly be seen as just one more instalment in 'the British Worker Question': the long-standing process of blaming labour for the ills of the British economy.[31] Certainly the TUC was alive to the extent to which a certain kind of essentially anti-union propaganda could be read off from the team findings. It responded very critically to the 'Fleming–Waddell' report, an internal AACP summary of the first fifteen team reports, which it saw as 'over-weighting atmosphere and psychological factors' and playing down the machinery and investment aspects of higher US productivity. This indeed was a general problem for the TUC, as it tried to balance support for the AACP with criticism of those who used the reports only for propaganda.[32]

However, it is worth emphasising that the reports generally contained a good deal of substantive material which is not about workers and their attitudes. Carew, whose main interest is in labour relations, and who relies largely on TUC sources for his discussion of the AACP, rather glosses over this other material, simply saying that it focused on 'scientific management'. Broadberry and Crafts similarly mention the AACP critique of British management, but focus on the restrictionism of labour since this fits in more with their economists' assumption about the importance of competition in labour and capital markets.[33]

An analysis of 58 team reports prepared in 1952/3 shows that the main factors that they deemed responsible for the US lead in productivity were as follows. Heading the list were 'extensive use of mechanical aids' and 'appreciation by work people of need for higher productivity', followed closely by three questions of 'managerial technique' – 'modern methods of costing', 'production planning and control' and 'work study'.[34]

Thus, alongside the almost mandatory reference to workers' attitudes, emphasis was placed on a range of factors which related either to low levels of investment in Britain (which, as we have seen, both the TUC and FBI accepted but regarded as unchangeable in the short run) or to managerial practices broadly defined. This was not, of course, the kind of finding which the FBI wanted from the AACP, though it had always been anxious that this might happen. As Middlemas remarks: 'In this sense, the FBI's fears were justified: the long-term thrust of the Marshall Aid experience highlighted management inadequacies, not those of the workforce.'[35]

The critique of management even comes across quite strongly in Hutton's *We Too Can Prosper*, despite the TUC's feeling that the author of this book had succumbed to the AACP disease of broad psycho-logistic generalisation without supporting evidence. Hutton's first substantive chapter was called ‘Better management, higher productivity’ and cited as evidence of the superiority of American management the summary of 22 team reports in the appendix of the AACP's *Education for Management*.[36]

The AACP concern with management raises a much broader issue about the forms of management that ‘Americanisation’ was held to entail in the late 1940s. This issue is considered later in the discussion of other components of government activity which also aimed at encouraging British industry to adopt (perceived) American methods. In many ways the questions raised there fell outside the institutional character of the AACP. However, that institutional character needs first to be considered in a little more detail.

General questions about the impact of Labour's initiatives on productivity, together with an overall assessment of the AACP, are considered in Chapter 8. Here the focus is on the peculiarities of the AACP as an agency for raising productivity. As so often with the impact of an institution, there are great difficulties of interpretation, because no one criterion can be applied. Clearly different actors hoped for different things from the AACP. The Government hoped to appease American criticism of British economic policy and performance and so help to secure the continuation of Marshall Aid, while at the same time encouraging union and employer enthusiasm for the productivity effort. The USA had high hopes of the AACP and felt that these were being realised. Its participating representatives recognised that the AACP formed a ‘temporary defensive alliance’ between the FBI and TUC rather than an enthusiastic partnership. This stemmed from what was seen as the defensiveness of the British participants about the causes of Britain's lagging productivity – allegedly demonstrated by the refusal to confront restrictive practices, the ‘over emphasis’ on higher investment as the key to progress and the general refrain of ‘British practice is suited to British conditions’.[37] However, these drawbacks were never serious enough to threaten what was seen as the major gain, the acceptance of the need to raise British productivity by following the American example.

Politically, the Government was committed to a ‘hands-off’ approach to the AACP. The difficulty with this from the Government's point of view was how to respond if the Council was seen to be insufficiently active or doing inappropriate things. This issue came to the surface in the autumn of 1949 when the US Government put forward proposals aimed at increasing technical assistance to Britain. The issue for the Government was how far this was to be channelled via the AACP.

Doubts on the desirability of using the Council were voiced by some senior civil servants, who noted that the AACP had not supplied government departments with its minutes, and indeed seemed to be working very hard to minimise any kind of liaison or contact. So the technical assistance proposal raised a dilemma: should the government reconcile itself to the various disadvantages of handing the whole thing over to the Council or should it think out some way of enabling the official machine to work openly with the Council and find a formula acceptable to industry to explain this state of affairs?[38]

In the event the Government channelled the increased assistance via the AACP, maintaining the earlier proposition that the Council was more likely to engage British producers, as well as to maintain America's support, if it were seen to be clearly working apart from Whitehall.

For the FBI, to repeat, the AACP was a means of getting government 'off its back'. The FBI used the Council as a basis for resisting the taking of decisions on productivity elsewhere. For example, it remained aloof from the work of the Ministry of Supply's committee on standardisation by arguing that this work should be done by the AACP. Similarly it suggested that the vexed issue of data gathering for productivity measurement should come under the Council – though this did not lead to any greater co-operation by industry in producing reliable data.[39]

Overall, therefore, it would seem right to characterise the FBI's response to the AACP as minimalist and defensive. It welcomed the Council as a means of combating US misperceptions of Britain and keeping the Government at a greater distance, rather than as a significant initiative in the battle to raise productivity in British industry.

Some of the same attitudes were shared by the TUC. But the productivity issue was more complex for the union side than for the employers. On the one hand, it was 'their' government which was setting so much store by raising productivity, and, as a central component of the Labour Movement, the unions could hardly ignore the political emphasis given to this objective. On the other hand, many union officials understood that Anglo-American comparisons were being used to attack trade unionism. The broad character of the TUC's response to this dilemma is clear. In public, it embraced the AACP with great enthusiasm. Yet, in private, it acted to try to restrain both the wilder rhetoric of the 'American Way of Life', with its usual anti-union implications, and the Left's criticism of some of the AACP material. Hence the TUC became politically committed to the idea of the AACP to a much greater extent than the employers.

As indicated in earlier chapters, the TUC was willing to go to unprecedented lengths in support of the productivity drive. Though not strictly part of the AACP, this support is well illustrated by the TUC's own 'Team Visit' to the USA in 1949. What was striking in the report which emerged from this initiative was the extent to which unions were encouraged to see productivity as their responsibility. As the document put it, the 'real problem confronting trade unions was to find ways and means of increasing productivity'. In pursuing this theme the role of American unions seems to have been substantially exaggerated, as when the report claimed that unions there made 'a major contribution to increasing the efficiency of less competent companies'.[40]

As Carew has persuasively argued, such conclusions were poorly supported by the evidence unearthed by the TUC. In fact, US pressure had produced a rather more 'up-beat' report which in effect recommended 'American' practices to the British even though these were rarely actually pursued by US unions. One result of the visit was the creation in early 1950 of the TUC's own Production Department, which focused attention on spreading the gospel of productivity amongst rank and file trade unionists, especially by providing training in management techniques for such people.[41]

In sum, union leaderships to a striking degree in this period saw their role as encouraging the productivity drive, though they often believed that this could be done more effectively by the unions themselves than by the heavy hand of government. Nevertheless, this attitude did not lead to a significant radical 'productionism', involving a challenge to managerial prerogatives on the grounds of management inefficiency. As the Director-General of the FBI reported:

> I must say I have been much impressed by the recognition by the T.U. members of that Council that each side has its own distinct function, and I feel there is no danger there of collaboration leading to encroachments by the trade unions on to the field of management.[42]

The AACP was created for a political purpose as much as directly to raise productivity. Equally, the support of the peak associations for it was part of a political 'deal' between them and the Government. Its economic impact (considered in Chapter 8) must be seen in the light of this political situation. In particular, the FBI continued to be quite successful in using the Council to keep government out of certain areas related to productivity, whilst resisting any enlargement of the unions' role in this issue. In this sense the AACP may be seen as a case study of the problems that were encountered by the Attlee Government in its pursuit of policies via 'corporatist' structures of close co-operation and indeed significant dependence upon the peak associations.[43]

For many, the crucial issue in the attempts at 'Americanising' British industry in the immediate post-war period revolved around 'scientific management'.[44] Carew's discussion of the AACP, for example, presents the key 'success' of that body in terms of the growing acceptance amongst British labour of scientific management, which it had previously resisted. Like many authors, Carew does not offer a definition of scientific management but tends to treat it as synonymous with Taylorism, in other words as concerned with the direct role of the worker in production, or what in recent years has often been called the 'labour process'.[45]

Whilst this equation of scientific management and Taylorism is appropriate for much of the early period of the scientific management movement before and after the First World War, it is very much less so in relation to the 1940s. Writers such as Urwick and Brech, for example, had incorporated much of the contemporary human relations approach into what they called scientific management.[46] Similarly, a major managerial ideologue such as de Haan could remark of scientific management that: 'increasing output and raising efficiency are its technical and economic goals, while its social purpose consists of careful treatment of the human factor in industry and of the raising of the standard of living of the community'.[47]

Even where the definition of scientific management did not include the whole human relations package, it usually referred to a range of issues beyond the focus on labour. It might therefore embrace subjects such as production organisation, production control and managerial techniques which fell between 'the labour process' on one hand and human relations on the other.

This background to the events of the 1940s is important because, in order to understand the significance of the debate about scientific management and Americanisation in that period, it is necessary to define the meaning and connotations of these terms with some care. To that end this chapter will schematically divide the package that was being proposed into three: standardisation (or, with simplification and specialisation, what were often called 'the three Ss'); standard costing and budgeting, commonly seen as a crucial accompaniment to standardisation; and work study, including time and motion study. Together, these techniques would seem to define the main thrusts of the Americanisation of production in this period, along with the human relations perspective, which was dealt with in Chapter 5.

Perhaps the longest standing adverse comparison of British and American industry was in terms of the scale of its units of production. The argument that British firms were too small to compete effectively with those in the USA goes back to at least the First World War, but came to prominence in the 'rationalisation' movement of the 1920s and 1930s. Very generally put, this movement proposed *inter alia* that Britain suffered from too many small units which were unable to realise the economies of scale that were available to larger scale firms. A key corollary of rationalisation was mass production of a standardised product.[48]

In the inter-war period the main focus of the rationalisation movement was on the depressed staple industries such as iron and steel, coal and cotton. But in the Second World War attention shifted somewhat to the consumer goods industries, encouraged by the policy of concentrating their production in fewer units, and only allowing the manufacture of utility (i.e. standardised) goods.[49]

This latter orientation was carried over into the Working Party investigations of the 1945–7 period. As Chapter 4 demonstrated, these were enquiries by tripartite (employer/union/independent) bodies into a range of consumer goods industries. Some proposed programmes of rationalisation or 're-equipment and consolidation' in order to gain the (alleged) economies of scale from larger units producing larger runs of output, and this was most strikingly so in the case of cotton.[50]

The cotton recommendation is a classic example of the proposed 'Americanisation' of an industry which was based in part on previous comparisons with US experience. The relevance of the American model was also vigorously disputed by a dissenting member of the Working Party, the economist John Jewkes. He argued that the production economies of scale in the industry were quite limited, and that the danger of inflexibility stemming from mass production was high. In sum, he felt that it would be 'a fatal mistake to allow the claims for mass production, standardisation or bulk selling to conceal the increasing reliance which ought to be placed upon the disposal in the markets of the world of quality products, fashioned in detail to suit the demands of the consumer'.[51]

Whatever the merits of the 'Americanisation' proposals in cotton or elsewhere, the idea of standardisation of production as a major route to productivity increase informed a great deal of the Government's policy in this period. For example, it was a major part of the idea behind Development Councils, Labour's most distinctive proposal for the reorganisation of the private sector.

Development Councils sprang in part from the Working Parties, several of which proposed a permanent tri- or bipartite organisation for their industry. One element in the Development Council proposals was that they would encourage 'rationalisation', in the sense of amalgamations and concentration of production. However, partly because of the very strong opposition of most employers (and the FBI) few Development Councils were actually created, with those that were being largely restricted to common service functions – research, marketing and the like. Thus, the high hopes held by both civil servants and some Labour Ministers of Development Councils as major instruments of industrial change were dashed. The whole episode had demonstrated a commitment to standardisation, but this was largely gestural.[52]

Whilst Development Councils were Labour's most original policy initiative for private industry, and an important channel for ideas on standardisation, they were by no means the only important initiative in this area. The Ministry of Supply had pursued standardisation in its military hardware purchasing during the war period, and carried this idea over into the Attlee years. The direct leverage of the Ministry declined as the volume of government purchases fell off, but standardisation continued to be pursued in such forums as the Engineering Advisory Council, which was dominated by the employers but in fact reluctantly created under union pressure.[53]

These efforts became focused on the Lemon Committee, which was set up to look at the whole issue of standardisation in engineering. Its report came out strongly in favour of the benefits to be gained from increased standardisation, and in particular advocated an expanded British Standards Institute (BSI) to pursue this objective. Whilst employers seem to have generally welcomed the Lemon findings, they were emphatic that any enhanced role for the BSI should not encroach on the voluntary nature of standard setting. Their insistence was based on two points. First, they argued that if standardisation were pressed too far it would threaten innovation and technical change. Second, it was felt that the BSI could become an agency for increasing government control of the private sector, about which employers were, of course, extremely sensitive, not to say paranoid, in this period.[54]

The BSI was expanded in the late 1940s, and this involved further government money pro rata with money from industry. The Ministry of Supply used the Lemon Committee to cajole engineering employers; some responded, but they continued to insist that this was a matter for the industry itself, and in particular the trade associations. Some of these associations had an existing concern with the issue, which may have been accentuated by government pressure. For example, the associations of locomotive manufacturers and aircraft constructors continued to be active in this area.[55]

However, these two examples point to a major issue in the standardisation debate. Locomotive manufacturers, almost entirely, and aircraft producers, to a significant extent, were dependent on the public purchasing of their output. Thus, in both industries standardisation was encouraged by the purchaser. In the case of the railways this occurred because of policies adopted by the newly created British Railways Board. In the case of aircraft, the position was more obscure; on the one hand, the aircraft trade association, the Society of British Aircraft Constructors (SBAC), stressed its independence from government while, on the other hand, there was a mandatory requirement by the Ministry of Supply for the use of SBAC standard parts in aircraft bought by the British government.[56]

There was a general attempt at Cabinet level to try to get public purchasing used as an instrument of standardisation, but the results seem to have been very uneven. Standardisation was successfully achieved in electricity generator sets, though how far this was economically desirable is debatable. For the full benefits of standardisation to be achieved there must obviously be utilisation of the most efficient design, without any inhibition of technical change. This is always a difficult balance to achieve.[57]

The publication of the Lemon Committee Report was timed to coincide with an AACP enquiry into *Simplification in Industry*. This, like so much of the material during these years, argued that 'any organised and determined effort to reduce our manufacturing variety still further could make a rapid and major contribution to increasing productivity and lowering costs in British industry'.[58]

The AACP document was followed up in 1950 by a report on progress over simplification. This gave a very general overview of activity in relation to the '3 Ss' which suggested that much was happening. Yet its recommendations also noted that 'a campaign should be launched at once in every industry in which a policy of simplification can be applied', which implied a need for very much more action.[59]

Another initiative concerned with standardisation was organised by the Special Research Unit (SRU) of the Board of Trade. This was a unit which was designed to apply operations research to industrial problems and which did a lot of work on productivity, particularly looking at how standardisation might improve efficiency. One of the most interesting SRU studies was of Glacier Metals, which also figured in the discussion

Table 7.1 Estimated savings from increasing batch size of bushes and bearings

Batch size	*% Saving/unit*
1–150	0
151–1,000	27.8
1,001–10,000	43.2
10,000–40,000	75.2
40,001+	80.8

Source: BT 64/2316

of human relations in Chapter 5. Here, the managing director, Wilfred Brown, approached the SRU with data on cost savings available from standardisation. He presented a table which was very much grist to the mill of the standardisers (Table 7.1). But it was also made clear that the achievement of such economies would require a radical change in the structure of demand for the products, in this case a change in the components policy of the car industry. Car manufacturers were, in fact, commonly regarded as slow to pursue component standardisation, though there was some movement towards model standardisation.[60]

Hutton called standardisation, simplification and specialisation 'the three charmed Ss of high productivity'. Alongside this went an equally hyperbolic emphasis on American management as essentially about cost measurement. American management 'is measurement', he argued, adding that 'all measurements are part of the planning, costing or reaching of targets . . . because *only* these measures are made which have relevance to these operations'. However, this was merely an extreme version of a common refrain about the deficiencies of British cost accounting, and the absence in particular of systems of standard costing and budgeting. Thus, almost all of the Working Parties reported unfavourably on the position in this regard. In cotton, for example, enquiry revealed that the industry as a whole lacked 'adequate knowledge of its cost structure'. A survey of the Working Party publications by the SRU concluded: 'The Reports find the system of costing in British industry to be, on the whole, hopelessly inadequate.'[61]

This was a theme, too, of many of the AACP industry reports. The AACP in fact sent a specialist team to the USA to report on management accounting. It argued that the key to American efficiency was US manufacturers' costing and budgeting procedures, and recommended that British management 'in considering the future and preparing plans, should make the fullest use of budgeting and forecasting, based on accounting and costing data'.[62]

The question of economic measurement and productivity engaged a great deal of attention in this period. Much effort was devoted to formulating and then proselytising direct measures of productivity at factory level for use as a management tool. However, this seems to have been largely a dead-end, meeting resistance from many managers who regarded cost rather than productivity measures as more helpful, a view that was supported by the AACP team, which emphasised that in the USA 'industry makes little attempt to measure productivity, preferring to rely on unit costs'. The AACP report went on to stress that what the Americans had was not different measurement techniques, but much keener attitudes on the intensity and speed of deployment of cost information, and its central role in everyday management activity. The keys were accurate costing, standard costing, and an understanding of their focal role in making production decisions.[63]

The response of British industry to this propaganda on costing does not seem to have been very enthusiastic. One letter to the FBI commented on the AACP report:

> It seems to me to have been compiled by a bunch of rather third rate accountants wearing the blinkers traditional to that profession, with the sole object of trying to magnify the importance of the accountant in industry.

There were more positive reactions, but overall the evidence suggests little changed. During the war costing seems to have improved in areas where cost-plus contracts required more accurate calculations, but after the war 'the thought in many entrepreneurs' minds that cost accounting was just another new-fangled administrative overhead could not easily be dislodged'.[64]

In his survey of British management at the end of the 1950s, Granick argued that:

> The single major managerial development of post-war Britain does not really violate the proposition that managerial professionalism is still rejected. For this development has been concentrated in the area of production efficiency and on the lowest level of managerial hierarchy. It is old-fashion work study, bearing the new name of 'O. & M.'. . . . While this is undoubtedly highly important for efficient operations, it represents a managerial movement which was

> revolutionary in American industry during the first decade of this century – but had been routinised into standard operating procedure in the US by the 1920s at the latest.[65]

Thus, work study represents the one clear 'victory' for Americanisation of the early post-war period, and one strongly encouraged in the late 1940s.

The major channel of such encouragement, was, like so much in the area of productivity, the brainchild of Stafford Cripps. Whilst Minister of Aircraft Production during the War he had become an enthusiast for motion study, and set up a Production Efficiency Board in the Ministry to propagate this. Post-war, he had pressed for transforming this into a Production Efficiency Service (PES), offering free and general management consultation to small firms, but with a considerable dose of motion study.[66]

Cripps's enthusiasm was very much for motion study, that is ergonomics, which he wished to keep sharply separate from time study, a much more contentious technique involving questions about the pace of work and wage calculations. In part this division reflected the peculiar if explicable desire to keep separate 'wage' and 'production' issues, as discussed in Chapter 5. But whilst motion study was being encouraged by the PES in the late 1940s, time study was also spreading, basically as part of the growth of piece-rate systems, encouraged by the British Institute of Management as a good management practice.[67]

The SRU was less inhibited about linking the two elements, and made investigations of time and motion study in the context of its research into productivity. A report by the SRU argued plausibly that most advocacy of time and motion emphasised the motion/ergonomic aspect, but that most adoption of it occurred as a basis for wage payment systems. In its view the discussion of time and motion as a device for aiding productivity had been bedevilled by the linkage with pay bargaining, as this involved controversial issues about how far unions would accept a 'scientific' basis for wage setting to displace collective bargaining. Generally the SRU saw merit in time and motion, but regarded claims that it was a crucial and scientific technique to be overblown.[68]

Work study emerged strongly in the 1950s, partly as a result of the example of particular firms, notably ICI, and partly because of the growing enthusiasm for piece-work systems. Nevertheless, it was also linked to the productivity drive of the 1940s and to the idea of Americanisation. Carew treats the spread of work study as a key index of the success of Americanisation, in the sense that it secured the support of workers for American-style scientific management, aimed at the subordination of labour. This general thesis is considered in the conclusion below, but it is important to note that by itself, work study was rather less radical in its implications than Carew suggests, because so little else in the package of 'scientific management' had been adopted. Enthusiasm for work study in the 1950s did *not* herald a radical restructuring of work and production organisation, but was more of an 'add-on' to existing production systems. As Granick implies, it was therefore rather limited in its implications for British firms, rather akin to the take up of just-in-time systems by British firms in the 1980s and 1990s.[69]

The clear implication of this chapter, to conclude, is that the extent of 'Americanisation' of British industry in the early post-war years was very limited. Whilst the precise content of what Americanisation might mean is disputable, it is difficult to argue that any of the possible aspects connected with such a process – standardisation of components or products, standard costing and budgeting, 'mass production' techniques in general – went very far in this period. Work study was, at most, a very pale imitation of Tayloristic practices and its significance remained largely confined to wage bargaining procedures.

Given the scale of Government and other efforts which went into propaganda for Americanisation, this very limited impact requires some explanation. Central here is the fact that many British industrialists were sceptical about the relevance of the American model for British conditions. No doubt in part this stemmed from a common gut reaction to the American model. But there was also a reasoned case which more than one authority made. The *Engineer*, for example, the trade paper of the engineering industry, was far from vitriolically anti-American, yet on a number of occasions it questioned just how relevant the US example was for British industry. One editorial thus argued:

> Britain, manufacturing for the world rather than for its home market alone, has to take into account . . . national tastes and likings. The consequence is that mass production methods cannot be so highly developed as in America, and output per worker is necessarily lower. Furthermore, many of the heavier engineering products of this country are made to special orders and designs, so that not even group productive methods are applicable.

On another occasion it pointed out that obsession with the American model had led to the neglect of the fact that, in many areas, Britain's competition came from Europe, not the USA: 'Much of real value to the industries of this country would, we believe, be learnt from a study of plants in Western Europe, which are confronting problems much more similar to our own than are those facing American producers'.[70]

Such scepticism was also evinced by some economists. Jewkes's view on cotton has already been noted, and he made similar points in a more general article in 1946. Another economist, G.C. Allen, expressed a parallel argument, though emphasising that he was not against learning from abroad. For Allen, the lesson was that 'an uncritical acceptance of foreign types of organisation as the norm' seemed 'as foolish as insular complacency'.[71]

But if a case can be made for the logic of some resistance to Americanisation in the 1940s, this line of argument has its dangers. Thus, for neo-classical economists (and historians who follow them), it is all too likely to lead to a Panglossian view that whatever industrialists did was for the best. This is a little hard to accept even in relation to cotton, where the significance of 'Americanisation' can be seriously questioned, but it is all the more so in areas where the most obvious forms of such 'Americanisation' would appear to have been only too relevant. For example, it is hard to believe that the engineering firm able to produce 20,000 different types of bearing would not have benefited from a dose of the '3Ss'.[72]

The simple point is that 'Americanisation' was differentially applicable to industries in Britain. In some cases markets could have been exploited with standardised products, in other cases this might have been a problem. In particular, standardisation of components would seem to have offered a much more fertile field for economies of scale than standardisation of some final products. This is brought out quite strikingly in the contrast between the clear market limitations in the standardisation of diesel locomotives in Britain as opposed to the possibilities in valve manufacture.[73] The important fact is how little this differential applicability was taken into account in the discussions – for example, it hardly seems to figure in FBI deliberations.

Finally, there is the question of 'Americanisation' in the more specific sense of work practices, and the idea that the AACP and other initiatives successfully sold an ideology of managerialism to the unions and the Labour Party in Britain, on the back of which 'Tayloristic' work practices were then introduced. It has already been suggested that work study, although undoubtedly popular in the 1950s, was a rather limited change in British industry. It was not a sign of 'Taylorism' being widely deployed. British resistance to Taylorism in the sense of systematic de-skilling, work fragmentation and machine-pacing of production seems to have remained strong. In part, this was because of the absence of the necessary parallel changes in product mix and production techniques.[74]

On an ideological plane, too, resistance to Taylorism was also significant. Carew is undoubtedly right in arguing that the AACP and Americanisation generally reinforced the spirit of 'class compromise' under the Labour Government. But this process surely had largely domestic roots, relating to the basics of Labour's electoral strategy, and can therefore be traced to the 1920s rather than the 1940s. Similarly with the trade unions, the acceptance of the productivity drive and its implications by union leaders was undoubtedly a striking feature of this period. But it seems much less clear that this owed much to American influence, as it fitted in with the whole union movement's conception of its role from, at least, 1941. So whilst Carew is right to suggest the importance of Marshall Aid for the political divisions in Western European Labour Movements in the late 1940s, it is much less apparent that it fundamentally affected the stance on economic and production issues that was taken by either the Government or the unions.

Chapter 8

Evaluation and implications

The previous discussion has focused on what Labour did about productivity between 1945 and 1951. It has demonstrated that the Government remained very concerned about the issue throughout the whole period and was willing to intervene in a number of different ways to stimulate improvement. In this chapter, the aim is to provide some perspective on Labour's initiatives, by asking questions about what was actually achieved in terms of the central policy objective – the amelioration of productivity. Did the administration's policies have any real impact on British industry's efficiency? And what were the factors that determined the efficacy, one way or another, of the various Government measures?

An obvious way of assessing Labour's record at this time is to look at the various quantitative analyses that are available about Britain's productivity record. Yet, before turning to these studies, it is as well to note that their methodology makes them of rather more limited value than might be imagined, not least for the problem being considered here. First, it must be emphasised that most of the quantitative estimates rely on either labour or total factor calculations, in which the ratio of change in labour inputs on their own, or in combination with capital inputs, is measured relative to changes in output. This approach always yields a large element of the productivity variation which cannot be accounted for by changes in factor inputs. Such 'residuals' of course need to be explained, and often open the door to a wide variety of *ad hoc* hypotheses. The end product is, therefore, all too often speculation rather than substantiated argument.

Second, there is also a problem of timescale. Many of the estimates deal with the grand sweep of Britain's long-run performance in the post-war period, rather than the 1940s as a single decade. To attempt a more limited perspective is fraught with difficulties. Productivity estimates for short periods must always be treated with reserve because, given problems with the data, changes in apparent performance over a few years may easily be statistical artefacts. This is even more so in relation to the 1940s, since the available series for these years are highly deficient by current standards.

With these problems in mind, what do the quantitative studies suggest about productivity at the time of the Attlee Governments? Cairncross, the author of the most authoritative macroeconomic survey of the period, accepts Feinstein's conclusion that GDP per head rose 1.6 per cent per annum between 1945 and 1951, and 2.5 per cent per annum in the three years 1948–51. Labour productivity in manufacturing apparently followed a similar pattern, rising at an average rate of 2.6 per cent per annum across the six years, but accelerating to 3.5 per cent per annum between 1948 and 1951.[1]

These recent calculations may be compared to those made at earlier dates. Rostas, writing in 1952, focused on labour productivity and measured output in physical terms. Using 1948 as a base year with value 100, he demonstrated that performance in large industries had been very variable, so that the index of output per head in 1951 ranged from 99 for cotton to 129 for steel tubes, with the (unweighted) average being 118.[2] Such estimates are broadly in line with those calculated by Nicholson and Gupta, who focused on the period 1948–54.[3] Finally, there is the pioneering study of what would later be called total factory productivity, published by Reddaway and Smith in 1960. These authors suggest that (allowing for increased labour and capital inputs) the rate of productivity increase changed positively between 1948 and 1951, allowing an average of 3.3 per cent per annum. This performance compared well with that achieved over the following four years, when the comparative figure was only 1.1 per cent per annum.[4]

Taken together, therefore, the figures do at least imply that, by any standards, productivity was tending to improve quite appreciably in the late 1940s. Indeed, Rostas referred to a 'general favourable development' during this period, while Reddaway and Smith noted that their data might appear 'too good to be true'.[5] But had this pattern been shaped in any way by Government policies? The latter authors felt that the acceleration of 1948-51 had reflected 'recovery from wartime organisation' and would prove unsustainable.6 Rostas accepted this point, but argued that an enhanced 'productivity consciousness' had also been important:

> This meant that the large potentialities for an immediate improvement of productivity were realised, that ways and means to improve

> productivity were expected and that positive measures were adopted in many factories and workshops for this purpose.[7]

In this light, at least, the Government was to be congratulated for its various efforts.

Reviewing the quantitative evidence does not, to conclude, yield any easy answers. A reasonable hypothesis is that productivity *did* grow somewhat exceptionally in the late 1940s, and that this *was* connected in some ways to Labour's initiatives. Nevertheless, the case here remains essentially unproven. Can any further light be cast on the whole matter by adopting a rather more detailed focus? What, specifically, can be said about the effectiveness of the different Government measures, case by case?

Evaluating some of the initiatives is fairly straightforward. Hardly anybody felt that the Tizard Committee had achieved very much.[8] By contrast, reactions to the Production Efficiency Service were generally favourable: in the words of an FBI source, the PES was not significant 'in a national sense', but nevertheless continued to undertake 'useful activity'.[9] However, as a brief review will demonstrate, reaching clear conclusions about many other of the developments that have been discussed in this book is much less easy.

Opinion about the impact that JPCs had made on productivity levels, to begin with, remained divided. The journal *Future* asked a sample of manufacturers about joint consultation in general during 1951, and found that only 6 per cent regarded it as 'really valuable', with the vast majority (57 per cent) stating only that it was useful 'as evidence of desiring good relations'.[10] The NIIP survey on JPCs, already referred to, also presented somewhat mixed evaluations. 'The majority of senior managers interviewed' supported JPCs, and the committees had clearly helped to solve a range of everyday problems, relating to questions such as 'hours, breaks and shifts' and holidays. Against this, discussion of, for example, 'work tempo' or 'methods of production' continued to be very much less successful. Moreover, even when good results were achieved on production questions, they usually involved only a small minority of the workforce:

> It was found that worker representatives who actually came in contact with management in the discussion of production problems did, in a number of cases, become really 'efficiency minded', but such individuals frequently complained in interviews that it was very hard to get their constituents to show any real enthusiasm.[11]

Opinion about the BIM was equally varied. Contemporary observers agreed that there was much to be proud of. The *Manager*, for example, noted in mid-1950 that 'the degree to which the BIM has been accepted in national affairs already, is the measure of its success'. The monthly journal *Business*, in a similar vein, applauded the 'un-doubted influence' won by the new institution. Yet, alongside these plaudits, there was a more general sense of disappointment, a feeling that, in the widest perspective, the BIM had not really lived up to expectations. It was observed that, if the Institute had gained a reputation, its real authority nevertheless remained limited, confined to an all-too-familiar circle of civil servants, management movement experts and progressive manufacturers. The great majority of industrialists and managers, by contrast, continued to be apparently unenthusiastic and certainly uninvolved. Symptomatic of this, as *The Economist* amongst others pointed out, was the situation over the BIM's budget, since, after five years of operation, the Institute still needed extensive Treasury support, with business subscriptions accounting for only around half of annual expenditure.[12]

Circumstantial evidence on the BIM offers no clearer picture. Observers noted that British management was becoming more professional in the 1950s but argued that there still remained much scope for improvement. As Mary Stewart reported in 1953, a good number of the defects associated with traditional, stereotypical 'captains of industry' remained depressingly intact; 'too many' of the 'old fashioned, mid-Victorian, high-handed backwoodsmen' continued in control.[13] Taken together, such evidence suggests that the conclusion reached by the 1960 Liverpool University study, *Management in Britain*, is probably about right. There could be no precise measure of the Government's various attempts to improve management standards, the Liverpool team decided, 'but their effects appear to be mildly encouraging rather than startling'.[14]

What, finally, of the two large-scale exercises in spreading 'know how', the Working Parties and the Anglo-American Council on Productivity? As regards the Working Parties, it is worth recording, first, that some of their reports were read in considerable numbers. About 4,000 copies of the pottery document were printed and over 3,000 sold. The cotton report proved even more popular, with two-thirds of a 14,000 print-run being bought in the first few months of availability.[15] Moreover, there can be no doubting the Government's resolve to ensure that Working Party recommendations were implemented. The Board of Trade, as has been noted, formed a special squad to check on progress here, and could provide the President with detailed lists of successes and failures, such as the one covering pottery that he produced in Parliament during late 1949.[16] However, when it comes to assessing how many of the Working Party recommendations were actually implemented in each case, the situation is very much less clear. Harold Wilson, in the House of Commons statement already referred to, claimed that action had occurred on 12 of the 30 measures outlined in the pottery report. A feature in *Business* presented a rather less rosy picture. Progress had been made over some questions, with, for example, the industry's wage structure being revised as the Working Party wanted. Yet, at the same time, there was still clearly much to do: only about one-third of the manufacturers, *Business* claimed, kept accounts in such a form as to allow detailed costing, despite all of the admonitions.[17] The fact that some of the issues discussed in the Working Party reports had to be raised once again during the British Productivity Council sector studies of the mid-1950s suggests that the impact of the earlier enquiries was at best uneven.[18]

The impact of the AACP proves equally hard to summarise simply. This organisation's reports were, once again, distributed in some numbers, with, for example, 300,000 of the first 20 documents being sold within a few months of publication.[19] Moreover, AACP teams spent a considerable amount of time publicising their findings. Typical here were the activities of the two printing teams, who visited the USA in 1951. Their reports sold 11,400 and 9,000 copies, but this was only the beginning of the publicity effort. In fact, the teams addressed over 200 meetings between them, explaining the position to, amongst others, the British Federation of Master Printers Congress, the Joint Industrial Council of the Printing Industry, the Printers' Managers and Overseers Association Conference, a Typographical Association delegate meeting and numerous print shops up and down the country.[20]

Nevertheless, it is clear that the AACP message was not always received with either favour or enthusiasm. Many on the Left, to repeat, argued that the teams had spent too much time enthusing about 'the American way of life' and too little on what was really going on in that country.[21] Less partisan commentators were equally uneasy, partly for the same reasons. The journal *Engineering* commented of one report: 'clearly the team was impressed . . . but it is impossible to avoid the suspicion that they were impressed as much by the USA as by the diesel locomotive industry itself'.[22] Others felt that, anyway, the USA did not make a good point of comparison. The *Manager* could thus conclude of the AACP reports:

> The results are demonstrably valuable and impressive. But it is not to decry them, and it is not to be churlishly unappreciative of a remarkably generous piece of international co-operation, if we say that some of the energy might have been spent in sending teams to countries whose problems are more nearly akin to our own.[23]

In this climate, sober assessments of what was actually being achieved by the AACP efforts were relatively few and far between. Some press comment was favourable and specific, as the *Business* feature 'Lancashire is Learning From Anglo-US Teams'. On the other hand, much was relatively cautious. *Future* felt that none of the reports was producing results 'as speedily as the idealists . . . would wish', though it added that this did not mean that the AACP had achieved nothing. *The Times Review of Industry* argued that the visits were 'significant' and their value 'certainly not negligible'. Moreover, the whole exercise was undoubtedly encouraging 'greater receptivity to fresh thinking on the subject'. Yet, in the end, it judged the effect on industry of all of the activity to be only 'marginal'.[24]

The AACP was, of course, keen to contribute to this debate itself, and produced a quantity of publicity material showing that team reports had changed attitudes and practices.[25] Some of this was of dubious value, aimed at maximising publicity, but there was also a series of more sober 'Follow up Statements', which tried to present a balanced and truthful reflection of what had been achieved. These were often cautious in tone. Thus, Statement 5, *Streamlining Production: A Review of Productivity in the Internal Combustion Engine Industry*, noted that the team report had encouraged 'the reorganisation of factory lay-out and, often, production methods', but it did not present the AACP document as the only agent of modernisation. What seemed to have happened was that 'many companies' had 'incorporated the recommendations of the report in policies of expansion which were already underway'.[26] The review of action taken on the reports by the electricity supply teams was equally careful to avoid exaggeration. The original documents had been 'accepted as a valuable contribution'. Moreover, there were examples, some spectacular, of new techniques being copied from the USA. But none of this was 'the real and important result of the productivity team programme'. Rather 'the dominant purpose' had to be about the 'fermentation of new ideas and the raising of keen interest to apply new ideas to British circumstances'. And measuring change here was a very much more intangible business:

> Success can only be reflected in the increasing efficiency of the

> industry in the years ahead. The proof of productivity puddings lies in their eating and this particular pudding affects the taste of all others.[27]

Taken together, the evidence on micro-performance offers no easy conclusion. Nevertheless, what seems to emerge from this and the quantitative data is a pattern of success and failure. In other words, it seems right to conclude that Labour's programme on productivity did produce some real gains. But it remains abundantly clear, too, that a number of the initiatives led only to cosmetic change, and that the overall impact of the Government's efforts was less than it might have been. What accounts for the gap between potential and reality?

Broadly speaking, three kinds of explanation have been produced on this point. Some have argued that Labour's policies were badly formulated, simply technically deficient. Others assert that the whole programme was poorly targeted, and therefore unsurprisingly ineffective. The barriers to efficient production in Britain largely originated with the unions, and took the form of restrictive practices. Labour should have been doing something about this, rather than tinkering with agencies such as the BIM. Finally, a third hypothesis contradicts the first two, and proposes that the seat of the problem was not in the strategy but rather in the party that was carrying out the strategy. Labour, in this view, simply lacked the will to enforce the modernisation that it perceived to be necessary. The Government capitulated before the employers, but it could and should have done better. Over the following pages an attempt will be made to assess whether any of these explanations is really consistent with the facts.

On the question of technical proficiency, it is quite evident that some of the initiatives were at least partly flawed. Taking the Working Party exercise as an example, a number of defects are immediately obvious. Individual enquiries rarely had access to current data, with the pottery team, for example, having to rely upon statistics from 1935.[28] On top of this, there was a noticeable lack of overall strategy. Indeed, *The Economist* noted, to repeat, that the Working Parties were 'apparently being sent off into the wilderness of industrial policy without any course to steer or any compass to assist them in holding to it'.[29]

There was, too, a range of more general problems with the whole programme. Translating recommendations emerging from the specific initiatives into practical steps that could be implemented by the ordinary employer or worker was never easy, as one observer found out:

> Sometimes when I heard two managers from opposite ends of the

> scale conversing with each other on productivity, I had the impression that they were talking at cross purposes, speaking different languages. Very often an employer with bad experience simply cannot understand the flood of good advice and high sounding moral formulas which are showered on him. [30]

At the same time, as the previous chapters have shown, policies on productivity were neither always consistent nor unaffected by other considerations. There was, for example, an obvious potential difficulty in trying to get industry to modernise and at the same time squeezing it for exports.[31] Moreover, political requirements might easily cloud an issue or affect a productivity equation: as *The Economist* remarked of these years, there was sometimes 'more industrial politics than industrial policy'.[32] Indeed, the commitments to tripartism and voluntary collective bargaining continued to set very definite limits on the Government's room for manoeuvre.

Accordingly, it must be admitted that the creators of the efficiency programme were to some extent themselves responsible for its rather chequered impact. Pressure on Labour Ministers was no doubt very great at this time, but it would perhaps have made a difference if a little more thought had gone into some of the initiatives. Nevertheless, it is also clear that this explanation alone cannot account for the whole problem. Even accepting the defects and inconsistencies, there was still an overwhelming amount of good in the programme. Indeed, even critical contemporaries were struck by the reasonableness and pertinence of much of what Labour was doing on productivity, and this judgement has been repeated in later, more scholarly accounts.[33] Technical deficiency may have blighted execution and policy muddle blunted impact, but these factors alone are insufficient to explain the various disappointments in performance.

What of the second argument, that the whole strategy was poorly targeted? The suggestion here is that trade union and worker restrictive practices were the biggest obstacle to faster growth in post-war Britain. If the Government had been really serious about productivity, it would, as a consequence, have tried to do something about these issues. Yet Labour's hands were tied here, because the unions were its allies, and vital power brokers in the post-war consensus. The end product was a set of half-hearted policies to deal with issues that were only ever marginal. In this scenario, the results could only ever be disappointing.

At first sight, this is all certainly very persuasive, not least because it seems to fit into a much broader literature linking Britain's economic decline to the pernicious influence of trade unions.[34] In these circumstances, it is hardly surprising to find versions of the core argument appearing in recent work by authorities as diverse as Barnett, Broadberry and Crafts (separately and together) and Middlemas.[35] Nor is it remarkable to discover that Olson's much cited *tour de force* also repeats a version of this thesis.[36] Is such endorsement sufficient to uphold the merit of arguments about restrictive practices?

This is not an easy question to answer. However, it is probable that what is being proposed here is much less plausible than its proponents would seem to believe, largely because the central proposition – that the unions were strangling the economy – is overexaggerated. This point can be established in two main ways. Firstly, it is worth noting that very few of the assertions about the prevalence of restrictive practices in the 1940s are actually grounded on hard facts. Broadberry, for example, cites work by Zweig and by Scott *et al.* in support of his argument, yet seems to have given these authors a highly perverse reading. Zweig, writing in 1951, offered a survey, largely based on interviews, of unions and productivity in five industries. He found that restrictive practices were prevalent in only one of these (printing) and he largely cleared the other four (iron and steel, building and civil engineering, cotton and engineering). Lest there be any mistake, he added a clear summary of his own viewpoint:

> When I started my inquiry I was under the impression that restrictive practices were increasing, because of the strengthened power of the unions. But fortunately the reverse is true.[37]

Scott and his co-authors produced a study of industrial relations and technical change in a Merseyside steel works during the early 1950s. The conclusion offered again contradicts Broadberry's reading, since it emphasises how *smoothly* technical change had occurred, and explains this partly in terms of the plant's high rate of union membership.[38] Neither case, certainly, gives much support to the view that labour's restrictive practices were immovable obstacles to changes in production.

This kind of muddle raises doubt, but a more damaging line of enquiry is opened up by simply returning to contemporary sources. What did observers and experts in the 1940s think about restrictive practices? Some, certainly, believed them to be prevalent.[39] Yet most of the evidence points to a rather different picture, as a brief review will demonstrate.

One kind of enquiry into restrictive practices at this time was carried out by journalists or academics and involved interviewing those in industry. Zweig's findings have already been referred to, but two other surveys are worthy of mention. The journal *Future* asked a sample of employers in 1951 whether trade union practices or trade customs restricted output or kept up costs, and found that neither was much of a problem. It commented:

> In management's view, restrictive practices of all kinds have little effect on British industrial efficiency. Possibly economists of the Right and of the Left will join forces to protest that such replies cannot be honest. However that may be, only 19 per cent of those replying alleged that trade union practices impeded output or put up costs, and only 14 per cent admitted difficulties in connection with trade customs.[40]

Also instructive is the work of the Oxford research group under R.F. Harrod.[41] This held regular meetings with senior businessmen between 1947 and 1949 and asked them, amongst other things, about restrictive practices. A majority of those questioned felt that such restraints existed. On the other hand, 'a number stressed how difficult it was to make a rational assessment of their effect'.[42] Indeed, actual instances of damaging action appeared hard to pin down. Asked whether the 'resistance of labour' had prevented the introduction of new machinery, most replied that it had not, leaving the group to comment:

> There was little evidence that resistance of labour to new machinery was important in preventing investment by a firm. Only 3 out of 18 who discussed this returned an affirmative answer, and only 2 felt it to be . . . an important factor.[43]

A second group of enquiries which cast light on the situation were those carried out by industrialists themselves. Again, the findings of these investigations hardly support the pessimists' case. Some of the Management Research Groups discussed restrictive practices in private during 1947, on the basis of a questionnaire answered by 22 firms. Again, the absence of problems was felt to be the most noteworthy feature of the situation. Thus, of the questionnaire, it was remarked:

> Only one firm mentions 'Trade Union restrictive practices' as an adverse factor, and then 'only in isolated instances'. This is surely most surprising in view of all that is being said on the subject today.[44]

More significant, still, were the facts uncovered by the BEC at the end of the 1940s. This organisation first contacted its 66 members (all trade associations) about restrictive practices in 1947, and received 22 replies. Of these, half stated that trade union restrictive practices were either absent or so small as to be irrelevant in their industries, while half made a variety of complaints.[45] This led the BEC to compile a much more detailed form for its members to fill in, which was circulated over the following year. The new enquiry generated 35 replies and revealed that 23 trade associations could identify one or more restrictive practices in their industries. Yet only 18 of the 23 felt such problems to be serious. Moreover, even here distributions tended to be rather skewed. Thus, 8 of the 18 complained of only one or two of the 15 possible types of restrictive practice, which meant that some important sectors (for example, engineering) remained virtually trouble-free. Similarly, some kinds of restrictive practice were comparatively unknown: 8 of the 15 categories appeared four or fewer times in the 18 questionnaires. The picture revealed, in other words, was of a small number of trouble-hit industries (cotton, shipbuilding, bleaching and printing) and a relatively limited group of recurring restrictions.[46]

Most of the available evidence, therefore, points in one direction. It is neither totally unambiguous nor fully comprehensive but it hardly supports a picture of rampant restrictive practices. This, in turn, makes the 'wrong target' thesis less than plausible. What of the third explanation for the gap between government effort and actual outcome, the view that the problem was really Labour itself?

There are a number of versions of this kind of thinking. Some would accuse the Government of simply lacking determination in its pursuit of reform. This was a point made by Labour left-wingers throughout the 1940s. Thus, Mikardo, in a debate about productivity policy during 1948, argued that:

> The problem is not that we want some doctor to prescribe some new medicine. It is the problem of getting the patient to take the medicine which he has already got, and which, in fact, is jolly good medicine. The real problem which the Chancellor has to face, and which with great respect, I say he always funks, is how to get people to apply better methods.[47]

On the other hand, there are those who would go further than this and suggest that the root of the Government's timidity lay in its ideological disposition. Social democracy, the argument runs, is always likely to compromise with private enterprise, perhaps even to the extent of allowing capitalists to set its real agenda. This is an interpretation favoured, for example, by Mercer, who draws on Miliband's wider work, *The State in Capitalist Society*, to understand how Labour failures on industrial policy in the 1940s came about. The central point for her is that the party and the Government shared a 'commitment to the private enterprise system'. Actual policy was, as a consequence, always going to be insipid:

> This [commitment] prompted an inevitable reliance on voluntary and co-operative methods of control, an inability to compel, and the necessity for retreat in the face of opposition.[48]

Again, a clear cut assessment of this hypothesis is far from easy. However, two reflections can be offered on what is being argued. One element of this case against Labour is that the party was not really serious about reform. Yet, as has been shown in this book, this is simply incorrect. With Labour, industrial modernisation and socialism went hand in hand, neither possible without the other. Nevertheless, it is accurate to state that the party *did* accept the parliamentary system and the existing rule of law. Moreover, as the preceding narrative has often shown, Labour was wedded to introducing reform by consultation, using tripartite discussions to establish consensus.

Of course, standing outside history, it is quite legitimate to quarrel with these dispositions. Indeed, a whole host of commentators have written books on the party, wishing that it was not what it was. However, a more interesting line of enquiry is surely to take Labour at face value, and ask whether it could in fact have done more to prosecute industrial policy in the particular circumstances of the late 1940s. This approach is really about political realities. Did Labour have enough support for a more radical pursuit of its policies? On the other hand, were its opponents solid or might they have been fractured with a little more pressure? It is to these questions that the next section turns.

Labour's greatest ally on the industrial modernisation question was, of course, the General Council of the TUC. This body had accepted the need to increase productivity in an important document ('Production Under Full Employment') of 1946, ratified its view with Congress,[49] and then done everything possible to aid official initiatives. The TUC had its own priorities in the productivity debate, but in practice fully supported Working Parties, JPCs and the BIM, and embraced the idea of the AACP and tried to make it work.[50] At the same time, there were numerous TUC attempts to get member unions fully behind this policy. Of note here were the special conferences on the subject for the various executives; the establishment of an in-house Production Department in 1950; and the support provided for a mission to the USA, which concentrated on discovering how American unions were responding to the productivity question.[51] Furthermore, all of this activity was conducted in a language which was both straightforward and uncompromising. The journal *Future* described some union officials' comments in favour of the AACP as 'remarkably outspoken', while the *Financial Times*, reviewing a TUC statement on the unions and productivity, noted that it contained 'a few home truths'.[52]

Labour could, therefore, count on the TUC and various other trade union leaderships. However, it is quite clear that support for its policies amongst rank and file workers was very much less secure. Certainly, when issues were taken to ordinary branch meetings, little enthusiasm was in evidence, as was noted by a number of observers.[53] Moreover, wider public appreciation of, and sympathy for, what Labour was trying to do on industry was hardly impressive.

To start with, most people did not think that production was the most pressing issue facing Britain. Gallup surveys found that everyday matters to do with living and eating were always at the forefront of people's minds, with other topics attracting very much less attention. For example, an enquiry of May 1948, asking 'What is the chief problem that the Government must solve during the next few months?', discovered that the popular choices for action were the cost of living (38 per cent), housing (31 per cent) and the food situation (21 per cent). 'Production' was seen as the key issue by only one per cent of those replying.[54]

Secondly, when people were asked specifically about productivity, their answers hardly indicated a yearning for more radical official measures. Government surveys revealed that many did not understand what the phrase 'increased productivity' meant. Indeed, of samples questioned between 1948 and 1951, only between 16 and 18 per cent provided unambiguously correct definitions.[55] On the other hand, when opinions were voiced about how productivity could be increased, the preferences which were revealed tended to encompass traditional solutions (for example, enhanced incentives) rather than imaginative departures.[56] This was partly because, for many, industrial under-performance was mostly a matter of personal laziness rather than systemic failure. A Gallup poll of July 1949[57] asked why Britain was not producing more and reported that answers could be ranked in the following way:

	%
People don't work hard enough/long enough	25
Shortage of raw materials	11

Incentives too few, wages too low, taxes too high	8
Strikes; industrial unrest	8
Inefficient management; bad organisation	4
Other; no opinion	52

In fact, there seems to have been a general feeling that the Government had gone as far as it should in interfering with business. A majority accepted existing controls of every kind as necessary and only 10 per cent or fewer thought them 'all bad'.[58] However, this did not imply a widespread belief that private enterprise was somehow failing the nation. Indeed, two comprehensive *Future* surveys of 1950 found that most people preferred to work for ordinary firms rather than nationalised industries; felt that business was generally efficient; and thought that their particular boss was 'a good chap'. Some clearly wished to have a greater say in how private companies were run, but there was no great discontent with the capitalist system as such.[59]

So much for those on, or potentially on, Labour's side. What of its enemies? Should the Government have been so circumspect with employers? Were they really as formidable an opposition as some of them liked to think?

This question has, of course, attracted a good deal of attention in the historiography, and remains somewhat controversial. Early commentators on the FBI's relationship with Labour asserted that business was sometimes not happy with what the Government was doing but never resorted to sabotage or unconstitutional opposition. Mercer argues that this kind of interpretation is entirely misleading, in that there were continuing attempts to derail official policy.[60] Reviewing the evidence that has become available suggests that Mercer is completely right on this point, though even she may have understated the problem. This conclusion can be supported by looking at various facets of business opinion about what Labour was trying to do during these years.

The first point to make is that in abstract terms few businessmen had very much sympathy even with the basic assumptions of the Government's approach. Thus, for example, most did not agree that management should be more professional. Indeed, there was a deeply ingrained belief that good managers were 'born and not bred' and that the only way to learn management was 'in the school of hard knocks'. Experts needed to be found a place, it was generally conceded, but they must never be allowed to dominate; in the memorable epigram of the 1950 FBI President, Sir Robert Sinclair, 'the specialist should be on tap but not on top'.[61]

Nor were many businessmen (as opposed to managers) really in favour of joint consultation. Some disliked the idea because they felt that it would open the door to union agitators. It was necessary, in this perspective, to reject 'peevish feminine socialism' and 'keep forcing [the unions] back'.[62] Elsewhere, the objection was that a consultative approach would compromise the manager's ability to manage.[63] Sinclair's views on this were, once again, very forthright:

> he stressed that in any business the line of authority must be kept clear, and stigmatized the practice recently adopted in Germany of having one or more of the directors appointed as representatives of the workers as sheer nonsense.[64]

Finally, there was, too, a more general dislike of the state's involving itself in business at any level. Examples of this have been referred to throughout the previous chapters, so that further elaboration is really unnecessary. The views of the managing director of a prominent Yorkshire firm were representative: 'I am strongly of the opinion that the Government should leave Industry to run its own business without so much interference and advice.'[65]

In these circumstances, when businessmen turned to address what Labour actually proposed for industry, it was inevitable that many would feel that the right course was outright opposition. Needless to say, this was expressed in different ways according to the precise issue at hand. One prevailing reaction was to seek methods of minimising change: to find out how little business could get away with in the face of Government pressure. The mentality at work here was captured by a disgruntled participant at a Conservative Party gathering for businessmen in Scotland during the Spring of 1947. His private account of the event included the following:

> I am sorry to say that the general impression which the meeting left on my mind was rather along the following lines – We, the Unionists, and we, the Capitalists, know what we want and what we think would be best for the country, but instead of asking the willing co-operation of the working man, the attitude seems to be, what concessions must we make to him to get him to come along with us. In other words how can we bribe him.[66]

On the other hand, if the situation was felt to merit it, the business community could take a very much more aggressive line. This occurred, most notoriously, in relation to Development Councils, where concerted action from manufacturers continued to frustrate Government intentions, as an anonymous civil servant's description of progress with the Hosiery Working Party's report of 1948 illustrated:

> Consideration of (and opposition to) a Development Council has absorbed practically all the attention the manufacturers' Associations have given to the Report. The Federation have gone ahead with certain work recommended . . . and have pointed to these activities as evidence that a Development Council is unnecessary. Apart from this it has not been possible to obtain their considered views on the recommendations or even on the production targets suggested by the Report.[67]

But it was also evident in some less publicised cases. Looking at the BIM's early history, for example, it is hard not to conclude that a large section of industry wanted the institution either made ineffective or else actually wound up.[68] The FBI's position was one of public support but, in private, its officials admitted that their objective was to keep the whole initiative 'in the hands of industry rather than of Government'.[69] Elsewhere, in confidential exchanges between firms, attitudes were expressed very much more bluntly; members of IMRA (Industrial Management Research Association, the new name of the old Management Research Group 1) were repeatedly advised, for example, that the Institute should be seen 'as a political weapon of the present Government designed to facilitate the process of nationalization'.[70] Nor was hostility simply confined to gesture. The BIM's opponents were active enough to engineer the resignation of the Deputy Director ('Members are aware that he had written for Communist papers and were not happy about him'); frustrate the spread of Local Management Associations, which Russell thought vital; and maintain a long-running whispering campaign against the BIM which was certainly damaging.[71]

All of this left Labour in a very difficult position. The party had proposed a set of policies and received a popular mandate, but it was evident that Labour supporters were least concerned about industrial modernisation. Opposite stood a determined foe, willing to conduct a tenacious and wearing campaign to limit change. In these circumstances, the only real option had to be a strategy of negotiation and even compromise. Labour might have done more to publicise its case and broaden support, as Crofts argues, but, on industrial policy specifically, it is not really clear that this would have made much difference.[72] A small but significant illustration sums up the Government's wider predicament. It relates, once again, to Development Councils. Industry argued vociferously in public that these were clearly a prelude to nationalisation – creeping and then outright state control. In 1951, Political and Economic Planning (PEP) examined this claim and reported that it was 'impossible to find in any Government statement any justification for . . . [it]'; the industries for which Development Councils had been proposed were all, without exception, outside the categories ever talked about as suitable for appropriation. Nevertheless, as PEP had also to remark, even without a rational basis, the idea of back-door nationalisation still persisted.[73]

It seems reasonable to opine, in the light of this discussion, that much thinking about Labour's problems over productivity policy in this period has been misleading. The Government cannot be accused of focusing on the wrong target or of lacking the will to pursue solutions. It certainly made mistakes and did not always harmonise objectives successfully. However, if the gap between effort and outcome is to be fully understood, due weight must be given to the actions of the employers; to repeat Mikardo's analogy, patients who remained unwilling to take their medicine, or even acknowledge the expertise of the doctor.

Four general observations may be offered as a conclusion to this study. The first concerns the Labour Party. Many historians have viewed Labour as essentially about redistribution. Typically, therefore, the Attlee years are described in terms of the creation of the welfare state. In this book, Labour has emerged in a rather different light, as a party which both considered the whole issue of production and attempted appropriate solutions to the manifold problems that existed in the area. The view presented here, therefore, confirms some recent scholarship on other periods, which suggests strongly that Labour's involvement with industrial modernisation throughout its history has been drastically underestimated.[74]

The second point relates to the wider historiography of the immediate war and post-war years. A number of historians have viewed this period as one of consensus, which bore fruit in a long-lasting 'post-war settlement'.[75] The evidence presented in the preceding pages, however, cannot be made to square with such an interpretation. Bluntly put, there was no general agreement on industrial policy during these years. In fact, dissonance and not harmony continued to be the most characteristic feature of discussion. Divisions existed between departments of state; between peak organisations; between management experts and industrialists; and, most importantly, between the main political parties. That this was the case must surely call into question the whole concept of 'consensus'. There may be some justification for using the term to describe the position in the higher echelons of Whitehall, but little reason appears to exist for its deployment elsewhere.

Finally, two comments need to be made about the long-running debate on Britain's economic decline. The first is about theories of causation. As Chapter 1 indicated, writing about the economy's chronic under-performance has tended to move in cycles, often fuelled by current fashion. During the last few years two explanations have been in vogue. Many have subscribed to the view that the real problem for Britain has continued to be its trade unions – creators of an inflexible market, police officers enforcing restrictive practices, opponents of any kind of constructive change. Elsewhere, in more liberal circles, such a partisan judgement is taken to be vulgar and one-sided. Blame should instead be allocated, as in the Ealing comedy, *The Man in the White Suit*, to all of Britain's institutions. The 'bolshie shop steward' is joined by the reactionary, venal entrepreneur and the bungling civil servant in a role call of stage villains.

These kinds of propositions may make good political propaganda, but they cannot be accepted as fully accurate representations of what happened in the past, at least not that part of the past that is covered in this book. Critics of the unions or 'big government' will find little comfort in the evidence that has been presented here. Only the liberals' stereotypical entrepreneur seems in any way grounded in fact. Indeed, it is, perhaps, ironic that the very group which in the end frustrated attempts at industrial modernisation in the Attlee years was also the one with most to gain from it. In some senses, more than a few of the nation's entrepreneurs gambled away their long-term commercial future after the war because of a pathological fear regarding state interference.

There is also an interconnected, if more general, point about the whole 'decline' literature, which relates to its common methodology. Many accounts about allegedly culpable institutions are presented with the political parties left out. The failures are explained by reference to 'the British disease', a peculiar culture, or even an unfinished revolution. Yet, as this book has shown, such an approach is really unjustifiable. Party politics did (and does) make a difference to industrial questions, as to many others.

Notes

References starting BT, CAB, ED, LAB, RG and T relate to files in the Public Records Office, London. References starting MRC relate to files in the Modern Records Centre, University of Warwick.

1 BRITISH INDUSTRY, STATE INTERVENTION AND LABOUR POLITICS, 1900–39

1 Important recent contributions include those in B. Elbaum and W. Lazonick (eds) *The Decline of the British Economy* (Oxford, 1987) and the *Oxford Review of Economic Policy* 4(1) (1988).
2 M. Shanks, *The Stagnant Society: A Warning* (London, 1961); S. Strange, *Sterling and British Policy* (London, 1971); N. Kaldor, *Causes of the Slow Rate of Growth of the UK* (Cambridge, 1966).
3 M. Wiener, *English Culture and the Decline of the Industrial Spirit* (Harmondsworth, 1985) and C. Barnett, *The Audit of War* (London, 1986). For good critiques of this approach see B. Collins and K. Robbins (eds) *British Culture and Economic Decline* (London, 1990), or, from a quite distinct perspective, D. Edgerton, *England and the Aeroplane* (London, 1991).
4 D. Marquand, *The Unprincipled Society* (London, 1988), p. 210. See also his *The Progressive Dilemma* (London, 1991) for a development of some of the same themes.
5 P. Hall, *Governing the Economy: The Politics of State Intervention in Britain and France* (Cambridge, 1986); S. Newton and D. Porter, *Modernisation Frustrated* (London, 1988); P. Hall, 'The State and Economic Decline', in Elbaum and Lazonick (eds), op. cit., pp. 266–302.
6 M. Barratt-Brown, 'Away With All Great Arches', *New Left Review* 167 (1988), pp. 22–51.
7 A.L. Friedberg, *The Weary Titan* (Princeton, 1988).
8 G.R. Searle, *The Quest for National Efficiency* (Oxford, 1971).
9 Ibid.; Newton and Porter, op. cit., Ch. 1; Marquand, *Unprincipled Society*, op. cit., Ch. 5.

10 S. Pollard, *Britain's Prime and Britain's Decline 1870–1914* (London, 1988).
11 E.H. Phelps-Brown, *The Origins of British Industrial Relations* (London, 1986), Ch. 7; A. Morrison, 'Businesses, Industries and Tariff Reform in Great Britain', *Business History* 28(1) (1983), pp. 148–78.
12 M. Freeden, *The New Liberalism: An Ideology of Social Reform* (Oxford, 1978).
13 Newton and Porter, op. cit., pp. 25–7.
14 The Board of Trade produced a series of reports on British industry, which were summarised in the *Final Report of the Committee on Commercial and Industrial Policy After the War* (Cd. 9035) (London, 1918).
15 Newton and Porter, op. cit., Ch. 2; K. Burk (ed.) *War and the State* (London, 1982); S. Armitage, *The Politics of Decontrol of Industry* (London, 1969).
16 R.D. Boyce, *British Capitalism at the Crossroads* (Cambridge, 1987), Chs 1–4.
17 Ibid., Ch. 3; A. Booth and M. Pack, *Employment, Capital and Economic Policy* (Oxford, 1985), Ch. 1.
18 J.M. Keynes, 'The End of *Laissez-Faire*', in his *Collected Writings* 9 (1971). Note that Keynes *did* take a keen interest in the rationalisation of the cotton industry: J.M. Keynes, *Collected Writings* 19 (1981), Ch. 7.
19 R. Lowe, *Adjusting to Democracy: The Role of the Ministry of Labour in British Politics 1916–1939* (Oxford, 1986), pp. 207–9.
20 M. Kirby, 'Industrial Policy', in S. Glynn and A. Booth (eds) *The Road to Full Employment* (London, 1987), pp. 131–5.
21 (Balfour) Committee on Industry and Trade, *Factors in Industrial and Commercial Efficiency* (London, 1927); and *Final Report* (Cmd 3282) (London, 1929).
22 L. Hannah, *Electricity Before Nationalisation* (London, 1979), Ch. 4; M. Bonavia, *British Rail* (London, 1971).
23 R.S. Sayers, *The Bank of England 1891–1944* 1 (Cambridge, 1976), Ch. 14.
24 M.W. Kirby, *The British Coal Mining Industry 1870–1946* (London, 1977), Ch. 6; L. Hannah, *The Rise of the Corporate Economy* (2nd edn, London, 1983), Ch. 4.
25 Kirby, op. cit., Chs 7–9. For a different view, see B. Fine, 'Economies of Scale and a Featherbedding Cartel: A Reconsideration of the Interwar British Coal Industry', *Economic History Review* 48(3) (1990), pp. 438–49.
26 J. Tomlinson, *Public Policy and the Economy Since 1900* (Oxford, 1990), Ch. 2.
27 F. Capie, *Depression and Protectionism* (London, 1983), Chs 8, 9.
28 Fine, op. cit.; A.F. Lucas, *Industrial Reconstruction and the Control of Competition* (London, 1939).
29 S. Tolliday, *Business, Banking and Politics: The Case of British Steel 1918–1939* (Harvard, 1987).
30 A. Booth, 'Britain in the 1930s: A Managed Economy?', *Economic History Review* 40(3) (1987), pp. 499–522.
31 W. Reader, 'I.C.I. and the State', in B. Supple (ed.) *Essays in Business History* (Oxford, 1977), pp. 227–43.
32 K.D. Brown (ed.) *The First Labour Party 1906–14* (London, 1985); D. Howell, *British Workers and the Independent Labour Party 1885–1906*

(Manchester, 1983); K.D. Morgan, 'Edwardian Socialism' in D. Read (ed.) *Edwardian England* (London, 1986), Ch. 6.

33 On the components of Labour at this time see J. Callaghan, *Socialism in Britain Since 1884* (Oxford, 1990), Chs 4, 5; D. Howell, *Social Democracy in Britain* (London, 1976), Ch. 1; R.E. Dowse, *Left in the Centre: The I.L.P. 1893–1940* (London, 1966), Ch. 1; A.M. MacBriar, *Fabian Socialism and English Politics 1884–1918* (Cambridge, 1962), especially Chs 10–12.

34 W. Clarke, 'The Basis of Socialism: Industrial', in B. Shaw *et al.*, *Fabian Essays in Socialism 1889* (London, 1948 edn), pp. 92, 95.

35 A. Besant, 'Industry Under Socialism', ibid., pp. 141, 146, 148.

36 For example, H.W. Macrosty, *Trusts and the State* (London, 1901); S. and B. Webb, *Problems of Modern Industry* (London, 1902).

37 V.I. Lenin, 'Imperialism: The Highest Stage of Capitalism', *Collected Works* 22 (London, 1964); J.A. Hobson, *The Evolution of Modern Capitalism* (London, 1894).

38 E.E. Barry, *Nationalisation in British Politics* (London, 1965), Chs 2–6. Much of the early discussion of coal mining nationalisation focused on mining *royalties*, seen as generating an unearned 'surplus' for landowners and an incubus on the development of industry (ibid., Ch. 4).

39 On the convergence of Labour and New Liberal thinking, see Freeden, op. cit., pp. 196–200; and on the Co-Efficients, the standard work is Searle, op. cit.

40 S. and B. Webb, *The Decay of Capitalist Civilisation* (London, 1923), p. 51.

41 S. and B. Webb, *A Constitution for the Socialist Commonwealth of Great Britain* (London, 1920), pp. 324, 328–30.

42 R. McKibbin, *The Evolution of the Labour Party* (Oxford, 1974), pp. 91–106; J.M. Winter, *Socialism and the Challenge of War* (London, 1974).

43 Labour Party, *Labour and the New Social Order* (London, 1918), pp. 19, 11–12.

44 Ibid., p. 17.

45 A. Oldfield, 'The Labour Party and Planning – 1934 or 1918?', *Bulletin of the Society for the Study of Labour History* 25 (1972), pp. 41–55; Labour Party, *Annual Conference Report* (London, June 1918), pp. 44–6. For a summary of the changes in Labour's constitution and programme see G.D.H. Cole, *A History of the Labour Party from 1914* (London, 1948), Ch. 2.

46 R. Skidelsky, *Politicians and the Slump: The Labour Government of 1929–31* (Harmondsworth, 1970); D. Winch, *Economics and Policy* (London, 1972).

47 A. Booth and M. Pack, *Employment, Capital and Economic Policy, Great Britain 1918–1939* (Oxford, 1985), Chs 1, 5, 6.

48 R. McKibbin, 'The Economic Policy of the Second Labour Government 1929–1931', *Past and Present* 68 (1975), pp. 95–123.

49 Booth and Pack, op. cit., Ch. 1.

50 J. Strachey, *Revolution by Reason* (London, 1925) (these proposals were largely the work of Oswald Mosley); H.N. Brailsford *et al.*, *The Living Wage* (London, 1926); on Mosley's memorandum, see Skidelsky, op. cit., Ch. 8, and R. Skidelsky, *Oswald Mosley* (London, 1975), Chs 9, 10.

51 Boyce, op. cit.

52 Hannah *Electricity* op. cit., pp. 88–9.
53 Labour Party, *Labour and the Nation* (London, 1928), pp. 23–4, 16.
54 Labour Party, *Labour's Reply to Lloyd George: How to Conquer Unemployment* (London, 1929), pp. 13, 14.
55 G.W. Macdonald and H. Gospel, 'The Mond–Turner Talks, 1927–33: A Study of Industrial Co-operation', *Historical Journal* 16(4) (1973), pp. 807–29; H. Gospel, 'Employers' Labour Policy: A Study of the Mond–Turner Talks 1927–33', *Business History* 21(2) (1979), pp. 180–97.
56 Macdonald and Gospel, op. cit., pp. 820–1, 823–4.
57 Skidelsky, *Politicians*, op. cit.; McKibbin, 'Economic Policy', op. cit.; D. Marquand, *Ramsay Macdonald* (London, 1977).
58 The LPTB was actually created under the Conservative Government of 1931, but largely on the model designed under Labour.
59 On the Morrisonian corporation see H. Morrison, *Socialisation and Transport* (London, 1930); Barry, op. cit., Chs 10–13; R. Dahl, 'Workers' Control of Industry and the British Labour Party', *American Political Science Review* 41(5) (1947), pp. 875–900; G.N. Ostergaard, 'Labour and the Development of the Public Corporation', *Manchester School* 22(2) (1954), pp. 192–226; J. Tomlinson, *The Unequal Struggle: British Socialism and the Capitalist Enterprise* (London, 1982), Ch. 4.
60 Skidelsky, *Politicians*, op. cit., pp. 129–32.
61 S. Tolliday, 'Steel and Rationalisation Politics 1918–50', in Elbaum and Lazonick (eds), op. cit., pp. 82–108; R.S. Sayers, *The Bank of England 1890–1944* (Cambridge, 1976); C. Heim, 'Limits to Intervention: The Bank of England and Industrial Diversification in the Depressed Areas', *Economic History Review* 37(4) (1984), pp. 533–50.
62 B. Pimlott, *Labour and the Left in the 1930s* (Cambridge, 1977), Ch. 1.
63 Tomlinson, *Unequal Struggle*, op. cit., Ch. 4; Dahl, op. cit.
64 Labour Party, *For Socialism and Peace* (London, 1934); Booth and Pack, op. cit., pp. 125–33.
65 *For Socialism and Peace*, op. cit., p. 15.
66 Booth and Pack, op. cit., p. 127.
67 *For Socialism and Peace*, op. cit., p. 16.
68 E. Durbin, *New Jerusalems: The Labour Party and the Economics of Democratic Socialism* (London, 1985), pp. 194–8, 276–7. Douglas Jay can also be said to have come into this camp; see his *The Socialist Case* (London, 1937).
69 Durbin, op. cit., Chs 6–8 and p. 277.
70 Ibid., pp. 175–9, 277–9.
71 Ibid., pp. 236–42.
72 On this theme see S. Brooke, 'Revisionists and Fundamentalists: The Labour Party and Economic Policy During the Second World War', *Historical Journal* 32(1) (1989), pp. 157–75.
73 Durbin, op. cit., pp. 274–6.
74 For example, Marquand, *Progressive Dilemma*, op. cit., pp. 65–6.
75 K.O. Morgan, *Labour in Power 1945–51* (Oxford, 1984), p. 135.
76 Marquand, *Progressive Dilemma*, op. cit., p. 106; R. Miliband, *Parliamentary Socialism* (2nd edn, London, 1973), p. 290; K. Middlemas, *Power, Competition and the State, 1: Britain in Search of Balance, 1940–1961*,

(London, 1986), p. 120; C. Barnett, op. cit., p. 275.
77 An obvious exception is A.A. Rogow and P. Shore, *The Labour Government and British Industry 1945–51* (Oxford, 1955).
78 Barnett, Marquand, Miliband and Morgan, in the works cited above, make no mention of the British Institute of Management. Middlemas (also already cited) refers in passing to the institution but does not discuss its creation or its relation to the government.
79 See Middlemas, op. cit., p. 118.

2 THE PRODUCTION CRISIS, PRODUCTIVITY AND THE RISE OF THE MANAGEMENT QUESTION, 1941–4

1 *Listener*, 15/5/1941.
2 G.H. Gallup, *The Gallup International Opinion Polls. Great Britain 1937–1975. Volume One* (New York, 1976), p. 41.
3 *Economist*, 12/7/1941 and 9/8/1941.
4 *The Times*, 2/1/1942.
5 Mass Observation, *People in Production* (Harmondsworth, 1942), p. 63.
6 Quoted in M. Edelman, *Production For Victory Not Profits* (London, 1941), p. 55.
7 'Argonaut', *Give Us The Tools* (London, 1942), pp. 1–2.
8 *Economist*, 5/10/1940.
9 *Twenty-First Report from the Select Committee on National Expenditure*, 6/8/1941 (P.P. 1940–1 III), p. 8; *Economist*, 1/11/1941.
10 These innovations, and the debates surrounding them, are reported on in most of the standard histories; see, for example, J.M. Lee, *The Churchill Coalition 1940–1945* (London, 1980), pp. 82–111.
11 See, for example, Oliver Lyttelton, Minister of Production, in *Hansard* 381, 14/7/1942, col. 1117; *Economist*, 18/7/1942.
12 *Listener*, 24/12/1942.
13 *Economist*, 20/6/1942.
14 G.R. Moxon, *The Growth of Personnel Management in Great Britain during the War 1939–1944* (London, 1945), esp. pp. 28–9.
15 H.M.D. Parker, *Manpower: A Study of War-time Policy and Administration* (London, 1957), pp. 411–19.
16 The following account is based on P. Inman, *Labour in the Munitions Industries* (London, 1957), pp. 376–83.
17 *Listener*, 15/7/1943.
18 BT 64/3537: Board of Trade Internal Reconstruction Department Report, 'War-time Measures To Raise The Standard Of Management In Industry', 19/7/1944, p. 1.
19 Ibid.; and BT 64/3324: H.A. Marquand, 'Ministry of Production. Note on Measures Designed to Improve Efficiency of Production in British Industry' [hereafter *Marquand*], 17/2/1944, pp. 9–10.
20 Inman, op. cit., p. 231.
21 *Marquand*, op. cit., p. 8.
22 For the PEB see Inman, op. cit., pp. 229–30; and A.G. Shaw, 'Motion Study in Wartime', *Occupational Psychology* 21(4) (1947), pp. 188–91.

23 Inman, op. cit., p. 229.
24 For the TCB see Inman, op. cit., p. 431; *Marquand*, op. cit., p. 6; and BT 64/3115: 'Discussion with Mr. James, Principal Technical Cost Officer of MAP', 21/7/1943.
25 *Marquand*, op. cit., p. 6.
26 BT 64/3115: 'Discussion . . . ', op. cit., p. 1.
27 Inman, op. cit., p. 433.
28 *Marquand*, op. cit., p. 6.
29 BT 64/3604: R.S. Edwards to Prof. G.C. Allen, 12/7/1944, p. 3.
30 Ibid., p. 1.
31 Inman, op. cit., p. 230.
32 BT 64/3324: Note by J. Maton, 15/7/1943.
33 Reported in *The Economist*, 17/4/1943.
34 *Business* 73(2) (1943), pp. 15–17, and 73(6) (1943), pp. 23–7.
35 Shaw, op. cit., p. 191.
36 BT 64/3115: 'Discussion . . . ', op. cit., p. 2.
37 Moxon, op. cit., pp. 28, 30.
38 BT 64/3537: 'Discussion of wartime experience in regard to industrial management – 21.6.44'.
39 BT 64/3537: Principal Director of Costing, 'Report by M/S Costings Department . . . ' [n.d.], enclosed with J. Zinkin to J. Maton, 6/6/1944.
40 BT 64/3604: Edwards to Allen, op. cit., p. 2.
41 Ibid., p. 4; and BT 64/3537: 'Discussion . . . 21.6.44', op. cit.
42 On this theme, see, for example, BT 64/3604: Edwards to Allen, op. cit., pp. 4–5.
43 L. Johnman, 'The Labour Party and Industrial Policy, 1940–1945', in N. Tiratsoo (ed.) *The Attlee Years* (London, 1991), summarises this kind of Board thinking.
44 For early Board discussion of the productivity issue etc., see material in BT 64/3115 and BT 64/3210.
45 BT 64/3210: Minute by J. Maton, 3/5/1943.
46 CAB 87/63: E.C. (43)4, War Cabinet Committee on Post-War Employment, 'General Support of Trade: Memo by Board of Trade', 15/10/1943, paras 39, 40.
47 The Steering Committee's terms of reference are in its final report: CAB 87/63: R.(44)6, 11/1/1944, p. 3.
48 CAB 87/63: E.C.(43) 10, Committee on Post-War Employment, 10th Meeting, 30/10/1943, p. 2.
49 See, for example, BT 64/3361: J. Maton, 'Industrial Management', 21/9/1943.
50 See letters in BT 64/3359; for example, G.L. Watkinson to B.S. Rowntree, 24/9/1943, and enclosure.
51 BT 64/3359: P. Lindsay to G.L. Watkinson, 10/12/1943.
52 BT 64/3359: 'Discussion with Mr Seebohm Rowntree, 30 September 1943'.
53 BT 64/3359: L.J. Cadbury to G.L. Watkinson, 8/10/1943; and J. Maton, 'Industrial Management – Progress Report', 11/11/1943.
54 BT 64/3455: 'Talk with Mr Lloyd Roberts . . . 29 September 1943'.
55 BT 64/3359: H.I. Bostock to G.L. Watkinson, 29/9/1943.
56 BT 64/3359: L. Urwick to G.L. Watkinson, 28/9/1943.

57 BT 64/3390: Paper 2, J. Maton. 'Industrial Management . . . ', 30/12/1943.
58 BT 64/3359: 'Discussion . . . with Mr John Ryan, Director of the Metal Box Co. Ltd, 5 October 1943'.
59 Information on the IIA comes from BT 64/3361: Memo by J. Maton, 11/10/1943; J. Maton, 'Conference on "Management in Action" . . . 22–24 October 1943'; and Letter from G. Marchand, 29/11/1943.
60 For the MRG, see material in BT 64/3361, esp. J. Maton, 'Discussion with . . . Ward . . . 28 September 1943'; and BT 64/3390, Paper 2, op. cit., p. 3.
61 Members included Babcock and Wilcox, Boots, Bristol Aeroplane, Courtaulds, Dunlop, Imperial Tobacco, Lever Bros, Pilkington Bros, Rowntree, Standard Telephone, Tootal Broadhurst Lee and United Steel: see the membership list in BT 64/3361.
62 BT 64/3361: 'Management Research Group No. 1' [n.d.].
63 BT 64/3361: Minute by G.C. Allen, 17/11/1943.
64 BT 64/3390: Paper 13 'Events leading up to the establishment of the British Management Council', 13/1/1944.
65 BT 64/3390: Paper 2, op. cit., p. 4; and BT 64/3210: J. Maton, 'Discussion with Mr Prescott – 2 November 1943', 6/11/1943.
66 BT 64/3361: Note by J. Maton, 27/10/1943.
67 BT 64/3390: Paper 2, op. cit., p. 4.
68 BT 64/3210: G.L. Watkinson, 'Industrial Management. Progress Report, November 1943', 25/11/1943, p. 1.
69 Ibid., p. 2.
70 BT 64/3210: Note by J. Maton 24/11/1943. For Weir's background, see his *Civilian Assignment* (London, 1953), and *The Times*, 31/10/1960. The Business Members were part-time advisers to the Board, who were drawn from industry and commerce.
71 BT 64/3210: Watkinson, 'Industrial Management', op. cit., p. 2. Loughlin was an ex-Chairwoman of the General Council and General Organiser of the National Union of Tailors and Garment Workers.
72 BT 64/3210: Note by J. Maton, 24/11/1943.
73 BT 64/3428: Minutes of 16 and 31/12/1943.
74 BT 64/3537: 'Report on Industrial Management' [hereafter *Weir*], 23/2/1944, p. 1.
75 Ibid.
76 BT 64/3390: Paper 14, 'Note of a meeting with Col. Urwick, 13 January 1944'.
77 BT 64/3390: Paper 23, 'Note of a meeting with Mr I.J. Pitman . . . 24 January 1944'.
78 BT 64/3390: Paper 21, Minutes of Meeting with MRG 2–8, 4/1/1944, p. 5.
79 BT 64/3390: Paper 27, 'Meeting with ABCC and NUM on 25 January 1944'.
80 BT 64/3390: Paper 36 'Note of a meeting with FBI, 1 February 1944'. Forbes Watson, of the British Employers' Confederation, was equally non-committal, stating at a later meeting that: 'He was in full sympathy with efforts to provide better opportunities for advancement for those qualified to make use of them' (BT 64/3390: Paper 41, 'Note of a meeting with . . . Forbes Watson . . . on 4 February 1944').

81 BT 64/3210: E.M. Pollock, 'Industrial Management', 8/1/1944.
82 BT 64/3390: Paper 14, op. cit.; and BT 64/3445: J. Maton to C. Weir, 27/1/1944.
83 BT 64/3390: Papers 27, 36, op. cit.
84 BT 64/3390: Paper 43, 'Minute of Meeting on Industrial Management . . . on 9 February 1944', esp. p. 9.
85 BT 64/3445: P. Lindsay to C. Weir, 16/2/1944.
86 Management Research Group Papers, LSE, Box 10, File headed 'Proposed British Management Institute . . . ': Note [unsigned] 'British Institute of Management', 10/2/1944.
87 BT 64/3445: C. Weir to P. Lindsay, 21/2/1944; and BT 64/3428: A. Kilroy to C. Weir, 5/2/1944.
88 *Weir*, op. cit., p. 3.
89 Ibid.
90 Ibid.
91 *Weir*, op. cit., p. 5.
92 Ibid.
93 *Weir*, op. cit., p. 6.
94 BT 64/3428: C. Weir to H. Dalton, 22/2/1944.
95 BT 64/3390: Paper 44, 'Note of a meeting . . . with representatives of interested Government departments, 21/2/1944'.
96 BT 64/3210: J. Maton, 'Note on Report', 26/2/1944.
97 MRC MSS 200/F/3/S2/38/1: Corr., Locock – Beharrell, 29/2/1944 and 8/3/1944.
98 MRC MSS 200/F/3/S2/38/1: 'Note from Sec., MRG No. 1 to J. Gough, FBI, 2/3/1944'.
99 BT 64/3428: Minutes by GEP [?], 10/5/1944.

3 DEBATES AND INITIATIVES, 1944–5

1 A useful compendium of what discussion there was is contained in C. Madge, *Industry After The War* (London, 1943).
2 Quoted in *Economist*, 23/6/1945.
3 S. Cripps, 'Management's Contribution to Post-War Prosperity', *Industrial Administration* 6(13) (1945), p. 3.
4 Ibid., p. 2.
5 *Daily Herald*, 23/5/1945.
6 *Daily Herald*, 20/8/1945.
7 See, on these macro policies, L. Johnman, 'The Labour Party and Industrial Policy, 1940–5' in N. Tiratsoo (ed.) *The Attlee Years* (London, 1991), pp. 29–53.
8 *Daily Herald*, 23/5/1945.
9 See, for example, speeches by Morrison and Attlee reported in *Daily Herald*, 20/3/1945 and 26/3/1945.
10 Cripps, op. cit., p. 4.
11 Ibid., p. 2; and A. Albu 'The Growing Demand for Security', *Industry Illustrated* 11(8) (1943), p. 21.
12 C.V. Plaistowe, 'Herbert Morrison on Industry', *Persuasion* 2(1) (1944), p. 7.

13 Labour Party, *Let Us Face The Future* (London, 1945), p. 7.
14 See, for example, S. Cripps, quoted in *The Times*, 19/8/1944.
15 For two very clear statements of this package, see ibid., and *Economist* 5/5/1945.
16 Quoted in *The Times Trade and Engineering*, 52(949) (1943), p. 1.
17 Cripps, op. cit., p. 5.
18 Ibid., pp. 4–6.
19 For example, A. Flanders, 'The Production Committee Experiment', *Socialist Commentary* (Aug. 1943), pp. 45–51.
20 Quoted in Anon., 'Discipline in Industry', *Labour* 7(10) (1945), p. 293.
21 Cripps quoted in *Economist*, 11/3/1944.
22 See, for example, E. Bevin, 'Works Managers and the War', *Industry Illustrated* 9(7) (1941), pp. 12–13; *Economist*, 22/5/1943.
23 Cripps, in *The Times*, 19/8/1944.
24 Cripps, in *Manchester Guardian*, 6/11/1944.
25 Cripps, in *The Times*, 19/8/1944.
26 A. Oldfield, 'The Labour Party and planning – 1934, or 1918?', *Bulletin of the Society for the Study of Labour History* 25 (1972), esp. pp. 53–4.
27 J. Burnham, *The Managerial Revolution* (Harmondsworth, 1942).
28 *New Statesman*, 13/11/1943.
29 Albu was a works manager by profession, while Cripps had been a factory manager in the First World War. See *Industry Illustrated* 16(3) (1948), pp. 14–15; E. Estorick, *Stafford Cripps* (London, 1949), pp. 46–7.
30 Albu presented this case on a number of occasions, but perhaps most fully in *Tribune*, 14/8/1942; and his *Management in Transition* (Fabian Soc. Research Series 68, London, 1942).
31 See, for example, A. Albu, 'How Soviet Factories Are Managed', *The Plebs* 36(12) (1944), pp. 151–3.
32 'Licinius', *Vote Labour? Why*? (London, 1945), p. 32; see also G.D.H. Cole, *A Letter To An Industrial Manager* (Fabian Society, London [n.d., but 1944?]).
33 Conservative Party Central Committee on Post-War Problems *Work: The Future of British Industry* [hereafter *C.P. Work*] (London, 1944). For the background to this report, see J.D. Hoffman, *The Conservative Party in Opposition 1945–51* (London, 1964), pp. 38–40.
34 *C.P. Work*, op. cit., p. 10.
35 Ibid., p. 42.
36 Ibid., p. 47.
37 Ibid., p. 43.
38 Ibid., p. 43.
39 Ibid., p. 15.
40 For example, *Daily Telegraph*, 3/1/1944; and *Onlooker* (Jan. 1944), pp. 4–5.
41 Quoted in *Industrial Administration* 5(10) (1944), p. 26.
42 Tory Reform Committee, *Tools For The Next Job* [hereafter *TRC Tools*] (London, 1945). Background on the TRC and this report can be found in Q. Hogg, 'British Industry After The War', *New English Review* 11(1) (1945), pp. 50–4; and Hoffman, op. cit., pp. 40–2.
43 *TRC Tools*, op. cit., pp. 22–3.
44 Ibid., p. 60.

45 Ibid., p. 59.
46 Hoffman, op. cit., p. 43.
47 O. Lyttelton, *Onlooker* (July 1945), p. 3.
48 *Industry Illustrated* 13(1) (1945), p. 11.
49 *Daily Telegraph*, 27/9/1944.
50 *Daily Telegraph*, 10/11/1944.
51 *Daily Telegraph*, 3/1/1944.
52 *News Chronicle*, 26/10/1944.
53 *Economist*, 19/8/1944.
54 *Economist*, 23/6/1945.
55 *Scope*, (Aug. 1944), p. 21.
56 E. Hulton, *The New Age* (London, 1943), pp. 174–85.
57 T. Fraser, *Business* 75(5) (1945), p. 35.
58 G.D.H. Cole, 'The Impact of Current Economic Changes on Industrial Relations and on the Demand for Labour', *British Management Review* 5(2) (1944), p. 42.
59 Ibid., p. 41.
60 For an assessment of the state of trade union thinking at this time, which emphasises its uneven character, see N. Barou, *British Trade Unions* (London, 1947).
61 TUC, *Interim Report on Post-War Reconstruction* (London, 1944).
62 Ibid., pp. 46–9.
63 Ibid., p. 8.
64 Barou, op. cit., pp. 190–205 summarises these plans.
65 National Society of Pottery Workers, *Reconstruction in the Pottery Industry* (Manchester, 1945).
66 A. Loughlin, 'The Responsibility of Management', *British Management Review* 4(4) (1943), pp. 50, 52.
67 *Asset* 2(9) (1945), p. 1.
68 MRC MSS 200 B/3/2/C698 Part 4: 'Walpole Lunch – 23 April 1942', p. 1.
69 Ibid, p. 3.
70 E.F.L. Brech, 'Management Lessons of the War', *British Management Review* 5(3) (1945), p. 49.
71 G. Chelioti, 'Management Lessons of the War', *Industry Illustrated* 12(6) (1944), p. 16.
72 See, for example, MRC MSS 200 B/3/2/C698 Part 4: 'Note. Institute of Industrial Administration. Conference at Waldorf Hotel – 23 October 1943'.
73 *Scope* (Sept. 1942), p. 26.
74 For background on the NUM, see BT/64/3072: Memo by C.K.H., 26/10/1945.
75 *National Union of Manufacturers' Journal* (June 1943), p. 193.
76 See above, pp. 31–43.
77 Johnman, op. cit.; N. Tiratsoo, *Reconstruction, Affluence and Labour Politics: Coventry 1945–60* (London, 1990), p. 17.
78 BT 168/169: Note by R.B., 13/3/1945, p. 1.
79 *The Times*, 26/10/1944.
80 BT 64/3465: G.L. Watkinson 'Reconstruction Committee', 18/2/1944, p. 1.
81 Ibid., p. 2.
82 BT 64/3597: G.L. Watkinson, 'Industrial Organisation and Efficiency. Stocktaking on Board of Trade proposals', 2/1/1945, pp. 1–3.

83 Ibid., p. 1.
84 Ibid. p. 1.
85 See above, pp. 38, 43.
86 BT 64/3537: BOT IRD Memo, 'War Time Measures To Raise The Standard of Management . . . ', 19/7/1944, p. 2.
87 CAB 87/14: R(1)(44)5, War Cabinet Reconstruction Committee, Ministerial Sub-Committee on Industrial Problems [hereafter *Sub-Com.*], Memo by President, 'Post War Exports', 23/6/1944, including Memo by BOT, 'Long Term prospects of British Industry', June 1944, pp. 1, 4.
88 Ibid.
89 CAB 87/14: R.(1)(44), Minutes of 2nd Meeting of Sub-Com., 29/6/1944, p. 1.
90 CAB 87/14: R.(1)(44)8, Memo by President, 'Measures to Promote Exports and Industrial Efficiency', 8/7/1944; and R(1)(44), Minutes of 4th Meeting of *Sub-Com.*, 31/7/1944, Minute 3.
91 BT 64/3428: 'Industrial Management', 29/9/1944.
92 BT 64/3604: S. Cripps to H. Dalton, 9/10/1944.
93 BT 64/3604: G.S. Owen to A. Kilroy, 9/10/1944.
94 T 228/624: A. Kilroy to P.D. Proctor, 24/8/1944 and A. Fforde to G.L. Watkinson, 5/10/1944.
95 Bruce-Gardner, a former iron and steel employer and Chairman of the Society of British Aircraft Constructors, was the Chief Executive for Industrial Reconversion at the Board.
96 BT 64/3428: Report by C. Bruce-Gardner, 15/1/1945.
97 B. Pimlott, *Hugh Dalton* (pbk edn., London, 1986), pp. 401–7 provides the background.
98 BT 64/3428: Minute by H. Dalton 16/1/1945; and Minute by [?], 22/1/1945.
99 CAB 87/15: R.(1)(45)9, Memo by President, 'Industrial Management', 6/2/1945.
100 CAB 87/15: R.(1)(45), Minutes of 5th Meeting of *Sub-Com.*, 7/3/1945, p. 2.
101 T 228/624: Note by A.F., 13/4/1945.

4 EARLY POST-WAR EFFORTS, 1945–7

1 See R.B. McCallum and A. Readman, T*he British General Election of 1945* (London, 1947), esp. pp. 51–61. It is important to note, in the light of recent criticism which portrays Labour as obsessed with New Jerusalemism at this time, that two out of the twelve pages in the party's manifesto, *Let Us Face The Future*, were concerned with 'Industry in the Service of the Nation' while less than one was devoted to 'Houses and the Building Programme'.
2 Labour Party, *Let Us Face The Future* (London, 1945), p. 6.
3 Quoted in F.W.S. Craig, *British General Election Manifestos 1900–74* (London, 1975), p. 119.
4 C. Chisholm, 'How Will Labour Deal With Business?', *Business* 75(9) (1945), p. 40.

5 *Financial Times*, 14/8/1945. See also N. Kipping, *Summing Up* (London, 1972), p. 16.
6 Anon., 'P.M.H . . . . Four Leading Industrialists Talk to The Editor', *Business* 76(1) (1946), p. 38.
7 C. Chisholm, 'Elbow Room for Free Enterprise . . .', *Business* (10) (1945), p. 43.
8 BT 13/220A: 52277, G.L.Watkinson, 'Working Party Programme', 22/10/1945.
9 BT 13/220A 52277: S. Cripps, 'The Work of the Board of the Trade', 7/8/1945.
10 BT 13/220A 52277/2: Minutes of President's Morning Meeting, 20/8/1945, 23/8/1945 and 27/8/1945.
11 BT 64/2180: Note by A. Kilroy, 21/8/1945; and material in BT 64/3607 and BT 64/3608.
12 BT 64/2180: Note by S. Cripps, 23/8/1945; M. Dupree (ed.) *Lancashire and Whitehall. The Diary of Sir Raymond Streat* 2 (Manchester, 1987), pp. 279–80.
13 CAB 71/21: LP (45) 152, President, Board of Trade, 'The Government Plan For Encouraging Industrial Organisation and Efficiency', 25/8/1945.
14 CAB 71/19: LP (45), Minutes of 30th Meeting Cabinet Lord President's Committee, 31/8/1945, Item 5, pp. 5–8.
15 *Board of Trade Journal* 18/8/1945; *Financial Times*, 14/8/1945.
16 MRC MSS 200 F/1/1/215: Meeting of President's Advisory Committee, 21/8/1945; and F/1/1/188: Grand Council Minutes, 22/8/1945, 1529.
17 BT 64/2622: L. Foyster to Ord Johnstone, 15/9/1945.
18 *The Times Trade and Engineering* 58(981) (1945), p. 43.
19 *Evening Sentinel*, 19/9/1945.
20 BT 64/1837: Sir Cecil Weir, 'Pottery. Visit to Stoke on 21 September', 24/9/1945, p. 1.
21 Ibid.
22 Schuster was Chairman of Allied Suppliers Ltd and a Director of the Westminster Bank and the Commercial Union Assurance Co. He had been a Director of the Southern Railway and a National Liberal MP. See *Industry Illustrated* 16(2) (1948), p. 23; M. Stenton and S. Lees, *Who's Who of British Members of Parliament* 3 (Hassocks, Sussex, 1979), pp. 318–19.
23 *The Times Trade and Engineering* 58 (981) (1945), p. 43.
24 BT 13/220A 52277/2: Minutes of President's Morning Meeting, 24/9/1945.
25 *Financial Times*, 5/10/1945.
26 BT 64/991: G.L.Watkinson, 'Working Parties. Progress Report, 9 October 1945', p. 1.
27 Wool was dropped from the first package of industries to be examined because consultation with the employers here took much longer than in other sectors (the trade was geographically spread and had several distinct manufacturers' associations).
28 *Hansard* 414, 15/10/1945, col. 693.
29 BT 64/2622: 'Report of a Meeting of all Hosiery Manufacturers . . . on . . . 8 October, 1945'.
30 T 228/624: S. Cripps to H. Dalton, 8/8/1945.
31 T 228/624: H. Dalton to S. Cripps, 14/8/1945; and Sir Alan Barlow to Sir E. Bridges, 4/9/1945.
32 T 228/624: A. Barlow to C. Weir, 11/9/1945.

33 BT 64/2192: LP (1) (45) 2, Lord President's Industry Sub-Committee, 24/10/1945, Memo by President, Board of Trade, 'Advisory Service on Production Efficiency', p. 1.
34 MRC MSS 292 557/1: TUC Circular 65 (1945–6).
35 MRC MSS F/1/1/215: Meeting of President's Advisory Committee, 4/10/1945.
36 BT 64/2192: LP (1) 45, Minutes of 2nd Meeting of Lord President's Industry Sub-Committee, 29/10/1945.
37 *Manchester Guardian*, 10/9/1945; *The Times*, 10/9/1945.
38 See, for example, a speech by H. Morrison, reported extensively in *Labour Woman* 33(10) (1945), pp. 220–2.
39 *Daily Herald*, 12/9/1945 and 2/10/1945.
40 *Industry Illustrated* 13(12) (1945), p. 11.
41 *Daily Herald*, 16/10/1945.
42 *Economist*, 20/10/1945; *Financial Times*, 16/10/1945; *Industry Illustrated* 14(1) (1945), p. 11.
43 *Daily Telegraph*, 13/9/1945; *Statist*, 15/9/1945.
44 *National Union of Manufacturers' Journal* (October 1945), p. 534.
45 BT 13/220A 52277/2: Papers for President's Morning Meeting, M/M/62 III: J.H.W., 'Working Parties', 22/10/1945.
46 BT 13/220A 52277/2: Minutes of President's Morning Meeting, 24/10/1945.
47 *Board of Trade Journal*, 8/12/1945, 16/3/1945, etc.
48 BT 13/220A 52277/2: Papers for President's Morning Meeting, M/M/62 II: G.L. Watkinson, 'Working Party Programme', 22/10/1945; S.E. Davson, *The State of British Industry* (National News-Letter Report 16, Autumn 1948), p. 4.
49 *Board of Trade Journal*, 16/3/1945.
50 *Hansard* 416, 5/12/1946, cols 2377–9; *Daily Herald*, 6/12/1945.
51 *Sunday Times*, 2/12/1945.
52 *Working Party Reports: Pottery* (London, HMSO, 1946).
53 Ibid., p. 10.
54 Ibid., p. 51.
55 Ibid., p. 51.
56 *Working Party Reports: Cotton* (London, HMSO, 1946).
57 On the cotton report in context, see J. Singleton, *Lancashire on the Scrapheap* (Oxford, 1991), pp. 30–3.
58 *Cotton*, op. cit., pp. 168–213.
59 Ibid., pp. 168–213, 218–38; Singleton, op. cit.; *New Statesman*, 1/6/1946.
60 *Cotton*, op. cit., p. 239.
61 *The Times*, 24/5/1946; *Economist*, 1/6/1946.
62 *National Union of Manufacturers' Journal* (Aug. 1946), p. 736.
63 *Financial Times*, 24/5/1946.
64 A. Roberts, 'The Cotton Industry Working Party', *Industry Illustrated* 14(10) (1946), p. 16.
65 *Economist*, 1/6/1946.
66 *New Statesman* 1/6/1946; J. Jewkes, *Ordeal By Planning* (London, 1948), p. 31.
67 BT 64/2205: Cable from Sir J. Woods to S. Cripps, 2/5/1946.

68 BT 64/2205: Cable from Woods to Cripps, 17/5/1946.
69 *Board of Trade Journal*, 8/6/1946.
70 Ibid. For the details of Streat's appointment and views about him, see Dupree, op. cit., *passim*.
71 See material in BT 64/2225, esp. 'Extract from Secretary's Office Meeting 21, 19/7/1946'.
72 BT 64/2225: Memo [unsigned], 'Consumer Goods Industries . . .', 6/7/1946.
73 MRC MSS 200 F/3/D3/10/14: 'Meeting of Employer Members of Working Parties held . . . 14 June 1946'.
74 MRC MSS 200 F/1/1/188: Grand Council Minutes, 10/7/1946, 1581.
75 MRC MSS 200 F/3/D3/10/14: 'Meeting of Employer Members . . . held . . . on 24 September 1946' p. 10.
76 MRC MSS 200 F/3/S2/14/34: Report of the FBI Trade Organisation Committee, 'Trade Organisation' (adopted by Grand Council, 9/10/1946), p. 2.
77 BT 64/2227: Personal note by [?] 2/10/1946.
78 See A.A. Rogow and P. Shore, *The Labour Government and British Industry 1945–51* (Oxford, 1955), pp. 80–1.
79 See *Economist*, 31/8/1946, 21/9/1946, 16/11/1946; and Davson, op. cit., pp. 47–8.
80 See, for example, material in MRC MSS 292 556/1: esp. A. Hollins to V. Tewson, 7/1/1947.
81 MRC MSS 292 556/1: Corr., G.H. Bagnall–G. Woodcock, 4/11/1946 and 5/11/1946.
82 MRC MSS 292 556/1: TUC Economic Committee 2/4, 'Report of Meeting with President of Board of Trade', 7/1/1947.
83 BT 64/2235: C.B. Reynolds, 'Industrial Organisation Bill . . .', 10/1/1947, p. 2.
84 BT 64/2227: W. Hughes, 'I.O.B. Memo by B.E.C.', 11/2/1947, p. 2.
85 BT 13/220A: M.M. (47) 18, P.M.M., 'Working Parties. Progress Report', 26/2/1947, p. 2.
86 See, for example, BT 64/2414: Memo [unsigned], 'Hosiery Working Party', [nd].
87 *Hansard* 433, 13/2/1947, col. 551.
88 Ibid., col. 547.
89 Ibid., cols 555–60.
90 Ibid., col. 565.
91 Ibid., col. 607.
92 *Hansard* 438, 3/6/1947, cols 53–64.
93 On the Bill, and Development Councils in general, see also *Economist*, 1/2/1947; *Planning* 17(326) (26/3/1951); and R. Brady, *Crisis in Britain* (Cambridge, 1950), pp. 547–68.
94 MRC MSS 292 556/1: Sec., Research and Economic Dept to G. Chester, 25/8/1947.
95 BT 64/220A: Minutes of President's Morning Meeting, 16/7/1947.
96 BT 64/2235: Memo [unsigned], 'Proposals for Future Action . . .', 2/1/1948.
97 Ibid., and MRC MSS 292 556/1: G. Chester to V. Tewson, 27/9/1947.
98 MRC MSS 292 556/1: TUC Economic Committee 1/7, 'Report of a meeting with the President . . .', 8/10/1947.

99 BT 64/2226: W.P.S. 21, W.P.S., Minutes of the 21st Meeting, 9/12/1947; BT 64/2226: M.M.(H) 47, 8th Meeting, President's Morning Meeting, 16/12/1947.
100 BT 64/2226: M.M.(H) 47, 8th Meeting, op. cit.
101 BT 64/2232: C. Weir to S. Cripps, 17/10/45. Baillieu had worked on various official supply and raw material bodies during the war and was on the boards of Dunlop, Zinc Corporation Ltd and the Midland Bank. He became Deputy President of the FBI in 1944–5 and was President 1945–7 (*Who Was Who* 6, 1961–70).
102 BT 64/2232: Note by Permanent Sec., 3/10/1945, and N. Kipping to Sir R. Wood, 5/11/1945.
103 Board of Trade, *A Central Institute of Management* (London, HMSO, 1946), p. 4.
104 Ibid., p. 6.
105 Ibid., p. 7.
106 Ibid., p. 5.
107 Ibid., pp. 8, 9, 12.
108 Ibid., p. 5.
109 T228/624: 'L.P.I. 46, 4th Meeting . . . 12 March 1946, Item 3'.
110 *Industrial Welfare* 28(305) (1946), pp. 41–2; *Engineer*, 22/3/1946; *Industry Illustrated* 14(4) (1946), p. 11.
111 MRC MSS 200/F/3/S2/38/1: N. Kipping to S. Cripps, 25/2/1946.
112 Management Research Group Papers, LSE, Box 24: 'Note by the Secretary on Proposed British Institute of Management', 24/7/1946; MRC MSS 292 570. 9/2: H. Ward to E.P. Harries 1/11/1946; Piercy Papers, LSE, File 15/13: Part 1, Copy Letter to L. Russell, 1/6/1949.
113 MRC MSS 200 F/3/S2/38/1: R.A.B. to Sir John Woods, 3/5/1946.
114 MRG Papers, LSE, Box 10: Confidential Memo 'BIM', 1/9/1948.
115 T 228/624: S.J. Campling to P.D. Proctor, 30/10/1946.
116 *Industry Illustrated* 16(2) (1948), pp. 21–3.
117 *Industry Illustrated* 15(6) (1947), p. 12.
118 *Industry Illustrated* 15(8) (1947), pp. 15, 20; *Sunday Express*, 26/10/1952.
119 See material in BT 64/2192; and BT 64/2324: NPAC1 (47) 55, BOT PES, 'Report on First Year's Working', 3/4/1947, p. 2.
120 Anon., 'The Production Efficiency Service', *Industry Illustrated* 14(8) (1946), p. 19.
121 BT 64/2324: 'Report on First Year's Working', op. cit., p. 1.
122 MRC MSS 200 F/3/T3/25/9: White to Hunnisette, 3/2/1948.
123 Anon., 'Training Within Industry', *Industry Illustrated* 13(12) (1945), pp. 14–15; MRG Papers, LSE, Box 17, 625: 'Report of Meeting . . . on . . . Training Within Industry', 12/7/1948

5 HUMAN RELATIONS AND PRODUCTIVITY, 1947–51

1 On the 'human relations approach' generally, see J. Child, *British Management Thought* (London, 1969) and M. Rose, *Industrial Behaviour: Theoretical Development Since Taylor* (London, 1975).

2 J. Tomlinson, 'The Politics of Economic Measurement: The Rise of the Productivity Problem in the 1940s', in A. Hopwood and P. Miller (eds) *Accounting in its Social Context* (forthcoming). Rostas was the leading contemporary expert on productivity measurement, and was hired as an adviser by the Board of Trade in 1946.
3 *The Times Review of Industry* 1(3)(1947), p. 10; *Nature*, 24/1/1948; W. Crofts, *Coercion or Persuasion?: Propaganda in Britain after 1945* (London, 1989), pp. 47, 57.
4 *New Statesman*, 15/2/1947; G.D.H. Cole, 'Trade Unions, Workers and Production', *Political Quarterly* 18(3) (1947), pp. 250–60.
5 *The Times Review of Industry* 2(20) (1948), p. 3.
6 CAB 124/1093: S.P.(47)53, Advisory Council on Scientific Policy, 'First Interim Report of the Committee on Research and Productivity', 17/9/1947, p. 1.
7 CAB 124/1093: A.R.M.M., 'Committee on Research and Productivity', 30/10/1947, and 'Note for Record . . .', 3/11/1947.
8 CAB 124/109: E.M.N., 'Note for Record', 9/12/1947, and E.M. Nicholson to H.P. Boon, 19/12/1947.
9 CAB 124/109: E.M.N., op. cit. and MRC MSS 200/F/3/T3/27/1: D.G. to President, 16/12/1947, and President to Sir William Griffith, 23/12/1947.
10 *Daily Mail*, 10/2/1948; *News Chronicle*, 29/5/1948.
11 *Industry* 16(9) (1948), p. 14.
12 Ibid.
13 For a full list of the projects of the 'human factor' panel, see the Ministry of Labour's *Human Relations in Industry* (London, 1952), Appendix 2.
14 Ibid.
15 *Manchester Guardian*, 2/4/1949.
16 *Industry* 17(4) (1949), p. 167.
17 *Manchester Guardian*, 25/7/1950; *Economist*, 29/7/1950.
18 LAB 10/655: JCC 183, 'Production Under Full Employment', 5/11/1946; MRC MSS 292/557/1/ NPACI: TUC General Council Side, 1/11/1947.
19 LAB 10/652: Minutes of NJAC, 5/6/1947.
20 Ibid.
21 TUC, *Report of Special Conference of Trade Union Executives, March 1946* (London, 1946); V.L. Allen, *Trade Unions and the Government* (London, 1960), Ch. 15.
22 TUC worries here seem to have derived from fear that such compulsion would lead to JPCs in non-union factories and thus to their use in an anti-union fashion: *Report of the Proceedings of the 1947 TUC* (London, 1947), pp. 433–5.
23 LAB 10/652: Minutes of NJAC, 5/6/1947.
24 For example, MRC MSS 200/F/1/1/189: FBI Grand Council, Discussion of 'Industry and the Way to Recovery', 27/8/1947.
25 See material in LAB 10/722.
26 Ministry of Labour and National Service Handbook on Industrial Relations, Supplement 3, *Joint Consultation in Industry* (London, 1949).
27 See material in MRC MSS 200/B/3/2/C961; LAB 10/652: Minutes of NJAC, 26/1/1949; and LAB 10/655: Meeting between PM and TUC, 7/5/1949.

28 L. Panitch, *Social Democracy and Industrial Militancy*, (Cambridge, 1976) Ch. 1; J. Tomlinson, 'The Labour Government and the trade unions, 1945–51', in N. Tiratsoo (ed.) *The Attlee Years* (London, 1991), pp. 90–105. On the employers' side, see, for example, MRC MSS 200/B/3/2/C443 Part 1: BEC, 'Industrial Organisation Act 1947'.
29 Allen, op. cit., pp. 281–2.
30 MRC MSS 200/F/3/D3/10/13A: FBI, 1st Meeting of Production Committee, 7/10/1948; and 200/F/3/E3/15/1, 2 and 3: FBI Home Economic Policy Study Group.
31 LAB 10/652: Minutes of NJAC, 5/6/1947.
32 See material in LAB 10/722 and LAB 10/724; and BT 190/2: Minutes of NPACI, 8/8/1947.
33 LAB 10/658: Minutes of JCC, 23/11/1949; and material in LAB 10/720.
34 LAB 10/721: Ministry of Labour, 'Machinery for Joint Consultation', 26/1/1949.
35 LAB 10/722: H. Stevens to G. Myrddin-Evans, 6/3/1948, and Lloyd Roberts to Secretary, 17/9/1948. Lloyd Roberts also wanted to play down JPCs and to focus on joint consultation more generally; see LAB 10/725: Lloyd Roberts to conference of officials, 19/8/1948.
36 Ministry of Labour, *Handbook on Industrial Relations* (London, 1953).
37 LAB 10/811: S. Cripps to V. Tewson, 3/8/1948. Cripps's threat in 1946 to impose JPCs was presumably intended to frighten employers into acting (and to a degree succeeded); see LAB 10/213: Speech, 12/9/1946.
38 F.W.S. Craig, *British General Election Manifestos 1900–74* (London, 1975), pp. 123–31; Labour Party, *Labour and the New Society* (London, 1950).
39 R.A. Dahl, 'Workers' Control of Industry and the British Labour Party', *American Political Science Review* 41(4) (1947), pp. 875–900; J. Tomlinson, *The Unequal Struggle?: British Socialism and the Capitalist Enterprise* (London, 1982), Ch. 3. Note that the TUC's *Interim Report on Post War Reconstruction* (London, 1944) endorsed the Morrisonian position. Workers' control was a very live issue in industries such as the railways: see P. Bagwell, *The Railwaymen* (London, 1975), p. 643.
40 H.A. Clegg, 'Nationalised Industry', in G.D.N. Worswick and P.H. Ady (eds) *The British Economy 1945–1950* (Oxford, 1952), pp. 424–51; R.O.V. Roberts and H. Sallis, 'Joint Consultation in the Electricity Supply Industry 1949–59', *Public Administration* 37(2) (1959), pp. 115–33.
41 Labour Party, *Labour Believes in Britain* (London, 1949), p. 7.
42 Labour Party Archive, Manchester [hereafter LPA]: Labour Party Policy Committee, Minutes of NEC, 25/10/1946; and Labour Party Research Dept. RD65, 'Industrial Democracy' (London, 1947).
43 J.M. Chalmers, J. Mikardo and G.D.H. Cole, *Consultation or Joint Management?* (Fabian Tract 277, London, 1949).
44 G.D.H. Cole, 'The Spirit of Democracy', in Industrial Welfare Society, *Joint Consultation* (London, 1948), pp. 8–12; A.W. Wright, *G.D.H. Cole and Socialist Democracy* (Oxford, 1979), pp. 135–7.
45 MRC MSS 200/B/3/2/C961 Part 4: BEC, 'Joint Production Committees', 29/9/1950; and LAB 10/722: 'Joint Consultation in Industry', 25/1/1950.
46 MRC MSS 200/B/3/2/C961 Part 3: BEC, 'Reply to Questionnaire from

Engineering Employers' Federation', 21/4/1950; F. Zweig, *Productivity and Trade Unions* (Oxford, 1951), pp. 148–9. A questionnaire to the Federation of Master Cotton Spinners' Associates in 1950 suggested joint consultation in this sector covered only 10 per cent of employees (MRC MSS 200/B/3/2/C961 Part 4: Letter from FMCSA to BEC, 5/5/1950). On the general problem of the reliability of surveys about the extent of joint consultation, see J. MacInnes, 'Conjuring Up Consultation: The Role and Extent of Joint Consultation in Post-War Private Manufacturing Industry', *British Journal of Industrial Relations* 22(1) (1985), pp. 93–114.

47 MRC MSS 200/B/3/2/C961 Part 3: Association of Chemical and Allied Employers to BEC, May 1950.

48 LAB 10/722: Minutes of NJAC, 26/10/1959; *Report of the Proceedings of the 1949 TUC* (London, 1949) pp. 201–3; and material in MRC MSS 200/B/3/2/C961 Parts 2, 3.

49 LAB 10/722: Lloyd Roberts to Secretary, 17/9/1948; LAB 10/725: J. Johnstone to Lloyd Roberts, 31/10/1949.

50 National Institute of Industrial Psychology, *Joint Consultation in British Industry* (London, 1952), pp. 63, 161.

51 MRC MSS 200/B/3/2/C961 Part 4: BEC, 'Joint Production Committees', 29/9/1950; Zweig, op. cit., pp. 108–11.

52 NIIP, op. cit., pp. 196–9, 211; W.H. Scott, *Industrial Leadership and Joint Consultation* (Liverpool, 1952), Chs 2, 3.

53 MRC MSS 200/B/3/2/C961 Part 4: BEC, 'Joint Production Committees', 29/9/1950; and LAB 10/655: PM's meeting with TUC, 7/5/1947. Morrison said that JPCs 'did a good job during the war, but have deteriorated somewhat. . . . some of them tend to get outside the sphere they were meant to cover and pass resolutions on high policy in foreign affairs which are not their business'.

54 MRC MSS 200/B/3/2/C961 Part 4: BEC, 'Joint Production Committees', 29/9/1950; and NIIP, op. cit., p. 85.

55 MRC MSS 200/B/3/2/C961 Part 4: BEC, 'Joint Production Committees', 29/9/1950.

56 Ibid.

57 On guild socialism see Wright, op. cit., Part 1; on Bullock, *Committee of Enquiry into Industrial Democracy, Report*, Cmnd 6706 (London, 1977); on France, A. Shennan, *Rethinking France: Plans for Renewal* (Oxford, 1989), Ch. 8; and on Germany, V.R. Berghahn, *The Americanization of West German Industry 1945–1973* (Leamington Spa, 1986), pp. 203–30.

58 LAB 10/723: Ministry of Labour Report to ILO on 'Co-operation at the level of the Undertaking', 7/7/1958.

59 Sir G. Schuster, 'Self-Government in Industry', in Ministry of Labour, *Centenary Lectures* (London, 1951), p. 68; TUC, *Public Ownership – An Interim Report* (London, 1953).

60 A. Flanders 'Industrial Relations', in Worswick and Ady (eds), op. cit., pp. 101–24; Tomlinson, *Unequal Struggle?*, op. cit., Ch. 3.

61 H. Clegg and D.N. Chester (eds) *The System of Industrial Relations in Great Britain* (Oxford, 1964).

62 Flanders, op. cit., p. 123; in support of the last point he cites C. Renold, *Joint Consultation Over Thirty Years* (London, 1950).

63 LAB 10/723: Ministry of Labour to Miss D. de Schwenitz, November 1957; W.E.J. McCarthy, *The Role of Shop Stewards in British Industrial Relations*, Royal Commission on Trade Unions and Employers' Associations, Research Paper 1 (London, 1967).
64 M. Terry, 'The Development of Shop Stewards' Organisation: Coventry Precision Tools, 1945–1972', in M. Terry and P.K. Edwards (eds) *Shopfloor Politics and Job Controls* (Oxford, 1988), p. 48.
65 I. Mikardo, 'Incentives in Industry', in D. Jay (ed.) *The Road to Recovery* (London, 1948), pp. 66–8.
66 Ibid, pp. 81–3.
67 For example, C.A.R. Crosland, *The Future of Socialism* (London, 1956), pp. 107–10; C.A. Mace 'Satisfactions in Work', *Occupational Psychology* 22(1) (1948), pp. 5–19.
68 LAB 10/652: Minutes of NJAC, 23/7/1947; LAB 10/723: Minutes of NJAC, 23/11/1949; MRC MSS 200/B/3//2/C1045: BEC, Minutes of Sub-Committee on Wage Incentives.
69 A. Cairncross, *Years of Recovery: British Economic Policy 1945–51* (London, 1985), Ch. 14.
70 R. Whiting, 'Taxation', in H. Mercer, N. Rollings and J. Tomlinson (eds) *Labour Governments and Private Industry: The Experience of 1945–51* (Edinburgh, 1992).
71 Cairncross, op. cit., Ch. 2.
72 Ministry of Labour, *Handbook on Industrial Relations* (London, 1953 edn), Appendix 6; V.L. Allen, 'Incentives in the Building Industry', *Economic Journal* 62(4) (1952), pp. 595–608; Ministry of Labour, *Wage Incentive Schemes* (London, 1951); and material in LAB 10/844 and 845.
73 MRC MSS/200/B/3/2/821 Parts 1, 2.
74 LPA: Labour Party Research Dept RD65, op. cit., p. 1; G.S. Walpole, *Management and Men* (London, 1944).
75 Child, op. cit.; I. Menzies, 'Psychological Aspects of Joint Consultation', in Industrial Welfare Society, *Joint Consultation* (London, 1948), pp. 13–19.

6 THE MANAGEMENT QUESTION AGAIN, 1947-51

1 *Industry* 16(4) (1948), p. 11.
2 The BIM's progress can be followed in its *Management Bulletin*, published every second or third month from December 1948.
3 L. Russell, 'The British Institute of Management', *Industry* 16(11) (1948), p. 16.
4 *Industry* 16(4) (1948), p. 18.
5 Russell, op. cit., pp. 15–17.
6 Information in this paragraph comes from various editions of the *Management Bulletin*. See also T228/626: S. Campling to F. Figgures, 11/1/1952, enclosing 'British Institute of Managers. Report on Organisation and Activities' [n.d. but 1951].
7 T.G. Rose, *A History of the Institute of Industrial Administration 1919–1951* (London, 1954), pp. 142–79; MRC MSS 292/570. 915/1: Meeting with Trade Union Subscribers, 11/10/1950; BIM, *Annual Reports and Accounts 1951* (London, 1951), p. 12.

8 *Report of Committee on Education for Management* (London, HMSO, 1947).
9 See, for example, reviews of Urwick in *The Times* and *Manchester Guardian*, 13/5/1947.
10 See material in ED 46/959.
11 *Report of Committee . . .* , op. cit., para. 1; L.F. Urwick, *A Short History of Industrial Management* (London, 1949), p. 23; F.W. Taylor, *Principles of Scientific Management* (New York, 1911).
12 Urwick, op. cit., p. 15; also L.F. Urwick, *Problems of Growth in Industrial Undertakings* (London, 1949).
13 P. Armstrong, 'The Abandonment of Productive Intervention in Management Teaching Syllabi: An Historical Analysis', University of Warwick Industrial Relations Unit Working Paper 15, (Coventry, 1987), pp. 3–20.
14 ED 46/959: L.F. Urwick to IEE, January 1947; Armstrong, op. cit., p. 13.
15 Armstrong, op. cit., p. 13.
16 LAB 10/966: 'Note of meeting, 5 January 1949, to discuss productivity publicity'.
17 Ministry of Labour, *Another True Story*, Works Information Series (London, 1951).
18 See material in LAB 10/601.
19 LAB 10/954: 'Work of the PMAS', 10/12/1952. Note that the PMAS was also involved in conferences organised by the Cotton Board to speed up redeployment in cotton; see material in LAB 10/953.
20 K.O. Morgan, 'The Rise and Fall of Public Ownership in Britain', in J.M.W. Bean (ed.) *The Political Culture of Modern Britain* (London, 1987), pp. 277–98. Compare E. Durbin, *New Jerusalems: The Labour Party and the Economics of Democratic Socialism* (London, 1985).
21 A. Albu, 'The Organisation of Nationalised Industries and Services', in W.A. Robson (ed.) *Problems of Nationalisation* (London, 1952), p. 76.
22 For references see Chapter 5, note 39. Ministerial sensitivity on this issue is shown by their hostility to the showing of the film, *Chance of a Lifetime*, because of its alleged advocacy of workers' control. See M. Dickinson and S. Street, *Cinema and the State: The Film Industry and the British Government 1927–84* (London, 1985), p. 202.
23 Some of this material is discussed in D.N. Chester, *The Nationalisation of British Industry 1945–51* (London, 1975), Ch. 9. See also BT 64/2416 and the records of the Ministerial Committee on the Socialisation of Industries, which are at CAB 134/687–691.
24 CAB 134/687: S.I.(M)(46)10, H. Morrison, 'Workers' Assistance in the Management of Socialised Industries' 26/3/1946.
25 CAB 134/689: S.I.(M)(48), 8th Minutes of Socialisation of Industries Committee, 3/6/1948.
26 CAB 134/687: S.I.(M)(46)10, H. Morrison, 'Workers' Assistance', op. cit., and S.I.(M)(46)19: Report by Official Committee on 'Workers' Assistance', 4/4/1946.
27 CAB 134/687: S.I.(M)(46)16, Ministry of Labour, 'Workers' Assistance', 28/3/1946.
28 CAB 134/687: S.I.(M)(46)19, Report, op. cit.

29 CAB 134/687: S.I.(M)(46)10, Minutes of Socialisation of Industries Committee, 8/7/1946.
30 BT 64/2416: 'Note of Meeting with Wing-Commander Cooper', June 1946.
31 CAB 134/688: S.I.(M)47, 3rd Minutes of Socialisation of Industries Committee, 27/3/1947, and S.I.(M)(47)15, 'Proposed Staff Advisory Council in the Post Office', 25/3/1947: CAB 134/689: S.I.(M)(48)65, 'Management and Men in the Socialised Industries', 13/12/1948.
32 CAB 134/691: S.I.(M)(50)39, H. Morrison, 'Workers' Attitudes in the Socialised Industries', 6/12/1950. This disillusion of workers with nationalised industries is strongly reflected in TUC discussion: see, for example, MRC MSS 292/560.1/65: TUC Economic Committee, 'The Public Control of Industry', 21/6/1950.
33 CAB 134/691: S.I.(M)(50), 9th Minutes of Socialisation of Industries Committee, 11/12/1950; CAB 134/592: S.I.(M)(51)25, 'Report of Sub-Committee on Relations with Workers in Socialised Industries', 10/5/1951.
34 CAB 134/689: S.I.(M)(48)62, Note by Morrison covering Attlee, 'Management and Men in the Socialised Industries', 4/11/1948.
35 CAB 134/689: S.I.(M)(48)65, Ministry of Labour, 'Management and Men in the Socialised Industries', 13/12/1948; CAB 134/690: S.I.(M)(49), 6th Minutes of Socialisation of Industries Committee, 26/4/1949, and S.I.(M)(49)21, 'Management–Worker Relationships in the Socialised Industries', 7/4/1949.
36 CAB 134/692: S.I.(M)(51)7, 'Training for Leadership in the Socialised Industries', 30/1/1951.
37 CAB 134/689: S.I.(M)(47)43, Ministry of Fuel and Power, 'Taking Stock', 13/11/1947.
38 CAB 134/688: S.I.(M)(47), 11th Minutes of Socialisation of Industries Committee, 19/11/1947, and S.I.(M)(47)50, 'Decentralised Administration in an American Business', 15/12/1947. This evidence indicates that Morrison was not such an unmoving centraliser as suggested by M. Chick, 'Competition, Competitiveness and Nationalisation 1945–51', in G. Jones and M. Kirby (eds) *Competitiveness and the State* (Manchester, 1991), pp. 66–7.
39 CAB 134/689: S.I.(M)(48)19, 'Progress Report on Socialised Industries', 17/3/1948.
40 CAB 134/688: S.I.(M)(47)32, H. Morrison 'Taking Stock', 18/7/1947; CAB 134/690: S.I.(M)(49), 2nd Minutes of Socialisation of Industries Committee, 25/1/1949; CAB 134/691: S.I.(M)(50)26, Minutes of Meeting with Chairmen of Boards, 27/6/1950. Similar lines of argument were pursued by Morrison in Labour Party discussions of nationalisation. See, for example, Labour Party Archive, Manchester: Labour Party Research Department RD253, 'Administration of Nationalised Industries', January 1949, and Minutes of Sub-Committee on Nationalised Industries, Sept.–Nov. 1948.
41 CAB 134/689: S.I.(M)(48), 14th Minutes of Socialisation of Industries Committee, 14/12/1948; CAB 134/691: S.I.(M)(50)21, 'Efficiency and Public Accountability of Nationalised Industries', 5/5/1950.
42 However, the long-standing debate on appropriate pricing policies for

nationalised industries continued with new relevance, now that the scope of nationalisation had so immensely expanded. See Chick, op. cit., pp. 68–71; and M. Chick, 'Marginal Cost Pricing and the Peak-Hour Demand for Electricity 1945–51', in M. Chick (ed.) *Governments, Industries and Markets* (Aldershot, 1990), pp. 110–26.

43 Albu, op. cit., pp. 77–81.

44 *Productivity: Report of the General Council of the TUC* (London, 1948), para. 37.

45 MRC MSS 292/S57.1/2: Meetings of General Council side of NPACI, 20/3/1950; E.P. Harries, 'Training of T.U. Officials', BIM Conference Series 8 (London, 1949), p. 10. The TUC was keen on encouraging trade unions to affiliate to and participate in the Local Management Associations of the BIM.

46 For example, CAB 134/691: Speech by Ernest Davies, MP; and MRC MSS 292/S57.1/2: General Council side of NPACI, 9/6/1950.

47 MRC MSS 292/S57.1/2: General Council, op. cit.

48 See editorials in *ASSET* 4(2) (1947) and 4(6) (1947); and Ian Mikardo, 'Blue Print for British Industry', *ASSET* 3(1) (1946), p. 34.

49 R. Crossman, M. Foot and I. Mikardo, *Keep Left* (London, 1947), p. 23; R. Acland *et al.*, *Keeping Left* (London, 1949), p. 37.

50 J. Schneer, *Labour's Conscience: The Labour Left 1945–51* (London, 1988), esp. Ch. 4; J. Eaton, *The Economics of Peace and War* (London, 1952), Ch. 6.

51 *ASSET* 4(4) (1947), p. 1.

52 A. Albu, *Management in Transition* (Fabian Research Series 68, London, 1942); Sidney Webb, *The Works Manager Today* (London, 1917). This latter analysis combined a discussion of 'human relations', which says most of what is worth saying on that topic, with a sophisticated attack on British managements' obsession with wages as the key variable to be controlled.

53 J. Burnham, *The Managerial Revolution* (Harmondsworth, 1942), esp. Chs 6, 11.

54 R.H. Crossman (ed.) *New Fabian Essays* (London, 1952), esp. essays by Albu, Crossman and Crosland (Crosland is most explicit in his discussion of Burnham on pp. 37–8, 47–9); C.A.R. Crosland, *The Future of Socialism* (London, 1956), Chs 3, 16, 17.

55 For example, Albu in Crossman (ed.) *Essays*, op. cit.; A. Albu and N. Jowett, *The Anatomy of Private Industry* (Fabian Research Series 145, 1953); Crosland, *Future*, op. cit., Ch. 3.

56 Albu in Crossman (ed.), *Essays*, op. cit., pp. 132–3; and Crosland, *Future*, op. cit., p. 339.

57 R. Brady, *Crisis in Britain* (London, 1951), pp. 563, 33. For a recent discussion of some of the managerial revolution literature, see S. Brooke, 'Atlantic Crossing? American Views of Capitalism and British Socialist Thought, 1932–1962', *Twentieth Century British History* 2(2) (1991), pp. 107–36.

58 *Industry Illustrated* 13(10) (1945), p. 11, and 13(12) (1945), p. 11.

59 BT 64/2360: R.M. Nowell, 'Minute of Meeting with BIM Representatives', 6/5/1948, and S.A. Dakin to G.B. Blaker, 29/7/1948.

60 H. Mercer, 'The Monopolies and Restrictive Practices Commission

1949–56: A Study in Regulatory Failure', in G. Jones and M.W. Kirby (eds) *Competitiveness and the State: Government and Business in Twentieth Century Britain* (Manchester, 1991), pp. 89–90.

7 THE 'AMERICANISATION' OF PRODUCTIVITY, 1948-51

1 S. Pollard, *Britain's Prime and Britain's Decline* (London, 1990), Ch. 4.
2 P.A. Clark, *Anglo-American Innovation* (Berlin, 1987), p. 326; see also W. Lewchuk, *American Technology and the British Vehicle Industry* (Cambridge, 1987).
3 CAB 134/222: EPC(49)92, 'US Private Direct Investment', 27/7/1949; G. Jones, 'The British Government and Foreign Multinationals before 1970', in M. Chick (ed.) *Governments, Industries and Markets* (Aldershot, 1990), pp. 199–202.
4 V. Berghahn, *The Americanisation of West German Industry 1945–1973* (Leamington Spa, 1986); J.B. Cohen, *Japan's Economy in War and Reconstruction* (Minneapolis, 1949); H. Mercer, *Constructing a Competitive Order: The Failure of British Anti-Trust* (Cambridge, forthcoming).
5 On Marshall Aid, see M. Hogan, *The Marshall Plan: America, Britain and the Reconstruction of Western Europe 1947–52* (Cambridge, 1987); A. Milward, *The Reconstruction of Western Europe 1945–51* (London, 1984).
6 C.A. Maier, *In Search of Stability: Explorations in Historical Political Economy* (Cambridge, 1987), Ch. 3.
7 T236/823: 'Note of Hoffman/Cripps meeting, 26 July 1948'.
8 The explicit economic conditions for receipt of Marshall Aid were limited to British commitments over balanced budgets and anti-inflationary policy. See CAB 134/215: EPC(47)34, 'Marshall Aid: Undertakings on UK Internal Finance', 29/12/1947.
9 MRC MSS/200/F/3/D3/10/11: Max Nicholson to Herbert Morrison, 25/6/1948, and F/3/51/1/11: 'Brief for the President on the AACP', 29/7/1048; BT 195/19: S. Leslie to E. Plowden, 19/8/1948.
10 MRC MSS 292/20/20: 'TUC General Council', 28/7/1948; BT 195/19: S. Leslie to S. Cripps, 27/8/1948, and 'Discussions with FBI and TUC on publicity about productivity', 24/11/1948.
11 MRC MSS 292/552. 3/5: Hornsey TC to TUC, [n.d.]; also BT195/61: AACP correspondence.
12 *Hansard* 454, 29/7/1948, cols 1566–1602. On anti-Americanisation more generally at this time see, for example, M. Dickinson and S. Street, *Cinema and the State: The Film Industry and the British Government 1927–84* (London, 1985), pp. 155–6.
13 *Hansard* 454, 28/7/1948, col. 1332.
14 AACP *Final Report* (London, 1952). Papers from the productivity measurement panel are in MRC MSS 200/F/3/D3/7/4.
15 MRC MSS 292/552. 31/1: 'TUC side of AACP', 26/10/1948; MSS 200/F/3/D3/7/1: 'FBI [input into] ACCP meetings', 25/10/1948, 29/10/1948; A. Carew, *Labour Under the Marshall Plan* (Manchester, 1987), pp. 135–6.

16 MRC MSS 292/552. 31/1: 'TUC side of AACP', 25/8/1948.
17 MRC MSS 200/F/3/D3/7/2: FBI to Trade Associations, 16/8/1948.
18 MRC MSS 200/F/3/E3/15/1, 2 and 3: FBI Home Economic Policy Study Group, 'Report on Economic Policy'; MRC MSS 200/F/1/1/189: FBI Grand Council Minutes, 8/9/1948 and 13/10/1948.
19 MRC MSS 200/F/3/S1/36/6: '2nd Draft Report on 3rd session of AACP', 3/10/1950.
20 MRC MSS 292/552. 312/1: 'TUC Verbatim accounts of AACP meetings, 28 and 29/10/1948'. This was a very different emphasis to that given at the TUC, where the General Council presented the AACP as a means of getting dollars for new machines: *Report of the Proceedings of the 1948 TUC Congress* (London, 1948), pp. 79–80.
21 BT 195/66: 'Productivity Teams', 19/1/1949, and E.P. Harries to L. Rowan, 24/2/1949.
22 BT 195/66: 'Fifth meeting of UK section of AACP, 1 February 1949'; Carew, op. cit., 138–9.
23 MRC MSS 200/F/3/S1/36/41: P.H. Cook, 'The Productivity Team Technique' (1951).
24 Ibid.
25 Carew, op. cit., pp. 138, 145; MRC MSS 292/577. 1/2 'Report of meeting between G.C. members of NPACI and Executive of Amalgamated Union of Foundry Workers, 13 January 1950'.
26 S. Broadberry and N. Crafts, 'Explaining Anglo-American Productivity Differences in the Mid-Twentieth Century', *Bulletin of the Oxford Institute of Economics and Statistics* 52(4) (1990), p. 387; N. Crafts, 'The Assessment: British Economic Growth Over the Long Run', *Oxford Review of Economic Policy* 4(1) (1988), pp. i–xxi.
27 Carew, op. cit., Ch. 9; A. Carew, 'The Anglo-American Council on Productivity (1948–52): The Ideological Roots of the Post-War Debate on Productivity in Britain', *Journal of Contemporary History* 26(1) (1991), p. 53.
28 *New Statesman*, 29/12/1951; AACP *Grey-Iron Founding* (London, 1950), p. 12. This kind of rhetoric was endorsed by commentators such as Graham Hutton; see his 'British and American Ways of Life – Diverging or Converging?', *Futures* 6(4) (1948), pp. 65–72.
29 AACP, *Building* (London, 1950), p. 54.
30 W. Campbell Balfour, 'Productivity and the Worker', *British Journal of Sociology* 4(3) (1953), pp. 257–65.
31 T. Nichols, *The British Worker Question* (1987).
32 MRC MSS 200/F/3/S1/36/28: 'TUC Note on Fleming–Waddell Report', 10/10/1950; Carew, *Labour* op. cit., p. 145.
33 Carew, *Labour*, op. cit., p. 155; Broadberry and Crafts, 'Anglo-American', op. cit., p. 386.
34 MRC MSS 200/F/3/T3/28/1: 'Analysis of 58 Team Reports', 22/1/1953. This was material prepared for the Crowther–Hutton report on the AACP, eventually published in much altered form as G. Hutton, *We Too Can Prosper: The Promise of Productivity* (London, 1953).
35 K. Middlemas, *Power, Competition and the State, 1: Britain in Search of Balance, 1940–1961* (London, 1986), p. 163.

36 Carew, *Labour*, op. cit., p. 147; Hutton, *Prosper*, op. cit., Ch. 2; AACP, *Education for Management* (London, 1951), pp. 21–24.
37 BT 195/66: 'Note on Conversation with American Representative on AACP, 25 November 1949'.
38 CAB 134/592: 10th Meeting of Productivity (Official) Committee, 30/9/1949; BT 195/53: S. Leslie to Hitchman, 26/9/1949.
39 BT 195/66: Meeting of AACP, November 1948; BT 64/2313: Special Research Unit, 'Meeting of 5 November 1947'; MRC MSS 200/F/3/D2/1/31: FBI Committee on Productivity Statistics, meetings 22/10/1948 and 22/11/1948.
40 TUC, *Trade Unions and Productivity* (London, 1950), pp. 5, 10.
41 Carew, *Labour*, op. cit., pp. 149–54; *Report of the Proceedings of the 1950 TUC Congress* (London, 1950), pp. 216–23; MRC MSS 292/557. 1/2: Meetings of General Council side of NPACI, 30/3/1950 and 18/5/1950.
42 MRC MSS 200/F/3/S1/1/11: 'Director General's Report', 8/9/1948.
43 J. Tomlinson, 'The Failure of the Anglo-American Council on Productivity', *Business History* 33(1) (1991), pp. 82–92.
44 For an interesting approach to this issue, see C. Littler, *The Development of the Labour Process in Capitalist Societies* (London, 1982).
45 Carew, *Labour*, op. cit., pp. 148, 155–7. This concept was popularised, to some extent, because of H. Braverman, *Labour and Monopoly Capital* (New York, 1974). For a telling critique, see T. Cutler, 'The Romance of Labour', *Economy and Society* 7(1) (1978), pp. 74–9.
46 On the general background, see J.A. Merkle, *Management and Ideology: The Legacy of the International Scientific Management Movement* (Berkeley, 1980); and L. Urwick and E.F.L. Brech, *The Making of Scientific Management, 2: Management in British Industry* (London, 1946), Ch. 12.
47 H. de Haan, 'Scientific Management to Productivity', *Manager* 20(9) (1952), p. 533.
48 For example, L. Urwick, *The Meaning of Rationalisation* (London, 1929); D.H. Macgregor, 'Problems of Rationalisation', *Economic Journal* 40(4) (1930), pp. 351–68.
49 M. Kirby, 'Industrial Policy', in S. Glynn and A. Booth (eds) *The Road to Full Employment* (London, 1987); W.K. Hancock and M. Gowing, *Civil Industry and Trade* (London, 1952), Ch. 10.
50 For surveys of the Working Party reports in these terms, see R. Brady, *Britain in Crisis* (London, 1952), Ch. 13; R. Edwards and H. Townsend, *Business Enterprise* (London, 1958), pp. 386–91; BT 64/2313: 'The Working Party Reports and Productivity' [n.d.].
51 See *Working Party Reports: Cotton* (London, HMSO, 1946), Note by Professor Jewkes, pp. 242–9. This analysis gains support from the failure of the US cotton industry to compete successfully after the Second World War, in comparison especially with other 'high wage' countries such as West Germany, Holland and Italy. See J. Tomlinson, 'Planning for Cotton, 1945–51: A Comment', *Economic History Review* 44(3) (1991), pp. 523–6; M. Dupree, 'The Cotton Industry', in H. Mercer, N. Rollings and J. Tomlinson (eds) *The 1945 Labour Government and Private Industry* (Edinburgh, 1992).
52 H. Mercer, 'The Labour Governments of 1945–51 and private industry', in

N. Tiratsoo (ed.) *The Attlee Years* (London, 1991), pp. 71–84; and pp. 83–4 above.

53 SUPP 14/138: Engineering Advisory Council Minutes 1947–52; and material in SUPP 14/141.

54 *Report of the Committee on Standardisation in the Engineering Industry* (London, 1949); SUPP 14/141: 'Employers' Comments on Lemon Report' [n.d.]; *Engineer*, 26/11/1948, 1/7/1949 and 4/11/1949.

55 SUPP 14/333: Cunliffe Committee Report on BSI and 'Reviews of action on Lemon Report', June and December 1950; *Engineer*, 28/1/1949 and 31/3/1950.

56 T. Gourvish, *British Railways 1948–73: A Business History* (London, 1986), pp. 85–90; *Engineer*, 31/3/1950.

57 CAB 134/640: Production Committee Minutes, 11/3/1949, 30/9/1949 and 4/10/ 1949; L. Hannah, *Engineers, Managers and Politicians* (London, 1982), Chs. 3, 4, 8.

58 Simplification was defined in this report as reducing the number of types and varieties of products, standardisation as standardising how those fewer products were made. Specialisation is concerned with producers that specialise in one or a few of these smaller number of products. Hence all three fit together ('the 3Ss') as embodying the idea of economies of scale from longer runs of a smaller range of products. See AACP, *Simplification in Industry* (London, 1949), pp. 1–2.

59 Ibid., p. 13.

60 See material in BT 64/2314-2322; J. Rosenhead, 'Operational Research at the Crossroads: Cecil Gordon and the Development of Postwar OR', *Journal of Operational Research Society* 40(1) (1989), pp. 3–28; SUPP 14/151: National Advisory Council for the Motor Manufacturing Industry, Minutes 1946–54; and material in BT 195/1.

61 Hutton, *Prosper*, op. cit., pp. 49, 96; *Cotton*, op. cit., p. 231; BT 64/2313: 'The Working Party Reports and Productivity' [n.d.], para. 22.

62 For example, AACP, *Cotton Spinning* (London, 1950), p. 26; AACP, *Management Accounting* (London, 1950), pp. 14–16.

63 AACP, *Management Accounting*, op. cit., p. 6; more generally, J. Tomlinson, 'The Politics of Economic Measurement: The Rise of the Productivity Problem in the 1940s', in A. Hopwood and P. Miller (eds) *Accounting in its Social Context* (forthcoming).

64 MRC MSS 200/F/3/D3/7/63: FBI, 'AACP Management Accounting'; N. Stacey, *English Accountancy: A Study in Society and Economic History* (London, 1954), p. 202; P. Armstrong, 'The Rise of Accounting Controls in British Capitalist Enterprises', *Accounting, Organisations and Society* 12(4) (1987), pp. 415–36.

65 D. Granick, *The European Executive* (New York, 1962), pp. 253–4.

66 See material in BT 64/2192 and BT 64/2324.

67 Ibid.; BIM, *Wage Incentive Schemes* (London, 1950).

68 BT 64/2419: 'The Use of Time and Motion Study in Industry', 27/1/1949.

69 Carew, *Labour*, op. cit., pp. 168–9, 207–8.

70 *Engineer*, 4/6/1948 and 6/5/1949.

71 J. Jewkes, 'Is British Industry Inefficient?', *Manchester School* 14(1) (1946), pp. 1–16; G.C. Allen, 'The Efficiency of British Industry', in his

British Industry and Economic Policy (first pub. 1948; London, 1979), p. 107. For a broad survey of the arguments about the relevance of US models to British industry, see G. Hutton, 'American and British Industry: A Comparison', *Futures* 2(1) (1947), pp. 2–11.

72 J. Singleton, 'Planning for Cotton 1945–51', *Economic History Review* 48(1) (1990), pp. 62–78; *Engineer*, 5/8/1949.

73 AACP, *Diesel Locomotives* (London, 1950), pp. 7–9; AACP, *Valves* (London, 1951) pp. 48–51.

74 Lewchuk, op. cit.; B. Elbaum and W. Lazonick (eds) *The Decline of the British Economy* (Oxford, 1986).

8 EVALUATIONS AND IMPLICATIONS

1 A. Cairncross, *Years of Recovery: British Economic Policy 1945–51* (London, 1985), pp. 18–19, citing C.H. Feinstein, *National Income, Expenditure and Output of the U.K. 1855–1965* (Cambridge, 1972).

2 L. Rostas, 'Changes in the Productivity of British Industry, 1945–50' *Economic Journal* 62(1) (1952), pp. 15–24.

3 R.J. Nicholson and S. Gupta, 'Output and Productivity Changes in British Manufacturing Industry 1948–54', *Journal of the Royal Statistical Society* (A)23(4) (1960), pp. 427–59.

4 W.B. Reddaway and A.B. Smith, 'Progress in British Manufacturing Industries 1948–54', *Economic Journal* 70(1) (1960), pp. 17–31.

5 Rostas, op. cit., p. 20; Reddaway and Smith, op. cit., pp. 29–30.

6 Reddaway and Smith, op. cit., pp. 29–30.

7 Rostas, op. cit., pp. 24–5.

8 See pp. 93–4.

9 MRC MSS 200/F/3/T3/25/9: White to Hunnisette, 3/2/1948.

10 Anon., 'Management looks at Labour', *Future* 6(3) (1951), p. 56.

11 National Institute of Industrial Psychology, *Joint Consultation in British Industry* (London, 1952), pp. 182–3, 198–9.

12 *Manager* 18(7) (1950), p. 311; *Business* (July 1950), p. 33; *Economist*, 18/10/1952.

13 *News Chronicle*, 19/1/1953

14 I. McGivering, D.G.J. Matthews and W.H. Scott, *Management in Britain* (Liverpool, 1960), p. 79.

15 BT 64/2738: 'Working Parties Progress Report No. 18', 17/7/1946.

16 *Hansard* 468, 25/10/1949, cols 123–5.

17 Ibid.; Anon., 'Progress report on Pottery', *Business* (Oct. 1948), pp. 37–43.

18 See, for example, British Productivity Council, *A Review of Productivity in the Footwear Industry* (London, 1953) and *A Review of Productivity in the Furniture Industry* (London, 1954).

19 Anon., 'The Productivity Reports', *Future* 6(3) (1951), p. 59.

20 British Productivity Council, *A Review of Productivity in the Printing Industry* (London, [n.d. but 1953]), pp. 4–5.

21 See, for example, *New Statesman*, 29/12/1951; I. Mikardo, 'Platitudes on Productivity', *Fabian Journal* 10 (1953), pp. 35–7.

22 Quoted in 'Productivity Reports', *Future*, op. cit., p. 60.

23 *Manager* 20(5) (1952), p. 271.
24 *Business* (Nov. 1951), pp. 41–6; 'Productivity Reports', *Future*, op. cit., p. 59; *The Times Review of Industry* 4(46) (1950), p. 33, and 6(64) (1952), p. 39.
25 The most famous associated publication was, of course, G. Hutton, *We Too Can Prosper: The Promise of Productivity* (London, 1953).
26 AACP, 'Summary of Follow Up Statement No. 3' (London, [n.d. but Aug. 1952]), pp. 1,3, 5.
27 AACP, 'Summary of Follow Up Statement No. 6' (London, [n.d. but Sept. 1952]), p. 5.
28 *Economist*, 25/5/1946.
29 *Economist*, 20/10/1945.
30 F. Zweig, *Productivity and Trade Unions* (Oxford, 1951), p. 46.
31 See N. Tiratsoo, 'The Government and Motor Cars', in H. Mercer, N. Rollings and J. Tomlinson (eds) *Labour Governments and Private Industry: The Experience of 1945–51* (Edinburgh, 1992).
32 *Economist*, 1/6/1946.
33 See, for example, Cairncross, op. cit., pp. 499–500.
34 This literature is reviewed in T. Nichols, *The British Worker Question: A New Look at Workers and Productivity in Manufacturing* (London, 1986).
35 C. Barnett, *The Audit of War* (London, 1986), p. 274 ('the trade unions . . . [were] possibly the strongest single factor militating against technical innovation and high productivity' in 1940s Britain); N. Crafts, 'The Assessment: British Economic Growth Over The Long Run' *Oxford Review of Economic Policy* 4(1) (1988), p. x; S. Broadberry and N. Crafts, 'Explaining Anglo-American Productivity Differences in the Mid-Twentieth Century', *Bulletin of the Oxford University Institute of Economics and Statistics* 52(4) (1990), pp. 375–402; S. Broadberry and N. Crafts, 'Britain's Productivity Gap in the 1930s: Some Neglected Factors' (Unpublished paper, University of Warwick, 1991), pp. 12, 36; N. Crafts 'Economic Growth', in N. Crafts and N. Woodward (eds) *The British Economy Since 1945* (Oxford, 1991), p. 283; S. Broadberry, 'Employment and Unemployment', in R. Floud and D. McCloskey (eds) *The Economic History of Britain Since 1700, 3: Britain Since 1945* (Cambridge, forthcoming), pp. 31–7; K. Middlemas, *Power, Competition and the State, 1: Britain in Search of Balance, 1940–1961* (London, 1986), pp. 94–5, 129–30.
36 M. Olson, *The Rise and Decline of Nations* (New Haven, Conn., 1982).
37 Zweig, op. cit., p. 21.
38 W.H. Scott *et al.*, *Technical Change and Industrial Relations* (Liverpool, 1956), *passim*.
39 See, for example, J.H. Richardson, 'Labour's Part in Britain's Economic Recovery', *Westminster Bank Review* (May 1949), pp. 1–8.
40 'Management', *Future*, op. cit., pp. 56–7.
41 P.W.S. Andrews and E. Brunner, 'Productivity and the Business Man', *Oxford Economic Papers* 2(2) (1950), pp. 197–225.
42 Ibid., pp. 216–18.
43 Ibid., p. 209.
44 Management Research Group Archive, Corby: File headed 'Enquiry Reports 1945–7', Report 7/1947, p. 2.

45 MRC MSS 200/B/3/2/C 821 Part 1: BEC N.C. 10487, 'Trade Union Restrictions' [n.d. but 1947], p. 1.
46 MRC MSS 200/B/3/2/C 821 Part 2: BEC, 'Restrictive Practices . . . Summary of replies received . . . ' [n.d. but 1950], pp. 1–3.
47 *Hansard* 454, 29/7/1948, col. 1581.
48 H. Mercer, 'The Labour Governments of 1945–51 and private industry', in N. Tiratsoo (ed.) *The Attlee Years* (London, 1991), p. 84.
49 LAB 10/655: JCC Papers No. 183, 5/11/1946; LAB 19/652: Minutes of NJAC, 23/4/1947; TUC, *Report of the Proceedings of the 1947 TUC Congress* (London, 1947), pp. 299, 325–8.
50 See J. Tomlinson, 'The Labour government and the trade unions, 1945–51', in Tiratsoo (ed.), op. cit., pp. 90–105.
51 Ibid.; TUC, 'Productivity Report of the G.C . . . . to the Special Conference of T.U. Executives', 18/11/1948; MRC MSS 292/557.1/3-4: TUC Production Committee Minutes 1950–2; A. Carew, *Labour Under The Marshall Plan* (Manchester, 1987), pp. 147–57.
52 'Productivity Reports', *Future*, op. cit., p. 67; *Financial Times*, 13/8/1948.
53 See, for example, G.F. Green, 'The Productivity Virus', *Socialist Commentary* 14(12) (1950), p. 269.
54 G.H. Gallup, *The Gallup International Public Opinion Polls. Great Britain 1937–1975 Volume One* (New York, 1976), p. 175.
55 RG 23/115: The Social Survey, 'Survey of Knowledge and Opinion about the Economic Situation', Feb. 1951, p. 1.
56 RG 23/103: The Social Survey, 'Survey of Knowledge and Opinion about the Economic Situation', Nov. 1948, p. 13.
57 Gallup op. cit., p. 203.
58 Ibid., pp. 189, 204, 211.
59 Anon., 'Does Britain believe in Business?, *Future* 5(2) (1950), pp. 13–17; Anon., 'What Do Workers Think?', *Future* 5(3) (1950), pp. 15–19.
60 For the historiography, see Mercer, op. cit.
61 Quoted in (anon.) 'The March of Business', *Business* (Jan. 1951), p. 33.
62 Management Research Group Papers, LSE, Box 6, Item 348: 'Report of Directors' Dinner . . . 19 April 1950'. The phrases quoted were used by Directors of British–American Tobacco Co. Ltd and Imperial Tobacco Co. Ltd, respectively.
63 See, for example, comments by a Dunlop Director reported in *Industry* 15(7) (1947), p. 13; editorial in *Financial Times*, 24/5/1948.
64 Quoted in 'March', *Business*, op. cit., p. 35.
65 Conservative Party Archive, Bodleian Library, Oxford, CRD 2/7/46: R.W. Guild to H. Macmillan, 20/3/1947.
66 Conservative Party Archive, Bodleian Library, Oxford, CRD 2/7/48(1): D.F.O. Russell to R.A.B. 4/3/1947.
67 BT 64/2414: 'Hosiery Working Party' [n.d.]. For the Development Council situation in general, see G.D.N. Worswick, 'Development Councils', *Socialist Commentary* 15(7) (1951), pp. 166–8; Anon., 'Development Councils', *Planning* 17(326) (1951), pp. 209–32.
68 See N. Tiratsoo, 'Labour and Management at Mid-Century' (Unpublished Paper, Business History Unit, LSE, 1992).
69 MRC MSS 200/F/3/T3/25/4: N. Kipping to L. Russell, 20/10/1948.

70 MRC MSS 292/57.912(1): Minutes of First (1949) Meeting of the BIM Council, 2/2/1949, Minute 8.

71 MRG Papers, LSE, Box 15 Item 9: 'Notes by the Secretary for the E.C. on 24/11/1948' (20/10/1948), p. 8; Tiratsoo, 'Labour and Management', op. cit., pp. 25–6.

72 W. Crofts, *Coercion or Persuasion?: Propaganda in Britain after 1945* (London, 1989).

73 Anon., 'Development Councils', *Planning*, op. cit., p. 226.

74 See, for example, J. Tomlinson, *Government and Enterprise: The Changing Problem of Efficiency* (Oxford, forthcoming), *passim*; M. Sawyer, 'Industrial Policy', in M. Artis and D. Cobham (eds) *Labour's Economic Policies 1974–79* (Manchester, 1991), pp. 158–75.

75 For a recent discussion of this concept, see R. Lowe, 'The Second World War, Consensus and the Foundation of the Welfare State', *Twentieth Century British History* 1(2) (1990), pp. 152–82.

Index